Time and Effort

~~~~~~

James E. Turner, M.D.
91B20

Burning Barn Books
El Dorado Hills, CA

Burning Barn Books
3941 Park Drive, Suite 20-712
El Dorado Hills, CA   95762
contact@burningbarnbooks.com
www.burningbarnbooks.com

The story, "Merry Christmas, soldier!" first appeared in The Greenville Advocate.
Library of Congress Control Number 2018964142
ISBN 978-1-7327289-0-5 (signed copy)
ISBN 978-1-7327289-1-2

Cover design: Natalie Rush
Cover Photo: author, age 14 mo.

Printed in the United States of America

To the combat veteran medical corpsmen of the
United States Armed Services.
Exceptional skill. Uncommon valor.

The author, circa 1957

Preface

I may be one of the most unlikely people to ever graduate from Northwestern University Medical School. I inherited attention deficit hyperactivity disorder from my mother's family and dyslexia from my father. When I was born, the syndrome of ADD/ADHD had not yet been recognized, and dyslexia was thought to consist only of an amusing oddity of speech. The more esoteric learning disabilities, of which I have a plethora, were completely unknown or only beginning to be explored by scientists. My parents noted early on that: I couldn't sit still, often did not seem to pay attention to what was said to me, and alternated between dreamy wandering and intense focus on something that inexplicably interested me. Probably because they were both teachers, Mom and Dad anticipated my entry into formal education with a good deal of dread. Their fears were well founded. In first grade, I was far below the achievement levels expected on standardized testing. A school administrator suggested the possibility of brain damage. This assessment resulted in consignment to the *slow track* instructional path and my introduction to thirteen years of educational torture.

After dropping out of college in 1967, the U.S. Army was eager to assist with my career choice and travel plans. What followed over the next ten years was an improbable series of adventures which culminated in acceptance to Northwestern University Medical School. This book is the story of my curious and circuitous path from brain damaged kid to medical student.

Table of Contents

Chapter I. Beginnings

Chapter II. Basic Training

Chapter III. Ft. Sam Houston

Chapter IV. The Pentagon

Chapter V. SIUE

Chapter VI. The Guad

Chapter VI. Summer of '74

Tail of the Dog

— Introduction —

I began this project with the intent of memorializing some frequently told stories and youthful adventures for my children. As the writing progressed, I took on several additional goals. I was encouraged by beta readers to describe in more detail what it feels like to navigate a world in which most other inhabitants play by a different set of rules and possess a different mental toolkit than I inherited. This required pulling back the curtain on aspects of my life I had not intended to share. I hope these stories will be beneficial to people who have differences in how they think and learn, such as I have, but don't yet believe the obstacles they face can be overcome.

Another intended purpose is to pay tribute to my brethren who served as combat medics. All of us who graduated from 91A10 medical corpsman training during the 1966-68 period served as subjects in an experiment to determine how much medical information and surgical skill could be taught to a nineteen-year-old soldier with no significant background in science, during a training program of only ten weeks. For our efforts, we earned a place in history that I don't think many of my Ft. Sam Houston classmates have ever realized. In combat, they performed procedures and made triage decisions previously reserved for physicians and surgeons. They solidified the value of aeromedical transport, and the benefit of having a medically trained crew to provide additional treatment during flight. The example provided by these men became the template for the creation of civilian trauma and emergency medical systems now used throughout the U.S.

For readers interested in a career in medicine and contemplating a path similar to my own, I believe I owe it to you to clearly convey this reality — the journey was sometimes dangerous, often unpleasant, and the outcome always uncertain.

I hope some of these stories help to describe the confusing array of information, opinions, events, voluntary choices, and involuntary demands that my generation experienced as we tried to grow into adulthood. Not surprisingly, some of the contradictions from that period of our national history have remained with us... and with American society.

The names of some individuals have either been changed or omitted for privacy. Others have been correctly identified in order to recognize their contributions to my life and career. My military experience included working at two highly secure locations. Regarding descriptions of that period, one must keep in mind the events occurred fifty years ago. Landscaping of the White House grounds, and the configuration of hallways and offices in The Pentagon have changed significantly since then, especially after the attack on 9/11. Although all of these stories are factual, I have altered or omitted a few locations and details as additional security precautions.

Likewise, the Autonomous University of Guadalajara has undoubtedly evolved significantly since I completed my first year of medical school in 1974. I have not returned there since, but my understanding is that conditions at the University, and in the city, now bear little resemblance to my experience in that distant past.

All of the stories in this book are taken from events occurring at least forty years ago. I have attempted to convey both the words and the emotions displayed in the context of the period described. Quotes are as close to verbatim as memory allows, but no one's memory is completely accurate. Incidents and circumstances are perceived and remembered differently by participants and observers. Although I have attempted to corroborate my recollection of public events through historical sources, most of these stories are personal experiences, and my perception of them. They belong solely to me.

I have omitted or substituted a few words from the narrative that would now be considered patently offensive, however I think efforts to sanitize history are misguided and dangerous. Readers who value political correctness over descriptive accuracy will, no doubt, find some subject matter objectionable. These stories are about how things were then, not how someone might wish they had been now.

I am dyslexic, and more than fifty years have passed since Margaret Warmbrodt tried to beat the rules of punctuation into my brain. I find the current plethora of recommendations contradictory and often nonsensical. I rely on commas, ellipses, and capitalized proper nouns to aid in the rhythm and associations of written information. The current trend of minimizing these cues makes comprehension of what I read, and the process of conveying my thoughts to the printed page, more difficult. The military stories are also from half a century ago. Abbreviations and rules of punctuation have changed, and several of the enlisted ranks, including my own, no longer exist. I have therefore chosen to stick with the military conventions of punctuation, capitalization, and rank I learned in 1967. On my arrival at The Pentagon, I was quickly instructed to capitalize the in all written references to the building. Until the DOD builds another one, it will always remain The Pentagon to me. My apologies to the arbiters of "proper writing." For better or worse, I write like I think.

And finally, I have relied on Mark Twain's advice to writers, "Tell the truth, or trump — but get the trick!"

Chapter I.   Beginnings

William Augustus Darnell,
circa 1900

Bertha Jane Miller,
circa 1905

— Heritage —

Apparently, I inherited some unconventionally arranged DNA, which may have been further impacted by my rather traumatic birth. It would not be inaccurate to say that I sort of skidded into life sideways, with a garbled set of instructions missing a few important paragraphs.

Aside from the genes I possess, the biggest impact on my life has been the social heritage gifted to me by my extended family. This book is a series of stories about the adventures I experienced while trying to turn the cards I was dealt at birth into a winning hand. My *genetic hand* may not have been all aces, but I also inherited a family who, by advice and example, showed me how to play those cards as best I could.

A friend once asked why I had made a particular choice in a matter of hospital politics and greed. I responded that in order to understand the answer to his question, he would need to have known my grandfather.

His reply was, "I don't have to know your grandfather. I know you."

For people who do not know me as well as Barry French did, what follows is an introduction to the actors who shaped my early life.

. . . .

My father was orphaned shortly after birth. Although his influence on me was considerable, his forebears and any biological siblings are a blank slate. His story will come next. My mother's family was her only dowry, and the polar opposite of Dad's. Heritage and tradition were rich and revered in the family, especially by her father.

William Augustus Darnell (Will) moved to Southern Illinois around the year 1900 from his birthplace near Lexington, KY. The Darnells are one of the *First Families* of Kentucky, having settled that wilderness with Daniel Boone in the 1770's. Grandpa was quite proud of his family history and maintained the manners and decorum of Old Kentucky throughout his lifetime.

Mom's mother, Bertha Jane Miller, was one of the youngest of thirteen children. After completing eighth grade at the top of her class, she returned to the same one room school the following term as teacher. She was fourteen years old, and the year was 1897. The next eleven years were filled with teaching, caring for ill family members, and one grand adventure out West, before she succumbed to the charms of the handsome man from Kentucky with the soft brown eyes and impeccable manners. The woman who would become my grandmother was then a bright and beautiful old maid of twenty-five and must have been considered quite a catch by the local bachelors. Her suitor had completed only three years of formal education, and financial success had so far eluded him, but he was intelligent, hard-working, imaginative, and ambitious, with a seriousness of purpose that attracted this bright, precociously independent-minded young woman with similar abilities and aspirations.

Will and Bertha married in 1908 and set up housekeeping in Fayette County, IL. Life was not easy for them. The promised opportunities in Illinois had not materialized for Grandpa. His new bride was a farmer, by instinct and ability, and encouraged her husband to give it a try. Will acceded to her wishes, but reluctantly.

In the second year of their marriage, my mother, Nellie, was born. Over the next eight years, four boys and one girl were added to the family: Rolland Leon (Rol), Jesse Ralph (Red), Helen Gertrude (Peg), (Lewis) Pope, and Richard (Paul). Grandpa worked long hours trying to coax a living from the marginal farmland available to him. Grandma tended the garden, managed the farm animals, and foraged in the woods for additional sources of food. She knew every plant in the Southern Illinois woodlands, including which were poisonous and which good to eat. As the eldest child, my mother spent most of her spare time caring for younger siblings. However, attending school, an activity regarded as a luxury by many rural families, was always a priority for the Darnell children. Country schooling was supplemented by reading at home and instruction provided by their mother.

Grandma was a prolific letter writer [...] also understood the concept of a teacha[...] before the idea became fashionable. The a[...] of the Miller and Darnell families with [...] shared at the dinner table, along with di[...] events, and the retelling of favorite (usu[...] the discussion related to events at a dist[...] required to find the corresponding locati[...] ly displayed in a central room. Grandma's favorite subject was always geography.

[Handwritten note:] Grandma would be happy you are doing geo... but disappointed you just listen to your dad @ dinner

Perhaps the most unusual characteristic of those conversations was the attitude of the parents regarding participation by the children. The opinion held by most people at the time was *children should be seen but not heard* when in the presence of adults. Grandma disagreed. Each of her children was encouraged to join in the discussion and describe his or her own experiences of the day. Their questions were answered forthrightly, and their opinions treated respectfully. Grandma believed, "when a child is old enough to ask a question, he or she is old enough to hear the answer." Careful observation and accuracy in reporting, appropriate to the age of the child, were expected, and the exercise of logic in reaching conclusions was prized most highly. Shortcomings in these markers were greeted with immediate laughter, but good-natured rather than mean-spirited, and provided a powerful stimulus to improve on those goals. I can only speculate, but I suspect the enlightened attitude toward children originated with Grandma. I'm told that Grandpa was a stern and traditional parent, however he accepted Grandma's opinions on childrearing and complied with her expectations. His contributions to the children's education, besides foregoing help in the fields during the times school was in session, were to demand unflinching honesty, to abide by respectful manners in debating ideas, and the importance of keeping one's word. Grandma had one other rule that perfectly matched my temperament as a child but got me into trouble regularly at school. If an adult corrected one of the children with a *do this* or *don't do that* type of declarative, and the child asked why or why not, it was impermissible in Grandma's domain to use *because I said so* as an answer. In my generation, if Grandma heard one of our parents, aunts, or uncles try to pull rank with that type of response, she would quietly say, "If you can't explain your reasoning to a child, your reason must not be very good." And, in our family, *no one* challenged Grandma.

In the early 1900's, country schools were generally mediocre, and travel was limited by the necessity of almost constant work. However, children were introduced to a wide world of ideas and experiences at the Darnell dinner table, and in the woods and fields beyond. I don't think anyone could have remained uneducated in the regular presence of my grandparents.

left to right: Rol, Peg, Red, Nellie
circa 1915

One should not assume the Darnell household was solely an oasis of serene thought, genteel conversation, and good works. Debate was lively and often loud. Only the difficult or tragic episodes were dealt with quietly. Grandma's philosophy was that life is hard, and fun should be indulged whenever possible. My mother's brothers were rambunctious and quite adept at finding mischief. Although Grandma and Grandpa both had dark chestnut hair, a Celtic streak ran through the Darnell lineage, and three of the eventual eight surviving kids bore the classic red mane of the Celts. Ralph was the first, and quickly acquired the nickname *Red*. By rights, his younger brother, Lewis (b. 1916), should have owned that descriptive. He had the reddest hair I have ever seen in my life! *It bordered on neon.* Baby sister Lola (b. 1924) was also a fiery redhead. All of my aunts and uncles had unique and very distinctive personalities, but the three with red hair always seemed larger than life and lived up to the rebellious reputation associated with their plumage.

According to my mother, home life was always a balance between Grandpa's expectations of decorum, and Grandma's insight and tolerance of the ways of children. Typical of an eldest child, Mom felt responsible for maintaining that equipoise. When I was a child, my cousins and I loved hearing our uncles retell the adventures of their youth, which we always thought were either amazing or hilarious. During those tales, Mom would often just sit there and shake her head in resignation.

By 1920, after several years of miserable weather and crop failures, Grandpa decided farming was not for him. With six children, and a seventh on the way, he took a job with the Egyptian Tie and Timber Company, supervising a crew cutting timber for railroad ties near the small town of Greenville, IL. Towards the end of that summer, a house was rented close to the work site, and the family moved to Bond County. Soon after their arrival, another daughter, Louella Faye was born.

The winter of 1920-21 was unusually harsh and deep snows came early. Grandpa and the new baby caught the Spanish flu, which had ravaged the world for the preceding two years. The nearest physician came to the house several days after being summoned by neighbors. He had ridden twelve miles on horseback because the snow was too deep for cars. By the time of his arrival, the baby had died, and Grandpa was delirious with fever. The doctor said people were dying all over the county, and he hadn't been home for three days. Neighbors simply tracked him down by word of mouth and informed him of the worst cases, so he could choose his next stop. The doctor concluded Grandpa had developed pneumonia. There was little to offer for treatment. His advice was to turn Grandpa in bed as often as possible and open the bedroom window to let in fresh air and help cool him. His final comment before leaving; if the fever broke, Grandpa might live, but if it persisted, he would most certainly die.

Logging had ceased for the winter. The woodsmen and their families were hunkered down on the rented tract of timber in temporary cabins built from pieces of wood and bark called slabs. These slabs were the first cuts applied to each side of the felled tree trunks to square their dimensions before cutting them into rail ties. The day after Louella Faye died, two of the woodsmen came to the house. They had built an oak coffin overnight for the baby. The snow was too deep for a hearse, so the men hitched a team of Belgian draft horses to a high-wheeled wagon used to haul logs out of the forest. The Belgians, accompanied by Grandma and a local minister, pulled the wagon and its small cargo through the drifts to a nearby cemetery for burial.

A few days later, Grandpa's fever broke. Over the next three months, he slowly recovered. By spring, he was back in the woods with the men.

. . . .

In 1922, Egyptian Tie and Timber moved their logging operation father west, following the railroad. Grandpa chose to stay in Bond County. He bought a used saw table and planing mill and began buying or leasing land with stands of hardwood timber throughout Southern Illinois and the Ozarks. His crew felled and limbed the trees, then used draft horses and sleds to drag the fallen logs to the nearest point negotiable by wagon. The logs were loaded onto the wagon and pulled by the horses to the nearest road. There, an ancient flatbed truck completed the journey to the mill. After arrival at the mill, most of the construction grade logs were rolled off the truck around the periphery of the property to await an order for specific sizes and quantities of sawed lumber. The mill was adjacent to Little Shoal Creek. Rains could be heavy in Southern Illinois, and the creek overflowed its banks several times each year. A stack of sawed lumber might disappear down the creek overnight during one of these rains. Intact logs usually didn't move very far, even when floated, and provided a barrier to prevent the escape of the stacks of newly-sawn lumber.

There was a steady market for specialty woods. Ash went to factories making baseball bats in Louisville and Chicago. White oak was cut into barrel staves, but since the bourbon distilleries in nearby Kentucky had closed or gone underground during Prohibition, the staves were shipped to France for wine barrels. Red oak was preferred for tongue and groove flooring in upscale homes, and walnut reserved for furniture manufacturers.

That year, William (Charles) was the newest addition to the family. He was followed in 1924 by Lola Mae, the last of nine children. The family lived frugally. Profits from the mill were reinvested in more land for logging. Even during the best of times, money was tight. Grandpa was a man of unbending principles, with a reputation for honesty and fair dealings with others. These traits made him a highly respected businessman and popular employer but didn't necessarily contribute to a profit margin. Mom and her siblings spent their childhood in a series of mostly rented houses around Greenville. Meanwhile, Grandpa, sometimes in partnership with his older brother John, slowly built up the inventory of undeveloped land and timber.

In 1928, Mom graduated from high school. She had reached the conclusion that hard work alone would not assure financial prosperity. Her father was living proof of that. In these modern times, a young person needed more of an education, and she was determined to get one. Sufficient money was found for tuition, and Mom enrolled at Greenville College, a small liberal arts school nearby. Her first year was everything she had hoped it to be, but by the summer of 1929, signs of the impending financial disaster were beginning to appear. Demand for hardwood was shrinking. Rol dropped out of high school to work at the sawmill, lowering Grandpa's labor costs, but there still wasn't enough money for Mom to continue her schooling. In an act of kindness, the college president arranged a job for her as a governess for a wealthy family at an estate in Missouri. During her one year of employment at Falicon, Mom saved most everything she earned, and with the help of a scholarship, resumed her education in 1930 at Johnson Bible College near Knoxville, TN.

Falicon - Clarksville, MO. circa 1928

That same year, Red convinced Grandpa to sign the waiver necessary to allow him to enlist in the Navy at age seventeen, although his birthdate had to be adjusted because he was actually still sixteen. On his first day in the Navy, an interviewer asked Red what he thought he might like to do in the Service.

Red shot back, "What pays the best?"

The Chief replied, "Well, the Submarine Service pays an extra $5 per month hazardous duty pay."

"Sign me up!" was my uncle's immediate response.

. . . .

Over the first few years of the Great Depression, Grandpa and Uncle John were unable to keep current on property taxes and all of the land they had accumulated was lost to tax sales. One by one, Mom's other brothers dropped out of school to look for jobs. By then, there was rarely enough work at the sawmill to engage the existing skeleton crew. Work was scarce, and times were hard. In 1933, Mom completed her degree in religious history and philosophy, but there weren't any more jobs for educated women than there were for able-bodied men. She moved back home to help Grandma while constantly seeking employment. In some months, not a single board foot of lumber was sold at the mill. The only sources of cash were selling butter from their milk cow, plus the military allotment Red sent home from his Navy pay.

After searching for a year, Mom found a job as a caseworker for a newly established federal program providing aid to destitute families. She hated the job, but the income helped keep the family afloat financially as the Depression dragged on.

In spite of these dire straits, Grandpa kept some men on the payroll at the sawmill because he felt their economic circumstances were even worse than his. To compound problems, the wife of one of his workmen died suddenly, and their two children were faced with going to an orphanage. When Grandpa announced the news one evening, Grandma's response was, "You bring those boys home with you tomorrow. They aren't going to any orphanage!" He did, and the boys stayed with our family until old enough to move out on their own. The lesson passed down was that doing the right thing wasn't always easy, but it was always expected.

For younger readers, who may have very little knowledge of the Great Depression, the effects of this catastrophe on the individuals who lived through it are difficult to understand. In a very short period of time, one quarter of the jobs in the United States ceased to exist. Hard working, highly motivated people could not find work anywhere. Many banks locked their doors and the assets they held simply disappeared, wiping out the life savings of their depositors. People like my grandfather lost homes and property, some of which was owned without indebtedness, simply because they couldn't afford the property taxes due each year. For average citizens, there seemed to be no safe haven. The terror and sense of helplessness these circumstances induced stayed with many people for the remainder of their lives. As a child twenty years later, my mother and Aunt Lola drove me like a rented mule. Anxiety remaining from the Great Depression was the reason why. The fear of once again losing everything never entirely left them.

In late 1941, Red was stationed at Pearl Harbor. He had been in the Submarine Service for eleven years. The Japanese attack on Dec. 7th caused immediate alarm for our family, and a seismic shift in the routine of daily life. Eventually, word was received that Red had been at sea during the attack and was still alive. The Navy, which had begun ramping up submarine construction before the war began, now desperately needed experienced officers to command these new boats. Red received a battlefield commission as an officer and started accompanying new subs and crews on their first wartime patrols in the Pacific.

Pearl Harbor Naval Base sometime prior to Dec. 7, 1941

Paul, impatient to try a new adventure, had joined the Royal Canadian Air Corps in 1940. He was allowed to transfer to the U.S. forces after we entered the war and served as an aircraft mechanic in the South Pacific. Rol, also an aircraft mechanic, was stationed in India. The youngest son, Charles, joined the Navy and volunteered for the Submarine Service, as his older brother had done. However, upon Charles' arrival at Pearl Harbor on the newly commissioned USS Razorback, Red wasn't allowed to escort his brother's sub on its first patrol. Relatives were not permitted to serve on the same submarine because of the risk of losing two members of a family at the same time.

Lola began dating a neighbor boy, LaMoine Brown, who was soon regarded as a de facto member of our family. After graduating from high school, Moine joined the Army, trained as an infantryman, and was assigned to Gen. George Patton's Army. Lola and Peg went to work for local companies producing war supplies. By then, my mother had moved to St. Louis for a job with the National Benevolent Association, a coordinating organization for the Disciples of Christ protestant churches.

The Darnell sawmill was designated a critical wartime industry. Contracts were signed to provide walnut blanks, called flitches, to various arms manufacturers for milling into rifle stocks. Suddenly, unemployment lines disappeared, and able-bodied men were in short supply for civilian employment. Accordingly, the family was offered a deferment for one son to help run the mill. Lewis was chosen, because he was the only one already married and with children of his own. In addition to Grandpa and Uncle Lewis, three local men beyond the limits of draft age, and another who was disabled by polio, now constituted the work force at the Wm. Darnell Lumber Company. From early 1943 until April 1944, this crew felled, milled, and shipped enough walnut timber to manufacture more than 200,000 gunstocks. Grandpa was sixty-nine years old.

Just do it! wasn't a sports slogan in our family. It was a way of life.

Uncle Lewis with a load of walnut

In 1945, Mom discovered that throughout the war, Grandpa had been selling walnut to the Army and its contractors at cost. He considered it his duty to help the war effort to the best of his ability, and felt it was unpatriotic for him, as a civilian, to make a profit from the enterprise. Consequently, he had been paying himself wages, just as he paid his employees, but without any percentage profit added to the invoices for the military. As a result, Grandpa was nearly as broke when the war ended as he had been when it began. He was now seventy years old, and he and Grandma were still living in a rented house.

Mom had an idea. She wrote to her brother, Rol, in India. If they pooled their savings, there would be enough to make the down payment on a house for their parents. After the war, if Grandpa couldn't keep up with the monthly payments, surely the eight children together would be able to contribute whatever was needed. Rol agreed, and on March 3, 1945, Mom signed the mortgage on a small farm just beyond the edge of Greenville. She then added Grandma's and Grandpa's names to the title. For the first time since the Depression began, Will and Bertha Darnell had a home of their own.

· · · ·

Over the course of the next year, all of my uncles came home. Miraculously, Mom's four brothers, plus Moine and another uncle to be, Marion Sussenbach, had all survived without physical injuries. Moine's brother, Benell, killed in the Battle of the Bulge, was the only person regarded as part of our extended family who had been lost in combat.

Red stayed at home for a few weeks, then returned to the Navy to continue his career. Paul joined a construction crew, building skyscrapers around the country. He took a job working *high steel*. It suited his skills and his temperament. He was agile and without any apparent sense of fear. Of equal importance to him, high above ground on those bare girders in a brisk wind, very few supervisors stopped by to tell him how to do his job. Rol and Charles joined their dad and brother, working in the timber and at the sawmill. Over the next few years, the unmarried siblings all gained spouses, and most started families, but the social center of gravity was still my grandparents, and the farmhouse at the east end of Main Street.

Christmas 1946.
Back row, left to right: Ralph (Red), Lewis, Rol, Paul, Charles
Front row: Lola, Grandma, Grandpa, Nellie, Gertrude (Peg)

— St. Louis Blues —

My parents met sometime in the latter half of 1945. They married in June 1946 and moved into an apartment in Edwardsville, IL. where Dad had a job teaching. Mom and Dad shared many interests besides their alma mater and religious faith, but their family backgrounds couldn't have been more different. Aside from religion, family was unquestionably the most important part of Mom's life. She regarded Dad as an addition to her existing family. For Dad, marriage presented an opportunity to create something he had never before experienced... a family of his own. But, suddenly becoming attached to the Darnell clan took some getting used to.

Dad's new family, 1946
Back row: left to right: Grandpa, Dad, Paul, Lewis
Front row: Jim, Billy, Jesse

Dad's early history is uncertain. His first memories were of living in a boardinghouse for boys run by two middle-aged, unmarried women. They told him that, as an infant, he had been left in their care by his parents, who needed to travel out of state for a family emergency. Allegedly, the parents never returned. (For a variety of reasons, this story is probably inaccurate.)

What *is* certain is that one morning at breakfast, a few months after his seventh birthday, the sisters announced, that because he was getting older, Dad was too much trouble and expense, and *would be going away that day.* (More likely, they had found a paying customer to take his bed.) Soon after, a county welfare agency worker appeared at the door. Unfortunately, there was no room available in the public orphanage, so Dad was taken to the St. Louis County Jail. For the next eight months, he lived in a holding cell in the basement of the jail with a group of other homeless orphans and boys who had been arrested but never claimed by family.

Old St. Louis County Jail 1955 (just prior to being razed)

He ultimately escaped this incarceration through adoption by a child-less couple struggling with a failed marriage. This new life, in the small town of Litchfield, IL, didn't prove easy, either. Predictably, the addition of a seven-year-old orphan did not improve the problems already present in the couple's relationship. Dad was described as a *sickly* child, and a skin test for tuberculosis was positive. The TB test result was presumed to explain his small stature and frequent bouts of illness. School had been hit or miss while at the jail, and he was plagued by stuttering and speech impediments common to dyslexia. These problems were interpreted as evidence of limited intelligence. Possibly, this combination of disadvantages influenced the attitude of his adoptive parents towards him. They didn't turn him out, as the boardinghouse women had, but the remainder of his childhood was characterized by ill-health, repressive rules of behavior, and emotional deprivation.

Dad was shy and reserved. He accepted his social circumstances, and the school's opinion that he wasn't very bright. His classmates teased him about his difficulties speaking, and his origins as an orphan. However, in spite of these challenges, he now had a place to live, and a chance to attend school regularly. He worked diligently to achieve an education because he believed it offered his best hope of escaping the environment so far experienced. Occasionally, other events also worked in his favor. A sympathetic Aunt and Uncle from his adopted family, Jess and Charlie Case, provided an emotional attachment that was lacking at home. Although his adopted mother allowed him only one friend, the boy chosen turned out to be a good one, and eventually, he was able to add another. Hiram Gooch, Garth Hendricks, and Dad maintained a close friendship for the remainder of their lives.

When it comes to people, quality beats quantity every time.

Dad graduated from high school, and with the help of a local church, was able to attend Johnson Bible College, the same school where Mom had received her diploma the previous spring. (At that point, they had not met.)

After graduation from Johnson, Dad entered Protestant seminary training and became an ordained minister, subsequently serving as pastor to a series of small, rural churches in Southern Illinois. As the Depression eased, a job teaching in the Edwardsville, IL public schools became available. This provided an important additional source of income.

When the U.S. entered WWII, Dad tried to enlist in the Army as a chaplain but was deferred because of his presumed medical history. When he protested the decision, the doctor who examined him said, "We need teachers and preachers at home, too. You just continue what you have been doing."

The facts of Dad's early life were revealed to me slowly over the course of my adult life. I did not learn the particulars of his childhood until I was twenty-nine years old. When I asked Mom why she hadn't told me the story long before, she explained that when Dad first described his childhood to her, during their engagement, he had asked that she never mention his background to anyone. His explanation was, "I just want to be normal." Dad's true medical history wasn't known, even to him, for several more decades. On review of his medical records while in his mid-fifties, there was no evidence he had ever had active tuberculosis. The positive skin test was probably gained during his time in the County Jail. He did, however, develop scarlet fever at some point in his childhood, complicated by inflammation of his heart and a chronically deformed mitral valve. Additionally, at the age of fourteen, he apparently suffered an episode of acute appendicitis. His adopted mother, who didn't believe in doctors, refused to seek medical attention. The result was a chronic appendiceal abscess, which wasn't discovered and removed until he was fifty-six years old. As it turned out, the man who was regarded as rather weak and sickly for the first fifty years of his life, was one of the toughest guys I have ever met, and the "Just do it!" approach to life clearly came from both sides of my family.

Charles E. Turner, circa 1923

— Trouble —

Some folks have observed that I began causing trouble before I was born. I am in no position to disagree. I arrived, pretty much on schedule, one year after my parent's marriage, although not much else about my debut went as expected. During her pregnancy, Mom developed steadily worsening high blood pressure. While in labor, she went into a coma, a pregnancy-related complication called eclampsia. At its most severe, eclampsia can cause permanent brain and organ damage, or death, for both the mother and infant. I was initially judged to have survived this tumultuous entry unscathed, but on the morning after my delivery, the doctor said to Dad, "You had better start figuring out what to do with this baby, because I don't think your wife is going to survive."

Mom remained in a coma for several days and was in the hospital for a number of weeks. In the interim, I went home to Grandma Darnell and the house at the end of Main Street. Mom eventually recovered, and within a few more weeks felt strong enough to assume my care. By that time, I had bonded to Grandma. I didn't recognize this misplaced phenomenon of infancy until I began paying close attention to the early development of my own children, many years later. With the exception of my mother, I don't think other family members were aware of this turn of events, either. However, for the remainder of her life, Grandma Darnell was the most important person in mine.

In recent years, a correlation has been noticed between several of the identified learning disabilities and a history of conditions during pregnancy or delivery, such as eclampsia, that may potentially cause periods of low oxygen levels in the baby.

One of my earliest memories is from December 3, 1950. At 4:00 p.m. the previous afternoon, a tornado struck Grandma and Grandpa's farm.

The wind demolished a small shed, no more than twenty feet from the house, and pulled the barn off its foundation. A neighbor watched the funnel cloud lift the roof of the barn about one hundred feet into the air. It then drifted over an adjacent field before suddenly dropping to the ground, where it shattered as if having exploded.

The house twisted on its foundation, interior door frames warped, and a portion of the upstairs ceiling buckled, but the old home remained otherwise intact. Grandma was in the middle room, reading, when the storm struck. She had developed increasing deafness since middle age and didn't hear the storm coming. Years later, she told me that she glanced through the kitchen door as the tornado passed the house, and realized she was now looking at the pasture, a view previously blocked by the shed.

The entire family gathered the following day to begin cleaning up the mess. My memory is of walking around the field where the barn roof had landed, picking up whatever pieces of splintered wood I could carry, and throwing them onto a large bonfire built for that purpose. My cousin Billy, four years my elder, was assigned to supervise my efforts. I remember the tug of his hand holding onto the back of my overalls, so I wouldn't fall into the fire, as I contributed small pieces of wood to the conflagration. Although two people were killed and twenty-five injured in the storm's path through Greenville, our family was very fortunate. The property destruction we experienced could all be repaired or replaced.

One loss from the storm became an oft-told family story. A milk cow had gone into the barn shortly before the tornado hit. When the building was uprooted, the cow's spine was dislocated near the middle of her back, but she was left standing on the site of her former home. Aside from her rather odd new silhouette, the shock to her psyche must have been considerable... she never gave milk again.

Dec. '50

Site of the former barn is in the foreground,
The house is in the background

About six weeks after the tornado, Mom and I were at Grandma and Grandpa's for the weekend. Billy had stayed overnight with us, much to my delight. Early Saturday morning, he and I were in the kitchen anxiously awaiting breakfast. Grandpa came in from doing the outdoor chores and sat down in a chair by the back door. He called to my mother, saying, "Nellie, will you help me take my boots off?"

Mom went to him, knelt, and began unlacing his boots. Grandpa leaned over, as if to say something, but his torso continued its forward arc until he landed on Mom's back. She called out to her mother, who was at the stove. Grandma hurried over and lifted Grandpa sufficiently for Mom to crawl out from under him. He wasn't moving or talking. The two women grasped his upper arms and dragged him into the middle room to a sofa. As they started to move him, Grandma looked up at Billy and me, still standing motionless in the doorway, and said, "Now, you children stay out of the way."

I had *never* heard my grandmother use that tone of voice before. We didn't understand what was happening, but clearly, it wasn't good.

A local doctor was called. Soon, we noticed a hearse coming up the lane. This was decades before dedicated ambulance service was available. Local mortuaries sometimes provided their hearse for emergencies when a stretcher was needed. My older, and wiser, cousin had nearly died six months before of a ruptured appendix. Upon glimpsing the ambulance, he said, "I know what that is. That's an ambulance! They take you to the hospital. I'm getting out of here!"

He bolted for Grandma and Grandpa's bedroom with me in hot pursuit. We hid in the closet and peered around the door, continuing to observe the proceedings. The two men attending the hearse lifted Grandpa onto a stretcher, then maneuvered it back through the kitchen and out the door. The last time we saw our Grandpa, we were looking through his bedroom window as the mortuary attendants slid the gurney through the rear door of the hearse. He had suffered a brain hemorrhage and never regained consciousness; dying six weeks later of pneumonia. Years later, while comparing our memories of that day, Mom remarked, "When he asked me to take off his boots, I knew something was wrong. My dad had never asked me to do anything for him in his life that he could do for himself."

. . . .

After Grandpa's death, the first question to be resolved was where Grandma would live. Although only sixty-seven, she was quite deaf and beginning to lose her sight from macular degeneration. She had narrowly avoided death in the tornado because of these limitations. On the other hand, she had now been in this home for nearly six years, the longest period of time in one place during her entire married life. Grandma was a farmer at heart. The house was surrounded by flowerbeds, the garden covered almost one acre, and there would soon be a new barn with chickens and one terrorized cow. She loved this place and refused to go anywhere else.

For her, there was only one reservation. As a child, her immediate family numbered thirteen. She left home at the age of fifteen to live with and care for the four children of an ailing older sister. Marriage to Will came soon after, followed by nine children of her own. She was not looking forward to living alone. A solution was soon crafted. Lola and Moine, now married, were assuming responsibility for a Ford Tractor dealership and would be quite busy. They offered to buy the groceries if Grandma would make dinner each evening. As things worked out, they frequently stayed until bedtime before leaving for their home, a few miles away.

One may wonder at the idea of a woman with serious impairments of both vision and hearing serving as the cook and caretaker of this property. These are examples of how independent and resourceful my grandmother was then and remained until beyond the age of ninety. The "Just do it" attitude was also shared by the women in my family.

There were now six grandsons. When Moine and Lola needed to be elsewhere, Billy and his older brother, Jim, would walk over from their house, do their homework under Grandma's tutelage, and stay overnight. Mom and I spent at least one weekend per month with Grandma, and after reaching school age, I became increasingly adept at finding reasons for additional days and weekends there. Two granddaughters and another grandson were added over the next few years. We helped her keep loneliness at bay and were blessed in return by her increased presence in our lives. Grandma was able to keep her farm, and the stage for the remainder of my childhood was now set.

Grandma & us, Thanksgiving 1955

— Brain Damage —

What I am about to describe is a combination of events and feelings I can re-member from the ages of four and five, enhanced by what I have learned in the past twenty years of studying the atypical syndromes whose labels are now affixed to children like me. I could not clearly articulate the feelings associated with those experiences then. I am somewhat better at it now.

I retain a searing memory of the smell of fresh varnish on wooden floors, and the feeling that I was entering incarceration as I stepped through the door for my first day of kindergarten.

.   .   .   .

By the age of five, I was discovering that my brain behaved in very different ways at different times. Sometimes, I could focus on single thoughts or stimuli sequentially and methodically, like most other people do. During these periods, I was able to resist random distractions but still shift my attention to a new, higher priority stimulus, such as my mother calling me. At other times, I could not seem to focus on anything! My consciousness was dominated by random memories, or the visual stimuli around me, all of which drifted by in a blur. My attention might even be drawn briefly to a color, texture, or pattern in my environment, but thoughts were mostly limited to sensations, not words. This mental state was relaxing and pleasant unless interrupted. If left undisturbed, I would exit my reverie slowly, like floating to the surface from deep underwater. When in this dreamy state, sounds were distant and muted, just as they are underwater. I could easily miss that same call from Mom. I would be vaguely aware of her voice, but somehow, it didn't penetrate far enough into my consciousness to trigger the recognition that this was a stimulus requiring a response. I would continue wandering about in my garden of sensation until she appeared directly in front of me with the usual question, "Jim! Did you hear me?"

This presented a considerable dilemma. We lived in a four room, six hundred square foot house. You could hear someone whisper in the next room. So, if I answered no, I was either deaf or lying... or so it would appear. If I answered, yes... well you can imagine.

Alternatively, I might occupy a very different mental environment in which I felt so excited that I could not sit still. Everything I encountered was interesting... at least for a moment... and usually not much longer. During these periods, I couldn't focus on anything, even favored activities, for more than a few minutes. My mind compelled me to search the surroundings for new objects of interest. After a short period, this quest for repetitive mental stimulation would evolve into an overwhelming urge for movement. I simply could not remain still. Sitting did not provide sufficient mechanical stimulus and *sitting still* would have required general anesthesia. I needed to *run*, or at least jump up and down. However, the practicalities of running or jumping in that small house meant almost as sure a path to trouble as ignoring a maternal summons. From experience with several of her younger brothers, Mom knew the only source of relief, for both of us, was outside... rain, shine or snow. Physical activity was usually an effective means of consuming the excess energy generated by my hyperactive urges and wasn't nearly as annoying to others as if I was confined to the same enclosed space they were inhabiting. Sometimes, Mom didn't even say anything. She would just silently open the door and stare at me patiently.

Rounding out my palette of cognitive variety was a phenomenon now associated with ADD called hyper-focus. This occurred, also unpredictably, when my attention was powerfully drawn to a thing or a thought. It was like suddenly changing my view from wide angle to high magnification. When hyper-focused, my mind felt nimble, rather than just fast. It scrambled over the terrain of information related to the source of interest, examining everything, then placing the pieces into a four-dimensional map of interaction and evolution. As I absorbed this information, the various pieces would assemble themselves in my mind, and I could see how potential interactions were likely to unfold. However, while in this state, I was oblivious to anything external to the subject of my attention. Interruptions of my thought process while hyperfocused would fragment my carefully constructed mental image, like kicking over a house of toy blocks. Re-establishing the details of the set, and the degree of concentration needed to make the movie restart, usually proved impossible. The intrusion causing this disruption invariably made me irritable. The combination of my oblivion to the adults around me and their commands, plus my irritability when interrupted, predictably led to conflicts. These same adults invariably presumed they outranked me; an assumption I did not necessarily share. Consequently, I was often regarded as "a willful child;" a descriptive not meant to be a compliment.

The syndrome of ADD/ADHD would not become widely recognized until the book Driven to Distraction *by Ratey and Hallowell was published forty years later.*

Dec. '44

By comparison, my parents were remarkably flexible in coping with the challenges of my idiosyncrasies. When I was in the midst of a hyper-focused examination of some curiosity in the back yard or circling that yard at a high rate of speed to burn off energy, unless we needed to depart for an appointment or the house was on fire, they usually found small delays in the daily schedule, while I completed these tasks, well worth the wait. The alternative of dealing with a cranky kid who possessed a voracious appetite for activity represented far greater downside potential than giving me a little more time to finish whatever I was doing or thinking about. Besides, when I was consumed by one of these hyper-focused periods, at least I was quiet.

Probably the only thing that helped Mom overcome the temptation to drown me, was *her* childhood experience of being the first born of nine, with five younger brothers. Her brothers drove her crazy, but she loved them dearly. Now, here was one more dreamy, impetuous, indescribable little boy in her life.

· · · ·

If I could have exercised any control over my varying states of cognition, they might have been a hell of a lot of fun! Unfortunately, the realm which my mind happened to occupy at any given moment was completely involuntary in those early years. Two things were clear: First, the existence or frequency of any of these states was not related to sleep, or lack thereof. I had a decidedly uncharacteristic sleeping pattern for a young child. Eight or nine hours per night was usually more than enough for me, even as a toddler. In fact, I literally couldn't sleep longer than nine hours under usual circumstances, and when I had absorbed this much rest, my battery was charged for the day! Mom had given up trying to make me take naps at the age of eighteen months, after I flung myself over the end of a bed and landed on my head in an attempt to escape an enforced nap time.

My parent's second observation, made with a considerable degree of certainty, was that my peculiarities offered unending opportunities for trouble in the regimented system of 1952-era public education.

. . . .

As a child beginning the task of social integration, the implications of my mental kaleidoscope were bewildering and frightening. Whether or not I unconsciously sensed the concerns of my parents, I certainly anticipated the start of school with dread. Almost daily, well-intentioned, coaching from them usually began, "Now, when you are in kindergarten, you will have to...." This only amplified my fears. As the school year approached, I became increasingly alarmed that I would not be a good *fit* with formal education. Two hours of Sunday school and church each week strained the limits of my ability to sit still and be quiet. How was I ever to manage four hours of kindergarten, five days a week? In kindergarten, I wouldn't be able to go outside and run around when I felt the engine of my hyperactivity race car roar to life. What would I do if the teacher wanted us to perform some task requiring concentration, when my mind was in that dreamy state where I couldn't focus on anything in particular? Coloring within the lines could be *hard*! Worse yet, I would have to take naps. I soon reached the same conclusion my parents had. School was likely to be a problem.

There were other challenges as well. According to my mother, the expectations of our social circles were a bit greater for me than most other kids my age. During the week, Dad was a schoolteacher, but he was also an ordained minister. On Sundays, we traveled to Atwater, IL, a small, rural community fifty miles distant, where he served as pastor of the only local church. Well before I was old enough for school, Mom had explained to me that teachers *and* preachers were looked upon with respect by other members of the community. Because of this notoriety, people sometimes paid particular attention to their families as well. The punchline was that any public misbehavior on my part would reflect badly on Dad, and we certainly didn't want that, did we. The comment was not voiced as a question.

Opinions and standards have changed considerably in the intervening sixty-five years, but in those days, a high school diploma was a proud possession, and people with college degrees were all treated with a measure of respect, although possibly a little more so for teachers and ministers. Mom's statement regarding public scrutiny certainly wasn't a delusion of grandeur. There was an enhancement to this public scrutiny on the playground, where we were labeled as PK's (preacher's kids) and TK's (teacher's kids) and singled out for teasing and taunting.

My suspicions regarding school were soon confirmed. At a get-acquainted meeting the evening before classes began, the parents were directed to send a small rag carpet to school with their student for nap times. The following morning, the boys marched to school with carpet rolls tilted against their right shoulders like rifle-bearing miniature soldiers. I suppose this high stepping little platoon was an endearing sight to many parents. For me, I might as well have been dragging a cross to Golgotha. (I don't recall how the girls carried their carpets, but they certainly didn't play soldier, like the boys did. Times have changed.) On that first day, and those to follow, I could *not* fall asleep during nap time. The teacher complained to my mother that, rather than sleep, I rolled around so vigorously I kept the other children awake.

Additional hurdles soon appeared. Whenever the teacher was giving us directions for our next assignment, my attention invariably wandered out the large windows; to a bird, or a tree, or a cloud beckoning me toward the freedom beyond. If I avoided looking out the windows, the voices of children racing through the hallway to recess proved equally distracting. Even when focused and paying attention, I *still* got into trouble. In learning about sharp objects, my family followed a pragmatic philosophy. Give the kid a knife or pair of scissors dull enough to only inflict cuts, not amputations. A few minor wounds would teach the fundamentals of safety with these implements far more efficiently than adult instruction ever could. I had been using scissors, unsupervised, for at least a year. During a brief interlude when I mistakenly thought that I was actually absorbing the teacher's instructions, she explained that the next activity would be to cut out the shapes we had traced on pieces of colored paper earlier in the day. My immediate reaction was, *Ha! I can do that!* As she hovered over a series of clumsy little urchins chosen for observation before reaching my desk, my next thought was, *why should I wait?* I began cutting out the traced images. *Wrong again!* Apparently, I had missed the part of the instructions about waiting for the teacher to arrive at each individual's desk before using the scissors. At the subsequent parent-teacher conference, the assessment was, *Jim doesn't seem to pay attention to instructions.*

. . . .

If it had been possible to flunk kindergarten, I'm sure I would have. However, in spite of nine months of failed attempts at educational regimentation and behavior modification, I was sent on to first grade.

In those days, I didn't understand and couldn't describe the four distinct realms of conscious thought that my mind might be inhabiting at any given time. And, I certainly had no idea why my inner world seemed to be in a different orbit than the people and organizations that ruled my universe. However, I was beginning to notice norms of behavior and social performance the other children seemed to accomplish with little effort, did not come naturally to me. What appeared as a reasonable and appropriate choice to me, whether in response to a classroom question, or a sudden urge to climb a tree, was frequently judged the wrong answer by the authorities. My growing recognition of these schisms created a self-perception that I was different than most other children; not special, just different.

— Time and Effort —

In 1953, the new big idea in education was that slow students held back the progress of gifted ones. Shortly after beginning first grade, and completing a rather perfunctory skills evaluation, we were assigned to educational tracks: gifted, average, or slow. My parents were informed that I had trouble learning, and the question was raised of possible brain damage. Because of Mom's history of eclampsia, she and Dad thought the brain damage theory quite plausible. It helped explain some of my behavioral eccentricities, as well as my inability to progress in reading, writing, or using numbers. However, they resisted the suggestion that I might be better suited for the group then referred to as *educable mentally handicapped.* These poor devils were completely segregated from the other students and rode a short yellow bus each day to an unknown destination. At my parent's insistence, I was mainstreamed with the normal students and assigned to the slow group, or *Dumb Track,* as we referred to ourselves.

Once the learning tracks had been established, the seating arrangement was reordered accordingly. Our group was moved to a rear corner of the room, further separated by a bookshelf. After this relocation, I remember the teacher telling us that as long as we kept quiet, and didn't disturb the other children, things would be fine. But, if we caused trouble or made noise... The remainder of the threat was communicated by a glare. Very little effort was applied to our instruction for the remainder of the year.

There was one consistency to my scholastic record during those early years. I failed everything the school system measured. In fact, probably the only reason that I, and virtually all of my colleagues in the Dumb Track, were passed on to second grade was because a new, equally large group of incoming first graders were awaiting our seats. The report cards diplomatically labeled most of my results as, *Time and effort needed to develop.* Although the intellectually segregated seating arrangement was relaxed in second grade, efforts to teach those of us deemed unpromising remained minimal. Our first-grade teacher had moved on to second grade with us, and her commitment to our instruction was unchanged. With the exception of reprimands for behavioral sins, she acted as if we weren't there, and questions from those of us in the lower caste were treated as unwelcome interruptions. We were simply empty chairs to her. In spite of this lack of focused instruction, near the end of the school year, I learned to read. This new skill developed rapidly and certainly without any assistance from the teacher. Up until then, I had seen only uninterpretable groups of letters. Now, those letters began to arrange themselves into recognizable words, and the words formed sentences that I could understand.

Just as my written language processing began to improve, we started reading a book about a wolf. In an interval that seemed like no more than one or two weeks, I progressed from being unable to read, to being impatient with the reading pace of my classmates. Each day, the other students took turns reading portions of the book aloud to the class. Those of us in the slow track were rarely, if ever, called upon. I was fascinated by the story, and wanted to know: *What was going to happen to that wolf?* I began reading ahead during these exercises. This seemed pretty safe, since the teacher generally ignored those of us on the back of the bus. One day she called on me, then immediately hesitated, as she realized her mistake. I was several pages ahead of the class at this point and didn't know which page they were on, so I also hesitated.

Within these few seconds, the teacher said, "Oh, never mind." and called on another student to continue. I desperately wanted to demonstrate that I could read. I glanced at the book of the girl sitting next to me, turned to the correct page, and found the proper paragraph. Just as the other child began, I also started reading aloud. The other student stopped, uncertain of what to do. Determinedly, I continued.

At the end of the designated section, the teacher said, "Why Jim, you read quite well!" Prior to this outburst, the teacher had been completely unaware of my progress. Foolishly, I thought this example would lead to more opportunities for me to participate in the reading exercises reserved for the normal kids. Silly me. I don't think the teacher called on me again for the remainder of the year.

In the educational system, once a label is affixed, the ink is usually indelible.

This incident in second grade was prophetic. During most of my twelve years in public school, I usually felt as though I was on the wrong page. Unfortunately, my mercurial attention span and difficulty sitting still were poorly suited to traditional teaching methods. As I labored through the lower primary grades, other aspects of the instructional standards presented more obstacles. In the elementary grades, the principle goal was the memorization of groups of facts or *building blocks*. The organizational plan was for these bits of information to be incorporated into a framework of knowledge at some point in the future. If a child happened to be thinking too far ahead and asked a prescient question, the response was usually, *You'll learn that next year*. This structure and presentation of information was the converse of how I learn best. I need to establish the relationship of the question to the framework of the subject, before I can make sense of the individual pieces of information. This method of organizing and incorporating new facts is a peculiarity of dyslexia.[1] An analogy would be a bricklayer who cannot figure out what to do with a pile of bricks until he sees the blueprint for the building. Unfortunately, I didn't discover an explanation of this trait until fifty-eight years after my head-on collision with the brick wall of the public school system.

To make matters worse, I have additional oddities associated with processing information. For instance, I input new data most efficiently

---

[1] *Eide, B and Eide, F, The Dyslexic Advantage Penguin Group (USA), 2012*

[2] *In the military, the term Command refers to an administrative unit comprised of members from multiple Services and/or civilians who are responsible for a large administrative task, usually affecting multiple Service lines or geographic areas. All members of the Command*

while moving. Educational theorists now describe this as kinetic learning. In the 1950's, the behavioral characteristics of: an inability to sit still for prolonged periods, difficulty paying attention on command, and continual fidgeting in your seat while thinking, were interpreted as misbehavior or stupidity.

Once I learned to read, it became my escape. I found that I didn't get in as much trouble if I was caught reading, as I would if engaged in more frivolous activities, such as my personal favorite, gazing out the window at cloud formations. Learning to read helped me in other ways, as well. With the exception of math, most subjects contained sufficient written instructions for me to gain an approximation of the goals to be accomplished. I might not be able to pay attention to the verbal instructions in class, but I could read the abbreviated version in the book, at my own pace... later. This usually provided sufficient information for me to bluff my way to a passing grade. Unfortunately, this workaround was a fail for math. Mathematics is described in symbols, from a language that I have never understood. More baffling, I couldn't seem to consistently arrive at correct answers in math, even for the basic processes which I thought I understood. Exercises and test papers invariably consisted of rows and columns of problems to be solved. My papers were usually returned with red slashes and circles, indicating incorrect answers, strewn across the page like crimson dandelions on an unkempt lawn. When the teacher or one of my parents reviewed the mistakes with me, I could often produce the correct answer.

At first, this elicited the response, "See, you know how to work these problems. Next time, do them just like this."

But, the next time, my results would be no better.

Eventually, the teacher, or my mother, would say something like, "*Jim!* You just aren't paying attention. Why else would you make so many mistakes, when you know how to do the work?"

I was at least as mystified and frustrated as they were, but I was guilty as charged of the accusation of not paying attention. The part of math that I hated the most was the repetition. We would do pages and pages of problems, all of them redundant. It was deathly boring! And, repetition clearly wasn't improving my results. At first, I really tried. I would force myself to stare at the pages of numbers, and work the problems repeatedly, until my eyes burned and my head ached. If I worked the same problem twice, I frequently arrived at a different answer the second time. Then, I would become even more confused and uncertain. At some point, I usually gave up. My most vivid memories of math homework are the frustration of persistent failure, and the headaches that would invariably develop as I attempted the problems over and over.

. . . .

I did learn one thing from these serial episodes of frustration. Up until then, the various states my mind might occupy seemed to be completely random and unpredictable. Now, I discovered that when presented with schoolwork that predictably resulted in failure, my mind would slide into a variation of that dreamy state where I couldn't concentrate on anything. Although my naturally occurring dreamy periods were relaxing and pleasant, these *induced* dreamy episodes were characterized by agitation and severe distractibility and were distinctly unpleasant. I just wanted to wander away and go sit under a tree until my brain could recalibrate. If recess happened to interrupt the punishment, allowing me to escape the classroom, I would sometimes seek refuge in the dense woods bordering one side of our playground. The exposed root of one of the majestic hardwoods residing there provided a seat from which I could stare at the ground, trying to minimize external stimuli. The brown color of the earth was somehow soothing. Eventually, an ant or other small trespasser, crawling across my visual field, would attract my attention, and I could slowly return to a receptive state for more demanding stimuli. My experience in school was continuing to confirm the anxieties I had felt before entering kindergarten. I had no idea why, but school presented an unending maze of questions with confusing, illogical answers that made little sense to me.

Interestingly, I found an explanation for my arithmetic misery forty years later when my daughter was suffering through the same experience in school. A wise math teacher reviewed several of her papers and suggested that she might have ADD, which we soon confirmed. People with ADD scan written information, as soon as it enters their field of vision, even their peripheral fields. This activity occurs in milliseconds, is involuntary, and subconscious. Some of this information is absorbed and processed, even if it has nothing to do with the subject of their primary focus of attention. Bits and pieces of this extraneous data may be incorporated into whatever the person was thinking about immediately before the distraction. The teacher suspected that my daughter was unconsciously transposing numbers from elsewhere on the page when trying to work individual problems. He said that kids with ADD have particular difficulty with standard arithmetic worksheets composed of columns and rows. His solution was a piece of cardboard with a cutout just large enough to expose only one problem at a time. He instructed me to place the cardboard over Heather's math paper, so she could only see the problem she was working on, then move it to the next problem upon completion. Her math grades went from C's and D's to A's, overnight. Here was the explanation for some of my own struggles with arithmetic. This insight was too late for me, but it had a huge impact on my daughter, and her success in school.

— **You're Not Stupid** —

Mercifully, 3rd grade brought a new teacher, who was young, enthusiastic, and worked diligently to undo the damage inflicted during the previous two years. If she thought I was slow, she never acted like it. In fairly short order, I mastered addition, subtraction and multiplication. By the end of the school year, we had reached long division, and I was actually performing better than some of my classmates. No doubt, some of the improvement was related to my recalcitrant brain finally maturing to the point that I was capable of learning the material, but I am also certain that the one-on-one attention and encouragement she contributed helped me significantly.

The following year, my luck with teachers once again turned south. Our teacher for fourth grade was *old school*. Her methods were long on repetition and short on creativity. If she felt a student was not exerting sufficient effort, her repertoire of corrective actions was limited to two. The first was to humiliate the offender in front of the entire class. The alternative was corporal. She patrolled the aisles like a drill sergeant, while clutching a wooden ruler like a DI's baton. Inattention or misbehavior by one of us boys earned a slashing downward blow from the edge of the ruler to the back of your hand that would have decapitated a chicken. Maybe she *had* been a drill sergeant? As best I can remember, the girls were spared the ruler, or at least the sharp edge of it. If one of them was found committing a minor transgression, a hand would dart out like a cobra, grasp a handful of the offender's hair, and give it a sharp yank.

Although I was now having a smattering of success in some subjects, I was still labeled as intellectually slow. Eventually the Drill Sergeant noticed my uneven performance and shared her opinion regarding the cause. While handing back test results for a project on which I had received an A, she announced in front of the class, "Why Jim, you're not stupid! You're just lazy!"

I remained assigned to the Dumb Track.

There were some good teachers at that school, and many of my classmates have fond memories of them. Some students would include teachers, who had a negative impact on me, amongst their favorites. Undoubtedly, I needed teachers with exceptional skills during those early years, and exceptional teachers were in short supply. Four of my first five teachers were ill-equipped to deal with a student such as me. If I had been the only person who did not fit the expected mold, I would regard it as just my tough luck. However, five or six other students in my class were similarly banished. We represented almost twenty-five percent of the class. At the level of the school district administration, I don't think the intended policy was to neglect our education, but the inadequacies and personal prejudices of individual teachers weren't monitored and had a negative impact on a significant number of students.

Beginning in 4th grade, my report cards contained a new criticism. *Jim doesn't respect authority.* Since both of my parents were teachers, conversation at our dinner table often revolved around their work. Although they were very careful not to criticize other teachers in the presence of my inquisitive little ears, I quickly learned to read between the lines. By 4th grade, I could read a teacher like a book—and I often found the book wanting. Respect them, *hell!* I may have been precocious in my assessments, but even at that age, I thought the mental acuity and teaching methods of some of our teachers contemptible. They certainly fell far below the example set by Grandma Darnell.

I was increasingly aware that school was filled with illogical rules and procedures, most of which were tilted against me. I was slowly beginning to understand that I could only concentrate on a specific subject when my mind felt *prepared* to take on the task. I didn't yet understand the association of this feeling to my unpredictable ability to focus, and I certainly didn't recognize my unusual sensitivity to how information was formatted, details of critical importance to kids with dyslexia.

However, I was becoming increasingly adept at recognizing tasks that would be futile for me to attempt at a particular moment. It seemed logical to me that as long as I accomplished the work by some point in the foreseeable future, the exact timing of my efforts should be immaterial. It also seemed illogical for a teacher to demand my best work and expect it to be produced when I knew I was not at my best. My idiosyncrasies did not blend well with standardized instruction, but their accommodation is absolutely essential for someone whose mind works in fits and starts, like mine does. These insights would eventually allow me to recognize some alternative explanations for my failures at school, other than just being stupid or lazy, but this knowledge was still decades away. In the 1950's, the only opinions offered by most of my teachers inferred inferiority in some aspect of my intellect or personality.

Driving *these* teachers crazy became my form of rebellion. I channeled much of my frustration with school into the process of pushing a mediocre teacher's buttons, and I got really good at it. This represented an evolution of the survival instinct I had initially sensed in 1st grade. When you are told repeatedly as a child that you are inferior, that you are bad or lazy, it is very difficult to resist assuming those roles. Even then, I sensed there were two choices available for those of us who had been prematurely banished. We could either accept the pronouncement of the authority figures, or we could resist. Initially, we weren't prepared to exclaim aloud, "No! You are wrong! I am not *all* bad. I am not inferior, or if I am, I *still* have some value!" We could only think it, if we dared do even that.

But after nine months with the Drill Sergeant, I was far less intimidated by teachers and began perfecting more direct means of resistance. If teachers were going to pronounce me dumb, I was going to do my best to expose their lack of imagination and effort in teaching. Some of my mates in the Dumb Track, mostly the boys, were also becoming less intimidated by teachers and more disruptive in class. In retrospect, I think their motivation shared elements with my own; frustration over the arbitrary pronouncements by school officials that we were less than the other students, not only in performance, but also in social value. In accordance with the social norms of the time, the girls in our little band of misfits simply suffered in silence.

I didn't dare be physically disruptive in class, as the other boys sometimes were. Dad had been promoted into an administrative job in the school district by then. Any physically disruptive behavior attributed to me would have been very awkward for him. My resistance had to be subtle. A strategically timed question that interrupted the class with laughter worked quite well. Although, I needed to devise an at least remotely plausible explanation for these unwelcome classroom questions or comments by dinnertime the same evening. Part of Dad's job involved traveling from school to school on an almost daily basis, and teachers rarely failed to report my transgressions during those visits. The mother of one of my friends was fond of saying that bad news always beats you home. I had ample experience with that homily.

There was another benefit to my classroom jousting with unpopular teachers, such as the Drill Sergeant. If I thought of something funny to say in class, people laughed, and they would talk to me at recess and lunchtime. Although I often felt like an outsider, it wasn't a role I sought. I desperately wanted to fit in, just like everyone else. I had managed to make some friends at school but remained unnoticed by most of my classmates. Now, my verbal sparring with unpopular teachers raised my visibility with the other kids and improved my popularity with some. This was a big step up.

I now understand that combativeness with these teachers was a subconscious response to my limited ability to adjust to the regimentation of the classroom. I didn't know why I was different than most of my classmates, but this resistance represented a first attempt to modulate my environment in order to compensate for those differences. I was also beginning to realize that when in the proper frame of mind, I could perform some tasks surprisingly well. I might feign nonchalance or in-difference, but in reality, *I hated* to do poorly on any assignment.

Since gaining my own experience as an adult and a parent, I marvel at Mom and Dad's patience. In those days, some people would have beat their kid half to death for causing them as much trouble as I caused mine. My parents were no fools. They may not have understood the reasons for my frustration, but they knew the purpose of my disruptive questions. Fortunately, they both possessed a well-developed sense of humor and enjoyed subtle word play. Sometimes, I think they may even have been impressed with my ingenuity.

But occasionally, Dad would say, "I understand your frustration, but could you tone it down a little. I'm getting a lot of complaints."

He had the proverbial patience of Job.

.   .   .   .

Regrettably, most of my mates in the Dumb Track internalized the judgment of the school authorities. A significant number of us were not dumb. We were simply in a different developmental time zone. How-ever, the stigma of our academic segregation remained. I was saved be-cause my family prized critical thinking, my parents resolutely believed in the value of education, and I had enough emotional resilience to par-tially withstand the subtle but repetitive slights from the teachers. But, over those first few years, I watched many of my friends become in-creasingly detached from the learning process. They were deprived of the *true* building blocks of early education. For them, the natural love of learning new things, inherent in almost all children, was extinguished. And for all of us, whether we rebelled or not, the accusation of inferiori-ty was indelibly imprinted on school records and on our perceptions of ourselves.

— Deaf and Dumb —

Until the age of seventeen, I had always assumed I would join one of the Darnell family businesses as my vocation. I certainly had no desire to choose either of Dad's careers as a teacher or minister. Although my first choice was the sawmill, by my thirteenth birthday, it was already sliding into oblivion due to changes in building techniques and the growing scarcity of hardwoods.

Farming was another option. Mom's sister, Peg, had married a farmer. From the time I was small, whenever we visited them, I would follow Uncle Marion around the farm while he did chores. As soon as I was old enough to hang onto the fender of a tractor unaided, I began going to the fields with him, as well.

Uncle Marion, Aug. 1967

Mom's other sister, Lola, was also involved in farming. She and her husband, Moine, combined farming with managing the local Ford Tractor dealership. Neither of these couples had children, so from 7th grade through high school, I spent summers and weekends during crop season helping out on their farms. When high school began, I registered for the agriculture track, which offered vocational courses directed toward a farming career.

Uncle Moine, circa 1970

During the middle years of K-12, I first became aware of another phenomenon sometimes associated with ADD. I had always gotten into trouble for not *hearing* things that were said to me. Many of the adults I encountered, especially at school, weren't very patient, and no one understood the vast range of receptivity my mind might cycle through on an average day. As a kid, it seemed like someone was always yelling at me. In fact, often they weren't *really* yelling, but it *felt* like yelling. The disapproving adult was displeased with something I had said, done, or forgotten to do. Usually, I didn't see it coming. I was unaware of my transgression until the authority figure became visibly angry. But now, it seemed as though I really *couldn't* hear them, even though they were staring me in the face and undeniably yelling. Actually, I could *hear* them, I just couldn't *understand* what they were saying. I was able to hear the sounds and see the person's lips moving, but rather than words, I heard incomprehensible noise. If I asked the person to repeat him or herself, I *still* couldn't translate the sound of their voice into recognizable speech.

Usually, this led to, *"What's the matter with you? Are you deaf?!"* or, *"Why don't you pay attention to what I am saying?!"*

So, I stopped asking, and instead, tried to guess. Predictably, that didn't always end well.

. . . .

These episodes were extremely confusing to me. I was only vaguely aware of the distinction between hearing and understanding, and of course, I knew nothing of neuroanatomy and physiology at that age. Intermittently losing the ability to understand my native language was inexplicable and frightening. Was I going crazy? That seemed like the only logical conclusion. I was fearful of talking to anyone else about this problem, assuming they would arrive at the same opinion. I had visited a nearby *insane asylum,* as mental hospitals were called in those days, while Dad made a pastoral visit to a patient related to the church congregation. The idea of being labeled as crazy and confined to a place such as that, terrified me. Therefore, I clung resolutely to the deafness hypothesis.

By the time I reached high school, the periods of *deafness* were occurring more frequently. I tried to avoid verbal interactions with people in public, out of concern others would witness my affliction. I lamented developing hearing loss to those around me, as a cover for anticipated future episodes. The ruse rarely worked. Most adults would counter that I just wasn't paying attention. Then, things got even more complicated. I began having verbal interactions in which I was unable to understand the other person's words as they were spoken, but in a matter of minutes, the meaning would slowly seep into my consciousness, and I could comprehend what had been initially uninterpretable.

On one of these occasions, I literally trotted to catch up with a thoroughly annoyed Uncle Moine, as he stalked off into the distance, after I had been unable to initially comprehend his instructions. Upon realizing there was no reasonable explanation for, *OK, now I understand what you were telling me to do,* I abandoned the pursuit. Who the hell would be able to make sense out of that? Yet, I was left with the dilemma of whether or not to proceed with the task he had described, since the last thing he said, in disgust, was, "Oh, never mind!"

Somehow, I always managed to understand *that* comment.

The phenomena of auditory processing disorders were not recognized for several more decades. Their complexities, and the profound impact they can have on social interaction, are still not fully understood or appreciated by physicians and neuroscientists.

When not needed in the fields, I worked as the go'fer for the mechanic at the Shop, as we called the tractor dealership. Moine and Lola were not the easiest of bosses. Lola had a legendary temper and was obsessive about how things were done. No one who knew her would have been surprised to see her trying to tell the grass how to grow. Uncle Moine was one of those people who could do everything well. He had been a star athlete in high school and a decorated member of Gen. Patton's Army during WWII. Since returning from the War, he had become nationally renowned in trap shooting competitions. I, on the other hand, was a clumsy, self-conscious teenager. Moine really couldn't understand why I was unable to do everything right the first time, and neither of us understood why I sometimes couldn't comprehend what was said to me when I got nervous. Uncle Moine had a reputation for being a happy-go-lucky guy who everyone liked. However, he could occasionally be pretty short-tempered with me, although not nearly as critical as his red-headed wife. He was one of my heroes, and his approval was of supreme importance. Naturally, when he was displeased, I assumed the fault was entirely mine.

John Merrifield was the mechanic during my first year working at the Shop. He had a reputation for being the best mechanic in the county, and the strongest. John was a giant of a man, and as patient and gentle as he was big and strong. While I did the menial tasks of disassembling and cleaning parts, he began teaching me about repairing tractors. He showed me the entirety of the power train, electrical and hydraulic systems, as we disassembled them. Because I could see what he was describing, I could understand it, and because he was invariably patient and never yelled at me, I could hear and understand what he said.

John Merrifield & son, Paul - circa 1968

He also taught me to ask the customer what was happening just before the tractor or implement quit working. Was there an unusual noise or vibration? Did it stop suddenly or lose power slowly? Then he would explain how these *symptoms* offered clues to which system; powertrain, electrical or hydraulic, was the most likely cause of the problem. Not surprisingly, this logical method appealed to me. John also offered encouragement whenever I mastered something new.

The default position for my youngest aunt and uncle, on the other hand, was that every task should be performed flawlessly, and anything less was subject to criticism. That summer, John was my oasis in what seemed like an unending sea of criticism. A few years later, his method and skill as a teacher would play a pivotal role in my choice of a career.

. . . .

Unfortunately, by the senior year of high school, I realized that my hopes of becoming a farmer were unrealistic. I would never make enough money as a farm laborer to buy a farm of my own. After working for five summers, I was now making $16 per day, with days usually lasting from ten to fourteen hours. It also seemed increasingly unlikely my performance would ever be sufficient to convince Lola and Moine to entrust their farm to me when they retired. Uncle Marion and Aunt Peg were considerably more patient *and* supportive. When I told them of my decision to give up farming, they asked me to reconsider and assured me their farm would be passed on to me in the usual family manner, if I stayed. I have always felt guilty about declining their offer. Marion clearly needed help as he got older. Unfortunately, the painful truth was that they were subsistence farmers, making just enough to get by financially from year to year. As much as I wanted to help them and continue in farming, I neither wanted to be a financial burden to them, nor spend my life living as frugally as they had.

Reluctantly, I dropped out of the agriculture program at school, prompting the teacher to change an entire year of my grades from C to F. In spite of the Ag teacher's treachery, I would still have enough credits to graduate, if I could get through two advanced level courses, American history and advanced biology. I was actually looking forward to the history class, but advanced biology threatened to be another major problem.

It required forty years for me to gain an understanding of the dynamics of my relationship with Uncle Moine, but that is a story for another day.

— Saved by a Rat —

During fall semester of my senior year, I took the standardized college entrance exams; the SAT and ACT. I wasn't enthusiastic about spending two of my Saturdays filling in little circles with a #2 pencil, but my parents insisted. They just couldn't abandon their belief in the utility of a college education, even though I hadn't shown much scholastic aptitude. They also insisted I take a county scholarship test, even though only one scholarship was awarded, out of the hundreds of students taking the exam. Using *my* name and scholarship in the same sentence was a non sequitur, but I chose the path of least resistance, and registered for all three exams. I had no interest in going to college. If college was going to be more difficult than high school, I predicted a brief and disastrous experience. College expenses would be a real hardship for my parents. In spite of these negatives, Mom and Dad were insistent. As a further nudge toward the college door, abandonment of a career in farming had narrowed my options for future employment. Two possibilities I emphatically did *not* consider were teaching and the ministry. I was pretty confident that I would find being at the front of either of those types of gatherings as distasteful as that experienced being in the seats located on the receiving end.

In those days, tutoring and other means of preparation for college entrance exams was not yet widely available. A study guide for the SAT, included with the instructions for the exam, was my sole source. I glanced at it briefly. Trying to study for a test like this seemed completely illogical to me. If the purpose of the exam was to measure what one had learned in three years of high school, how could you go back and learn it now? Either you had retained something from your education, or you had not. For this reason, and because expectations for my performance hovered somewhere near the altitude of Death Valley, I went into each of these tests completely relaxed. The three exams were given several weeks apart. The SAT came first, then the ACT, followed by the county test. Soon after the county test, I received a letter from an SAT official. The letter began with condolences, explaining that because I had not scored within the top one half of one percent of examinees, I would not be eligible for a scholarship. The author then went on to congratulate me for scoring in the top two percent of students in the U.S. He concluded with an assurance that I would receive a certificate of commendation for my performance. I think my parents must have each read the letter three or four times. They simply could not process this inconsistency in my scholastic achievement.

Nor could I.

. . . .

One morning in the following week, I passed a high school administrator in the hall. He motioned for me to stop, then approached me. As we came face to face in the crowded passage, he scowled, and said, "I saw the SAT scores. I don't know how you did it, but when I figure it out..." Just as the teacher in 1st grade had done, the remainder of his threat was delivered by a glare.

A few weeks later, my ACT scores arrived, and were similar to the SAT results. On the county scholarship test, I ranked fourth out of several hundred examinees.

. . . .

In spite of these unexpected results, the fact remained I had barely passed freshman biology and had no idea how I was going to bluff my way through the advanced course. My salvation turned out to be a skilled and compassionate teacher named Gayle Day. He gifted me with a C for the first semester, and it was truly a gift. During the third quarter, I was so far below a D that the pass mark was over the horizon. Midway through the quarter, Mr. Day warned me he could not continue to be as generous as he had been the previous semester. Somehow, I worked my way up to a D+. After spring break, Mr. Day informed the class that since many of the students were thinking of majoring in biology in college, he was going to increase the course complexity to approximate the first year of college. Until then, there was a glimmer of hope I might squeak through the semester with a D, thereby meeting all the requirements for high school graduation. Now, a heavy feeling settled into my chest as I contemplated the embarrassing prospect of not even graduating with my class.

Mr. Day continued his announcement with a reminder that the subject matter for 4th quarter would be anatomy and physiology, with most of the laboratory portion of the course devoted to the dissection of a rat. Groans went up from a number of my classmates. I had been suffering the news in silence. Now, some of my classmates seemed to be sharing in my misery. Conversely, I had no aversion to examining the innards of a rat. I had witnessed farm animals butchered for meat, and I had been cleaning the game I shot while hunting since age nine or ten. This last detail of our assignment actually buoyed my spirits a little. Misery loves company. If I was going down in academic flames as the finale to this biology course, I could at least enjoy watching some of my more delicate classmates squirming and sweating at the anatomy table.

To my surprise, the anatomy and physiology portion of the textbook was interesting and largely understandable, probably because of the illustrations. As soon as we started the dissection, I was mesmerized. I could actually see and touch organs and tissue very similar to those in my own body. This was just like learning about tractors from John Merrifield. I could trace out blood vessels, as I had followed the hydraulic lines on a tractor. Most of my classmates were complaining that the dissection was repulsive, and the physiology difficult. To me, it was logical and fascinating. Who wouldn't want to know about their own body, and how it works? The lectures and dissection were timed to cover the same structures at the same time. The majority of our grade would be determined by a laboratory test asking for identification of various items, paired with written explanations of their functions. The big test was on a Friday. After class, the mood of almost the entire group was dark. I was unnerved. I had thought the questions straightforward and relatively easy to answer. Obviously, I had completely misinterpreted the test.

. . . .

On Monday, Mr. Day's countenance was uncharacteristically gloomy. His voice was listless as he admitted grading the test had made him question himself as a teacher. Then, it got worse. He went on to say almost everyone's performance had been dismal and much of the material would need to be repeated. My heart sank. If this was true, I wasn't going to graduate on schedule. He then mentioned there had been one exception to the otherwise poor showing. After confirming his belief in maintaining the confidentiality of student grades, he speculated that in this case, the student probably wouldn't mind being recognized. With his voice now approaching its usual animated style, he walked down the aisle to my desk and held up my test paper. It was marked 95% with a big red circle and exclamation point. I was numb. He stood there until I stopped staring at it. Then, very quietly, he said, "Congratulations, Jim."

I don't remember much about the rest of the semester. I received a B, and it wasn't entirely a gift. One day, toward the end of the school year, Mr. Day was chatting with me and Paul Meyer, one of my friends who was also a farm kid. He asked about our destinations for college. Paul was a certified genius, and one of the smartest kids in our graduating class. He was headed for the University of Illinois to study physics. Mr. Day asked if I was also going to U. of I.

"Oh, no." I replied, "I'm not that smart."

Mr. Day looked directly at me, and with a kindly demeanor I will never forget, said, "Jim, you're smart enough to do anything you want to do."

It is difficult to overstate the impact those words had on me. They didn't erase the cumulative damage done during the past twelve years, but they provided a counter-balance which helped me get through a lot of dark days ahead in college and graduate school.

During my years in the Edwardsville Public Schools, I had several exceptional teachers who I have never forgotten: Mrs. Catalano, Lillie Pearl Helm, Wally Draper, and Margaret Warmbrodt in particular. But, when I hear the comparison of a great teacher to the wind beneath your wings, I immediately think of Mr. Day.

— Goodbye, Dean —

In September of 1965, I reluctantly headed off to college. Although my performance on the scholarship tests the preceding autumn had resulted in some additions to the choice of schools, my parent's financial situation did not. I could either stay at home to attend the newly opened campus of Southern Illinois University, or I could go to Blackburn College, a small liberal arts school which provided student jobs in exchange for cut rate tuition and fees. I *really* wanted to experience more of the world than the small farming towns of my youth. Blackburn was located in Carlinville, IL., a farming town with which I was quite familiar... but at least it was fifty miles away, and the price was right.

Some things went as planned; others... not so much. As expected, I was not prepared for the increased academic expectations of college. What surprised me though, was the rapid onset of homesickness. For the first month, I thought I would die of melancholy. The term helicopter parents hadn't been coined when I went to college, but if it had, my parents would not have been flying. My first trip home was for Thanksgiving.

The only scholastic recognition I garnered during the first semester was to land on academic probation. Second semester, my grade point average inched up 0.1 to a lofty 1.7. This meager sign of improvement saved me from expulsion. Freshman year confirmed my impression that college wasn't the right place for me, but neither did I relish the idea of leaving involuntarily. The only thing at which I had excelled was my campus job. I was assigned to the construction crew, learning the skills of bricklaying and finish carpentry. Although costs were nominal at Blackburn, they were still more than my parents could afford. I felt like I was wasting their money.

During the summer of 1966, career choices for draft-age boys were limited. The U.S. was beginning a large build-up of troops for the war in Vietnam. All male citizens were required to register with their local

Selective Service office at the age of eighteen. The Draft was compulsory; if they needed you, off you went. Aside from deferments for medical conditions, exemptions were being given to high school students and college undergraduates, and to married men with children. If you were not in any of those categories, the choices were to join one of the military services voluntarily or wait until the Draft Board found you, which usually didn't take long. In the latter half of 1966, the Army and Marine Corps were vacuuming up just about every able-bodied male (and some not so able-bodied) not sufficiently wealthy to obtain a deferment for bone spurs.

The previous summer, I had replaced farm work with a job in a local aluminum foundry. The owner was an entrepreneur and family friend. Until then, I was of the opinion that the hottest working conditions possible involved stacking bales of hay in the loft of an Illinois barn during the month of August. I was wrong. On the worst of days, the foundry temperature could exceed 130°F. But, the boss and his wife, Charlie and Harriet Starnes, were wonderful people, and I enjoyed learning this new job. Following that first year at Blackburn, Charlie was kind enough to again provide me with summer employment.

Unbeknownst to my parents, I left work early one afternoon and made a visit to the local Navy recruiter. I was particularly interested in the Submarine Service because of my uncles, Charles and Red, who had served on subs during WWII. The recruiter was a wise old Chief. After a lengthy conversation, he had me sized up pretty well, and probably sensed my remaining uncertainty about the military option better than I did. He talked me into trying one more semester of college, with the promise to help me enlist if I was still dissatisfied with school at the end of that time.

. . . .

For the rest of that summer, and probably the first time in my life, I exercised critical thinking, as I examined the choices confronting me. I had no idea what I wanted to do in life. None of my college classes had interested me. I liked the construction jobs but was pretty sure I would tire of them quickly enough. However, I was becoming increasingly certain not all smart people attended college. My mechanic mentor, John Merrifield, seemed as smart as any professor I had met to date, and he was certainly a skilled teacher. My new boss, Charlie, was a mechanical genius. He had dropped out of high school during the Depression. While working as a pipefitter, Charlie invented several items for the after-market automotive industry. He then built the components of an aluminum foundry to produce these products and started his own business. Employees joked that the only things on the property Charlie hadn't built were: the welder, drill press, metal lathe, and Harriet. He could create amazing designs and build almost anything, working from complex mechanical drawings kept in his head, rather than on blueprints. Surely there must be a niche for me somewhere that did not involve going to college. I still didn't understand why I was different than many of my peers, who had acclimated to college and were progressing with their education, but at least my recognition of circumstances where I would either flourish or flounder was improving. Uncertain of where I wanted to go in life, I was increasingly confident that, at this point, college wouldn't get me there. Even if I ultimately discovered a career requiring a college education, I was skeptical of finding it in my current environment. Besides, I was bored with college, and when bored, I usually got into trouble.

I needed more information before making any career plans. The ingredient lacking was life experience, but because of the Draft, my only option to see the world was the military. I also suspected the Vietnam War would drag on for a very long time. Many of my classmates privately admitted similar uncertainty about their long-term goals but felt strongly that they wanted to avoid the military for as long as possible, hoping the war would conclude first. (The college deferment was limited to four years.) That sort of plan didn't appeal to me. My parents couldn't afford for me to waste time in college without a pretty defini-

tive goal... and betting this war would be over within thi.
looked like a losing wager to me. On the other hand, the alternative
volved serious risk. The evening news was already dominated by stories about Vietnam; increasing numbers of soldiers weren't making it
back alive. However, I also had convincing evidence that life could be a
lethal adventure, even at home. My cousin Billy, my hero and surrogate
older brother, had been killed in an automobile accident, five years before. Several of my high school classmates were also dead, none of them
as a result of the war. Still, there was a big difference between being
dragged into the Army because you didn't have a Draft deferment,
compared with throwing away the deferment you had. Several of my
friends from high school had also experienced difficulties with college.
They were now in the military and strongly recommending I stay in
school. It boiled down to several unpalatable choices.

After serious introspection, I reached the conclusion that, of the
choices available, wasting more of my time and my parent's money on
college was the most disagreeable. From that perspective, the decision
seemed clearer. In spite of occasional successes at school and on the national aptitude tests, my default position still seemed to be I couldn't do
anything right. I had failed at establishing a pathway into farming. I
had been a mediocre student for the twelve years ending with high
school. I was now just a hair's breadth away from flunking out of college. It was time to try something different.

*Blackburn College was a good quality school, offering a small college environ-
ment to students of modest means. Most of the faculty were highly motivated
as teachers and devoted to the students. It was simply the wrong place for me
at that particular time in my life.*

By the time I returned to Blackburn in September, my decision to drop
out of school was almost complete. I had also reconsidered the choice of
a service branch. My efforts at introspection were proving useful. I now

ouldn't find the military experience enjoyable, no
ce I chose. I really wasn't very good at regimenta-
sounded a lot like *Because I said so* to me. Better to be
alistic. The time commitment for the Submarine Ser-
rs, compared to two years if drafted. The experiences
my frien... e having in both the Army and Air Force seemed to confirm my suspicions; military service was best viewed as a necessary un-
pleasantry to simply endure. Choosing the shortest time commitment
seemed the most logical. There was only one more question for me to
address, and it was a deeply personal one.

Instinctively, I valued the role of tradition in our family. Grandpa's
death in 1951 had left me with only fleeting memories of him. However,
Mom spoke of her dad so often, and with such unmistakable reverence,
I have always felt as if I knew him. Many of her stories related to the
traditions of family-life in Kentucky, and Grandpa's unyielding belief in
doing what one thought was right, whether or not it was easy. She also
spoke of his generosity towards other people in need. It came as no
surprise that over the course of my childhood, strangers would occasionally approach me, confirm I was his grandson, and then tell me a
story about him. Those stories invariably concluded with the narrator's
opinion, *He was a good man* (a significant complement in Southern Illinois society), or even, *He was a great man.*

All of our family members from the WWII era had served honora-
bly. At the frequent gatherings of kinfolk during my childhood, conversation was suffused with stories of the recently concluded war. After
dinner, my uncles would invariably move to the front porch to relive
some of those experiences. My cousins and I sat with our feet dangling
off the porch deck, listening intently. I was in awe of these men. The
tales of their exploits set a standard for what I felt was expected of me.
As I contemplated entering the Service, their examples weighed heavily. My performance so far had been an accumulation of disappointing
results. I wondered if I would ever be able to measure up to the accom-

plishments of the two generations before me.

The stories we heard as children carefully omitted sordid details but were sprinkled with harrowing events, where fear was readily admitted. I had no illusions of the glory of war and could vividly imagine its misery and terror. The possibility of dying in Vietnam was very real to me. Conversely, the possibility of joining the military, but not going to Vietnam, never entered my mind. I assumed a line company would be my destination. The question now absorbing much of my thought was whether I would be able to prove worthy of the family legacy. Those before me had served bravely and well. Could I meet the same standard?

I remained without confidence in my abilities but ultimately reached a decision. The men of the previous generation, who I most admired, had all gone to war when needed. In my generation, several friends were now in the military, and several others were preparing to go. My childhood neighbor, Gary Lane, was en route to Dau Tieng, near the terminus of the Ho Chi Minh Trail. If my friends did their duty, while I stayed comfortably at home in college, I would always regret my failure to take my turn. It was time to pay my dues. I would go, and I would endeavor to do my best. I began mentally preparing for war.

. . . .

My deadline for decision was November 1. When a student was no longer eligible for deferment, the process of notifying the Draft Board took weeks. Further processing by the Draft Board and Department of Defense (DOD) was equally methodical. A Notice of Induction from the DOD would typically appear about three months after loss of one's deferment. I saw no reason to waste the three months, and I had never been very good at waiting anyway. The college semester would conclude the last week of January. During the first week of November, I took a deep breath and mailed a letter to my local draft board, informing them of my decision to leave college as of January 31.

During the summer, my college roommate, Rodney, had reached a similar conclusion. He subsequently enlisted in the Marines but wasn't scheduled to report until February, so decided to complete one more semester of school. We were unaware of each other's decision until our return to campus. Both of us seemed to have found a new seriousness of purpose. We were determined not to continue schlepping along, doing poorly in everything, until the school decided our fate. We resolved to study diligently, even outlining a study plan; a revolutionary departure from our previous style. The new schedule included uninterrupted study from the conclusion of dinner until 10:00 or 10:30 each evening. This period was followed by an hour of relaxation with the beverage of our choice, then bedtime before midnight. The only logistical difficulties with the plan were: the college prohibition of alcohol on campus, the legal drinking age of twenty-one, and a lack of transportation. Almost all underage college students had a source of alcohol, but without a car, travel to a compliant merchant and then finding a safe site for consumption were persisting problems.

With an ingenuity driven by need, we crafted several utilitarian solutions. This was the cusp of the Age of Aquarius. Putting candles in empty wine bottles was all the rage, even in rural Illinois. The college administration had grudgingly agreed to allow students to have *empty* wine bottles in their dorm rooms for this purpose. Room searches of anyone suspected of possessing contraband were routine, and usually carried out by the Dean of Students, while the suspect student was away at class. Upon investigation, we determined that our outside window ledge was just wide enough to accommodate several wine bottles. Our dorm window faced the dean's office in the administration building. We secured two bottles of wine and dutifully emptied them one weekend. Then, we placed the empty bottles, with candles atop, on the ledge in full view of his office. We also placed shims between the bottles and the window, so if either was disturbed, we would know. Sure enough, the day after the bottles were positioned, the shims were lying flat on the sill when we returned from class. Since an inspection had now been confirmed, we filled the bottles with our favorite alcoholic beverages and reinserted the candles for stoppers. The autumnal Illinois weather provided refrigeration. My roommate built a dummy speaker cabinet to house bar supplies. For the remainder of the semester, cocktail hour began no later than 10:30 p.m. A few select friends began joining us, and were quite willing to replenish our supplies, in return for the convenience of being able to drink in the dorm. Otherwise, we told no one.

When not studying, working, or enjoying cocktail hour, I spent most of my time mentally preparing for what I assumed lay ahead. I read a magazine article discussing one of the books in the classic trilogy of WWII novels by James Jones. In the article, the author compared green troops to seasoned veterans with the observation that in order to be most effective in combat, one needed to have already given oneself up for dead. In a fire-fight, the immediate necessities could be best accomplished if the soldier was not distracted by thoughts of self-preservation. I certainly didn't want to die, but I was more fearful of not performing satisfactorily when called upon. Neither did I have fantasies about being a hero. I just wanted to live up to family expectations. In combat, that would be hard enough. I did not want to end my days as some quivering mass of terror, huddled in a trench, paralyzed by fear and unable to function. Yet, I could easily imagine how that could happen to anyone. This possibility conjured a vision of my uncles or friends sitting around talking and looking at the floor in silent embarrassment when my name was mentioned, if I proved to be a coward.

Interestingly, my grades improved significantly that semester, as did my roommate's. In three classes, I had solid C's, a considerable improvement over the preceding year. My fourth class was Introduction to Psychology. I had the highest grade in the class, earning an A. More than increased effort, it seemed that having a finite quitting time each evening allowed me to concentrate more effectively and accomplish more. Regarding the A in Psychology, some things hadn't changed. If I was interested in a subject, I usually excelled in it. My last exam was on January 31. Earlier that week, I received the standard letter from the Department of Defense, ordering me to report for induction on Feb. 10, 1967.

Nui Ba Den (Black Virgin Mt.) Tay Ninh Province
Vietnam, circa 1967. Photo courtesy of Gary Lane

On the last day of finals, my roommate dropped by the Dean of Student's office. Later that afternoon, he related the conversation to me with relish, as we were packing to leave.

"Hello, Dean. I'm leaving school as of today, and just wanted to stop by to say goodbye."

Best wishes were offered perfunctorily, as the Dean indicated his need to get on with other matters.

"One other thing, Dean." Rod sauntered across the ornate office to a window, then pointed to our window in the dormitory across the street.

"Yes, yes, I see it!" was the impatient reply.

"Do you see those two wine bottles in the window?" continued my roomie.

"Yes, I see the wine bottles!" The school official clearly wanted to end this conversation.

"Well, the one on the right is filled with beer; the one on the left with whiskey. My roommate and I plan to leave a little... just in case you want a drink after work this afternoon. And, by the way, they've been kept full all semester.

Goodbye, Dean."

Grandma & me Feb. 8, 1967

Chapter II. Basic Training

– Greeting –

I reported for duty to the United States Army on 10Feb67 at 06:30. (As of then, I was on military time.) The day began with Dad delivering me to the Greyhound bus stop in downtown Edwardsville. Although my destination, the St. Louis military induction station, was only twenty-five miles away, I had been given specific instructions to take the bus and a voucher for the fare. As the day wore on, several of us concluded that the Army's reason for insisting on bus transportation was to avoid a scene of weeping mothers and other family members in front of the military facility in downtown St. Louis. Who says the Army knows nothing about public relations.

George Washington described the farmers, laborers and craftsmen who formed the Continental Army as *citizen-soldiers*. After the Battle of Concord, these Colonials either responded to notices asking for volunteers, or simply showed up at Army encampments. When I entered the Service, 191 years later, the method for raising a military force during time of war had changed very little. Mostly, we were kids recently graduated from high school, although some had attended college or even completed advanced degrees. Our average age was nineteen. Although a portion of "recruits" had actually enlisted, committing to a three-year period of active duty, the majority of us were simply responding to a summons from the Department of Defense. Curiously, the greeting at the beginning of the induction notice was exactly that; Greeting. For reasons never explained, this salutation failed to include an s at the end of the word.

Approximately two hundred of us were inducted at St. Louis on 10 February. Almost the entire day was spent standing in line, waiting our turn to enter a succession of small offices where various tests and exams were performed to determine our fitness for military service. We carried our examination form from room to room and handed it to the examiner, who performed his/her designated function, checked the appropriate boxes and handed the form back to us. We then rejoined the serpentine column of soon-to-be soldiers. We were instructed not to talk, other than when answering the questions of examiners. This was our first experience with military boredom, and whispered comments persisted in spite of the orders. The only humor I can remember was speculation regarding the infraction one poor doctor must have committed to result in his assignment; sitting in a tiny, windowless office, performing rectal exams on two hundred recruits. At some point, I absent-mindedly turned the multi-page examination form over. There, stamped in large print on the line identified as Assessment, was the word ACCEPTED. Apparently, the Army needed recruits pretty badly.

. . . .

Early in the day, someone with a felt-tipped marker had walked down the line of inductees, placing a very prominent purple slash across the top of the examination form of every 9th person. At the conclusion of our inspection, we were escorted into a large room with a podium, flanked by the American flag and flags of the various military services. Our escort then announced that the lucky devils in possession of an examination form bearing a purple slash would be going to Marine Corp Basic Training. The Marines were evidently also short a few good men. My examination form did not have a purple slash across the top.

The two groups were then separated and led through a recitation of the Pledge of Allegiance to the service branch assigned and to the United States of America. This marked our official entry into the military. Following the induction ceremony, we were treated to our first Army meal. The cafeteria resembled a prison; the food maybe a little better. After enjoying this gastronomic delight, we boarded buses for delivery to various Basic Training facilities. I was directed to a bus heading southwest on I-44 to Ft. Leonard Wood, MO.

Once on the bus, I settled into a seat and listened to the rise and fall of the clatter from the diesel engine as the driver maneuvered his cargo of fresh cannon fodder through city streets and onto the highway. Absentmindedly, I gazed out the window. A car slowly pulled alongside in the next lane. Through the windshield, I could clearly see a teenage boy and girl who looked to be dressed for a date. My induction into the Army was on a Friday. I suddenly realized that it was Friday night. For the first time in many years, I was not out on some adventure, or eagerly awaiting one. The entire day had passed without a single thought of what I would be doing this evening. The best part of Fridays had always been anticipating the fun to be had that night. Usually, it involved hanging out with my friends. Dates were reserved for Saturdays. Friday was *boy's night out*. We rarely did anything very exciting. Most often, we piled into someone's car and drove around Edwardsville, waving at passing carloads of our classmates, doing exactly the same thing. After an hour or so spent orbiting Main Street and Troy Road, anchored by a drive-in restaurant on one end, and an ice cream shop on the other, we would head for one of the neighboring towns, to cruise *their* Strip in search of excitement.

There was an undeniable favorite end to those evenings; one we enjoyed as often as luck smiled upon us. Until the late 1960's, alcohol was overwhelmingly the drug of choice for teenagers in Southern Illinois, and liberally enjoyed. For most boys, beer was the preferred method of fermentation. Small bars located in the tiny towns and crossroads which dotted the landscape of surrounding farmland were usually the most accommodating source. These neighborhood taverns, a custom brought from Europe by the early settlers, were regarded as a necessity of local society. Although, in the more sparsely populated areas, many of these watering holes struggled to survive economically. Satisfying the thirst of underage imbibers from cities and towns nearby was a common means of supplementing income. Every self-respecting adolescent male knew which joints were currently *open for business*. Local police departments made half-hearted attempts to discourage this commerce, knowing their efforts were futile. However, in order to satisfy the neighborhood blue noses, the police would periodically stake out a joint suspected of serving under-age patrons. As you can imagine, police stake-outs in a town consisting of a half dozen streets were laughable. Everyone knew the cops were watching the place before the cruiser's engine had cooled. If a teenager didn't see the lurking patrol car and wandered inside, he or occasionally she, was turned away, often with a request to inform their friends the place was being watched. Since manpower was in short supply, no county sheriff was willing to waste more than one patrol car for this surveillance, which meant that it was clear sailing for other miscreant purveyors to slake the thirst of the area's youth. This cat and mouse game clearly favored the mice.

To be sure, many tavern owners refused to serve underage drinkers for the usual variety of upstanding reasons, but a significant minority felt no such compulsion. So, as social activities slowed on Friday nights, if our network information was accurate, we could find a tavern willing to meet our needs. If one or two six packs could be had, we would repair to a nearby country road with the booty. There, we would listen to a favorite Top 40 radio station, talk about recent happenings at school, and tease each other, while sipping our purloined brew. Simple pleasures... but I have never laughed harder, or been happier, than I was on those Friday nights under the stars, enjoying the taste of forbidden hops, and the camaraderie of good friends.

. . . .

My attention now returned to the couple in the passing car. She was sitting near the passenger door, the vast expanse of vinyl front seat between them protecting her reputation at school. They apparently hadn't been dating for long. I imagined their evening itinerary. The couple looked to be sixteen or seventeen, so probably dinner and a movie. Then home, a quick peck on the cheek, and an escort to the front door, where at least one parent would be stationed in the living room. I imagined the boy's thoughts as he drove home, remembering the excitement I felt when beginning the dating ritual just a few years before.

My reverie swiveled back to my friends. I mapped their current whereabouts. One was already in Vietnam, in the infantry. Two others had also joined the service ahead of me, and another was awaiting a draft notice. For us, the rituals and fun of high school were over. The adventures we now faced had much higher stakes. The young man in the car would almost certainly end his evening back home in his familiar bed. I would end my evening in an entirely new bed, in a completely unfamiliar environment. The sight of the couple's car, slowly pulling away from us in traffic, felt like my life as a child and adolescent, also pulling away as I headed into an uncertain future. This bus was a spaceship, transporting me to the next chapter of my life in an unknown world. We would be landing in a few hours.

— Ft. Lost in the Woods —

We arrived at our new home away from home, shortly before midnight. A tired and cranky Sergeant led us to an empty barracks. He directed us to pick any open bunk, mentioned that the latrine was down the hall, and warned us not to leave the building until another Sergeant arrived in the morning to take us to the chow hall. I was in the Army now!

Ft. Leonard Wood covers 97.6 square miles of Ozark forest in southeastern Missouri. It has been a major site of Army Basic Training since WWII. In the Army, Ft. Leonard Wood had two nicknames. The more benign was *Ft. Lost in the Woods*. The other descriptive, *Little Korea*, had been earned because of the surprisingly bitter cold spells, considering its southern latitude, that sometimes occurred in winter. During February and early March of 1967, temperatures on the parade ground dropped as low as the mid-teens. In spite of the temperature, and the nickname, when uniforms were issued the morning after our arrival, they did not include cold weather gear, field jacket liners, insulated gloves, and insulated caps, designed during the Korean War in response to the high number of casualties inflicted by the cold. We were informed that since the current conditions were not expected to last more than four weeks, we weren't eligible for this supplementary clothing.

In 1967, all soldiers joining the U.S. Army underwent basic combat infantry training. This phase of Army life had several goals. The first was an attempt to reprogram trainees to follow orders unquestioningly, rather than engage in the independent thinking usually praised in civilian life. The methods consisted of repeated reminders: that we had left civilian life behind, that we literally *belonged* to the Army, that we were simply a piece of military equipment, and were in fact, the lowliest piece of equipment the army owned. This mindset was reinforced by near-constant harassment and humiliation. Our days began at 05:00 and ended at 21:00. An Army regulation specified Basic Trainees were to be allotted eight hours of sleep per night. We soon learned that in the Army, *sleep* was rather loosely defined. Specific sets of physical exercises were interspersed throughout the day. The goal was to produce a soldier with the minimal level of physical conditioning needed to perform on the battlefield. For those of us accustomed to rigorous physical activity, the exercise routines were not particularly difficult, but the couch potatoes amongst us paid a dear price for their previous slothful ways. What none of us were prepared for, was the combination of constant activity, sleep deprivation, and exposure to cold.

The barracks used for Basic Training were steel frame structures covered with corrugated metal sheeting. The Army can erect these units faster than the concrete floor slabs can dry. With the war in Vietnam intensifying, the outskirts of the occupied portion of FLW looked like the military version of a subdivision under construction. The rectangular buildings had a single door at either end. Two small, walled rooms were located just inside the front door. One was used for armament storage and was always locked. The other served as personal space for the Platoon Sergeant. The remainder of the building was an open space, accommodating a row of twelve metal bunk beds placed perpendicularly against each of the long axis walls. Between each four rows of bunks were a row of wall lockers, also placed perpendicularly, which served as partial room dividers. The buildings were just wide enough to fit the bunks, wall lockers, and a walkway down the center of the room. Windows provided direct ventilation for every bunk. Plywood foot lockers were placed at the ends of bunks, and between bunks against the wall. Each of these wooden boxes served as the storage area for all clothing and personal items for one soldier, and as a seat. The wall lockers held field equipment. Every time we changed locations, which occurred frequently during the months of training, all clothing and footgear had to be fitted into one duffel bag. If you mashed the contents as flat as possible, there might be two or three inches of space at the top for *personal gear*, not an inch was wasted. The civilian clothes worn on the day of enlistment had been mailed home the day after. Almost all soldiers smoked, so gallon coffee cans, half full of water and fondly referred to as *butt cans*, were placed about every ten feet down the center aisle of the room. This completed the furnishings. The buildings had no running water, and restrooms, called latrines in the Army, were located in a separate building.

Each barracks housed forty-eight men. So many people in an undivided space invites the spread of communicable diseases. Armies have a long and lethal history of such problems. Shortly before our induction, an outbreak of meningococcal meningitis had occurred at a training facility elsewhere. The Army, from painful past experience, takes meningococcal outbreaks very seriously. At the time, there was no vaccine available, and the mortality rate from this infection was high. The military was desperate to find preventative measures. An unknown epidemiologist, with no idea of the implications of his observation, mentioned to someone in the command hierarchy that the Meningococcus organism doesn't grow very well at low temperatures. Viola! The Army had its solution. Our barracks did not contain wall insulation, and if equipped with furnaces, they were never turned on. To further discourage transmission of the bacterium, we were ordered to leave our windows open at all times. For the first month of Basic Training, the water in the butt cans had a skim of ice on top most mornings.

— Five Hundred Miles —

Our first week at Ft. Leonard Wood was an orientation to life in the Army. Everything about *the Army way* was new and different. Things as simple as walking were now governed by rules. The first rule was that you didn't walk anywhere, unless you were off duty; you marched. As Basic Trainees, we were *never* off duty. So, a bunch of nearly grown men had to be taught the acceptable way to travel from one point to another on foot. Marching and formations (the shape and position of a group of soldiers when standing still) were called field exercises and practiced outdoors. Although this regimentation seemed stupid and unnecessary at the time, its utility became clear as we gained more experience as soldiers. When not practicing how to walk, i.e. march, or performing a series of calisthenics called Physical Training (PT), we were herded into a large auditorium for lectures on Army rules, regulations, and history. Some of the tidbits shared during these lectures included the fact that we would cover more than five hundred miles on our feet during the next eight weeks. We also learned that our Company Commander would be an Army Ranger, that Rangers had a tradition of never walking anywhere, and therefore, we could anticipate covering most of those miles at an accelerated gait.

Typical cadence when marching is one hundred twenty steps per minute with a thirty-six-inch stride. Double time is actually one hundred eighty steps at thirty-six inches each. When marching long distances carrying our packs and rifles, we assumed a gait of one hundred forty steps/minute. This is sometimes referred to as the Ranger's Gait. Civilians would describe it as a trot. Over reasonably smooth terrain, a speed exceeding four miles per hour can be maintained by a physically fit soldier, with the gear we were carrying, for hours. This may seem like minutiae to non-military readers, but armies have devoted considerable effort over the past several thousand years to studying how fast a man can travel on foot, and for how long, under certain sets of conditions. That knowledge and its reliable performance sometimes determines which side wins a battle, or even a war.

One class was an introduction to the set of laws governing the military, called the Uniform Code of Military Justice (UCMJ). This session was taught by a very stern looking Drill Instructor. First, he informed us that military law varied from civilian law in many ways, and we could forget about any protections we might assume under civilian law. He went on to state that the United States Military regarded the conflict in Vietnam as a State of War. This turned out to be incorrect, but we were in no position to argue, even if we had known the relevant statutes. He went on to say that any soldier leaving his post against orders was guilty of desertion. The penalty for desertion in time of war was death by firing squad.

As a footnote, he added, "By the way, Ft. Leonard Wood abuts the Mark Twain National Forest; 182,000 acres of dense, uninhabited wilderness. If any of you dick heads (a favorite descriptor used for soldiers who have just enjoyed their first Army haircut) decide you don't like it here, or you don't want to be in the Army, these are your choices. If you go that way (he pointed east), you will be in the forest. We won't bother to look for you, because you will starve to death before you get to the other side. And, if you go that way (he pointed in the opposite direction), we will hunt you down and send you to Ft. Leavenworth, Kansas, for execution."

That really took the shine off the rest of the day.

Another Drill Instructor then took the stage. He was somewhat older, and his sleeve displayed the rank of a Master Sergeant. Although probably no more than in his mid-forties, his face was lined and weathered from constant outdoor exposure. His manner was relaxed. He actually leaned on the podium, rather than standing ramrod straight behind it.

He began his comments, "Some of you are p
how you will ever get through the next eight we
haven't yet figured out how difficult a task you a
been in the Army for seventeen years. I have beer
eight of those years. I am here to tell you some thing
help in your transition from civilian to soldier over the course of basic
Training."

After a pause, in which he slowly scanned the room, as if assessing
each of us individually, he continued, "I imagine all of you played cowboys and Indians when you were younger. Basic Training is a gauntlet
that you must run. It will be difficult, it will be painful, but most of you
will complete it successfully. The trick is this: accept the challenge of
each day, put the yesterdays behind you, and don't worry about the
tomorrows. Over the next eight weeks, do what you are told, master the
skills you are taught, and don't let the inevitable one or two trouble-
makers in the company pull you into the shit they are going to find for
themselves. If you follow this advice, you will become a good soldier."

Another pause. "Some of you may be wondering what I consider to
be a good soldier."

He visually surveyed the audience once again, "For the next eight
weeks, your Platoon Sergeant is going to be your mother, your father,
your big brother and your confessor. You will get to know him well,
but he will only get to know you if you can't keep up the pace or you
cause trouble. Last week, I graduated a company of Basic Trainees. As
they were returning their gear, a man in my platoon stepped forward to
present a piece of equipment. I had to look at his name badge in order
to find his name on the list. That is my definition of a good soldier in
Basic Training."

I decided right then that my goal for the next eight weeks would be
for my Platoon Sergeant to never learn my name.

of senior enlisted men (and now women) provide the instruction and vision in Basic Training. These non-commissioned officers (NCO's) hold e title of Drill Instructor (DI), in addition to their rank. Besides teaching much of the material learned over the eight weeks of Basic Training, a Drill Instructor is assigned to each platoon. This person is referred to as your Platoon Sergeant. He supervises your activities during the time you are not in a specific class or exercise. During the first few weeks, the only time the Platoon Sergeant wasn't our constant companion was for trips to the latrine or when we were sleeping. After the first month, his presence gradually became less constant. None of us had experienced this much supervision since we were toddlers.

— Thee Queek! —

After orientation, our first weeks of Basic Training were devoted to: learning to march, conditioning exercises, and some basics of infantry combat. No order prompts more fear and dread for a foot soldier than, *Fix bayonets!* This means hand-to-hand combat with the enemy is expected and may require using your rifle as a spear. Practicing the methods of fighting with a bayonet brought home the reality that, within a few months, our lives might end in a painful and terrifying death.

Fortunately, one of the redeeming characteristics of our species seems to be the ability to find a sliver of humor in almost any calamity, and so, in spite of the morbid prospects of bayonet fighting, we did. The director of the Bayonet Committee happened to be my Platoon Sergeant, Staff Sergeant (SSG) Rosario. We actually liked Sergeant Rosario, an unusual sentiment for Basic Traineess when applied to a Drill Instructor. He never engaged in the harassment or sadistic behavior displayed by some of the other DI's, and he was the only DI who occasionally smiled during interactions with us. Sergeant Rosario was of Puerto Rican heritage, and the irony of a Puerto Rican teaching the art of knife fighting was not lost on us. He would begin each bayonet exercise with the same chant, shouting from an elevated podium, "There are two kinds of bayonet fighters!"

After a slight pause, he would add, "*The quick...*"
followed by another pause, "*...and the dead!*" his black eyes slowly scanning the group of trainees before him.

Then came the question, "*Which kind are you?*"

At this point, we were expected to shout back, as loudly as possible, "*THE QUICK!*"

Sergeant Rosario had a rather pronounced Puerto Rican accent, so, phonetically, his question during the chant sounded like *thee queek* to a bunch of Midwestern white boys.

Even in our downtrodden mental state, we couldn't resist shouting back at the top of our lungs, "*THEE QUEEK!*"

Our instructor never failed to smile at this pronunciation, and it became one of our rituals. I'm sure he recognized the subtle joke, and probably realized the utility of distracting our terror with a bit of humor, so we could better concentrate on what he was teaching. At least for me, the ruse worked.

When addressing, or referring to, an NCO of any rank, the generic term Sergeant was used, with the exception of a First Sergeant or Sergeant Major, who were always addressed by their full rank. Although the currently recommended writing style has changed, calling an active duty soldier of superior rank or an officer by their last name, without including their rank, was regarded as disrespectful when I was in the Army, and it still feels that way to me.

This word play during bayonet training was about the only humor present during that first month of Basic Training. As the days dragged by, superficial friendships amongst the trainees formed, but they never evolved in the manner typical of adolescent male group behavior. During breaks, small groups began to coalesce, formed largely around personal interests, such as hobbies or sports, but personal relationships were not encouraged. We were frequently reminded that this was not a social club. In fact, conversation was discouraged. The purposes of these ten-minute breaks were to rest and to smoke. With a solemn countenance, a DI would remind a trainee whose voice he detected, "A chatty soldier is a dead soldier."

This wasn't harassment. He was teaching a survival skill. In dense cover, two opposing forces could sometimes pass within yards of each other, undetected. However, a single word could reveal one's position. If discovered, the unit who became aware of their adversary first gained both the choice of engagement and the advantage of surprise.

In general, we used only last names to address each other, but nicknames were popular, and some guys could make everyone laugh no matter what the circumstances. In our platoon, this role was filled by PVT Tuma, who quickly became *Tuma Fish,* and then, just *Fish.* He could think of something funny about even the crappiest of days.

Soon, we would be joining a war on the other side of the world, in an environment that sounded more nightmarish with every story the DI's recounted of their own experiences. But now, our war was very personal, and the enemy was the U.S. Army. Our mission was to survive Basic Training. Sometimes, the success of that mission seemed in considerable doubt.

We were outside almost continually from 06:00 until 19:00 each day. Temperatures were usually in the twenties, even at mid-day. Icy winds blew in gusts and changed direction unexpectedly, constantly searching for a gap in your outer clothing to fill with its companion, a light dusting of snow.

We weren't any better equipped for the cold at night. We had been issued one set of sheets and one army blanket. The frigid barracks and inadequate bedding made sleep difficult. Although the Meningococcus may not thrive at low temperatures, influenza viruses do quite well. The cold, exhaustion, and crowding took their toll. By the end of the third week, half of the trainees and one Drill Instructor were in the hospital with either pneumonia or frostbite.

The Senior Drill Instructor (SDI) informed us that if Company strength fell below fifty percent, the training cycle would be cancelled. *If one more person* went to the hospital, we would *all* be required to start Basic Training over again. Those of us still on our feet, myself included, were almost all sick. In retrospect, I unquestionably had pneumonia. I felt as though I might die. However, going to Sick Call was not an option for two very compelling reasons. First, most of us would have chosen the firing squad over having to repeat the previous three weeks, and one more hospital admission would trigger that nightmare. Second,

Sick Call occurred during morning formation at 06:00. If you believed you were ill, you were to notify your Platoon Sergeant, sign out of formation, and walk to the medical clinic for examination by a corpsman. The times of arrival and departure from the formation and the clinic were noted, and results of the medical assessment were reported to your Company Commander. (So much for medical confidentiality.) Ten minutes was allowed to travel the one mile to the clinic.

On the day the SDI announced the possibility of the training cycle being halted, he added a new rule for reporting to sick call. Before leaving the company area, we would now be required to retrieve all our gear from the barracks, place it in our wall locker (weighing over eighty pounds when packed), and carry it to the Orderly Room to be stored for safekeeping. Furthermore, if transit time to or from Sick Call exceeded ten minutes, we would be considered AWOL (Absent Without Leave) and referred to the Battalion Commander for court martial. Additionally, if the examining corpsman concluded that the trainee did not have a significant illness, the trainee faced possible court martial for malingering.

Fortunately, before any of us still standing became too ill to march, several people were discharged from the hospital. Company strength never fell below fifty percent, although the term was a misnomer for the next several weeks.

— **Six Hundred Pounds of Potatoes** —

Army mess halls are models of efficiency, if not gastronomic excellence. Our mess hall could feed six hundred soldiers in approximately one hour. Tables were circular, belly button high and did not come equipped with chairs. We entered the mess hall about twenty-five at a time. Food was served on metal trays in a military version of cafeteria style called a mess line. You walked down the line with tray out-stretched. Mess Sergeants (the Army term for their professional cooks) dispensed the food with large metal spoons. Although items could be refused, they rarely were. The Army spent little effort on food quality, but a great deal of attention to protein and total caloric content. Amounts provided were carefully calculated to be modestly protein positive and calorie neutral for the ideal-sized soldier. In eight weeks, fat guys reliably lost weight, thin guys gained weight, and everybody increased muscle mass, provided you ate everything available. Once you arrived at a table with your tray, you had six minutes to consume the meal. You then scraped your tray clean over a garbage can and exited the mess hall immediately. Those lingering over their meal were re-warded with an extra day of KP.

To accommodate these thrice daily bursts of activity, each Basic Trainee was periodically assigned to work in the mess hall, assisting the cooks. This was referred to as Kitchen Police (KP) and was a hated as-signment. In the Army, to police something usually refers to a defined space, and means to clean and straighten the area and its contents. Du-ties included washing dishes, handling garbage, prepping foods for the cooks and constantly scrubbing or hosing down every square inch of the kitchen and food serving areas. The Army was just as afraid of food poisoning as they were of other communicable diseases. Those assigned to KP arose at 04:00, rather than 05:00, in order to prepare breakfast. The cooks were notoriously ill-tempered, and punishment for displeas-ing them was additional time assigned to this duty. A day on KP typically ended about 22:00-22:30. These days were even more exhausting than regular training days.

To get an idea of the quantity of food served, our mess required six hundred pounds of potatoes be peeled each day. This was all done by hand. Fifty-five-gallon stainless steel garbage cans were filled with potatoes. Three guys stood around a can. You grabbed a potato, peeled it, and dropped it into another can filled with water. Midway through my day on KP, I actually fell asleep while standing, peeling potatoes. I was falling head first into one of the cans of water and potatoes when the other two guys caught me.

. . . .

Just as our company was beginning to recover from the Army attempts to *protect* us from the deadly Meningococcus by freezing us to death, we received one last assault, courtesy of military medicine. A new outbreak of meningitis erupted at another military facility. For patients suffering from acute meningococcal infection in 1967, gamma globulin was sometimes given in hopes that antibodies contained in the solution might provide some immunity to the infection. This was unproven but had theoretical validity... That was good enough for the Army. The government must have vacuumed up every available dose of gamma globulin.

One afternoon, after spending a very cold day outside, our formation was diverted toward an unfamiliar building, merged from four columns into two, and marched through a set of double doors into a long hallway. At the far end, another set of doors led back outside. Halfway along this passage, each pair of trainees was stopped in front of two medics with needles, syringes, and a table full of glass vials. The leading two soldiers were instructed to step forward, drop their pants and a medic administered a shot containing five milliliters (one teaspoon) of gamma globulin into an exposed buttock. The gamma globulin was administered as fast as the medic could push the plunger of the syringe. It hurt like hell! The two victims were then ordered to pull up their pants, run out the doors ahead, and continue running in circles in the yard. Meanwhile, the remaining victims were assaulted, two by two, until the entire company had been similarly wounded.

The recommendation of running after the injections only worsened the pain. By dinner, a few hours later, almost everyone was limping. Double time from the mess hall back to our barracks was accomplished in a gait similar to that of little boys, imitating galloping horses. If it wasn't *your* ass involved, I imagine it looked pretty funny. That night, some of us developed shaking chills and high fevers. Throughout the night, the rattle of metal bed frames identified the afflicted. Upon urinating in the morning, several of us produced red urine which looked as though it contained blood. In spite of these infirmities, no one reported to Sick Call. Over the next few days, the symptoms resolved.

Gamma globulin (GG) is a generic term for a component of blood that includes antibodies to bacteria. In 1967, this technology was still relatively new. Antibodies are large protein molecules with a propensity for binding to foreign substances in their environment, bacteria and viruses in particular. Gamma globulin has a consistency similar to maple syrup. At body temperature (98.6F), it is relatively fluid; at the temperature of an unheated hallway on a cold winter day, it is almost too thick to pour. In our case, the rapid injection of a teaspoonful of this material through a large bore needle caused the muscle near the tip of the needle to tear sufficiently to create a space about the size of a marble, in order to accommodate the thick ball of GG. In those days, the source of the GG and methods of purification were considerably less sophisticated than now. Impurities in the solution frequently caused allergic reactions, including shaking chills, fever and severe body aches. Forcing the muscle fibers apart during the administration of this very thick fluid resulted in the muscle being torn. The orders we were given to begin running immediately after receiving the injection worsened the tearing of the muscle fibers. Torn muscle leaks another protein, called myoglobin, into the bloodstream. This phenomenon probably accounted for some of us noting the appearance of red, bloody urine the next morning. Myoglobin has the same color as hemoglobin. When filtered through the kidneys, it produces urine which looks like blood. During Combat Medic School, a few months hence, we learned the correct method and precautions for administering GG, which contradicted virtually everything that had been done during our injections in Basic Training.

By the end of week four, life in Basic Training was slowly improving. Insulated Korean service hats, insulated gloves, and liners for our field jackets had finally been issued. We were also settling into the daily routine. We made fewer mistakes, which provided fewer targets for harassment by the DI's. The physical conditioning regimen was producing some visible results, especially for the guys who had entered the service overweight and out of shape. Now, most members of the company were approaching ideal body weight. Strength and stamina had also improved noticeably. Private Sal, who had lost over forty pounds in four weeks, was the most dramatic example. His uniform now hung on him like a sack. One morning, we were called to an unscheduled formation. The Drill Instructors and Company Commander (First Lieutenant [1LT] Baisden) were all present as Sal's Platoon Sergeant presented him with an entire new set of uniforms to match his newly acquired physique. The Company Commander congratulated him for his hard work and determination and led a round of applause by the entire group. I think this was the first positive feedback any of us had received since Basic Training began.

— Know Your Weapon —

The next month was devoted to weapons training and life in the field. Oh boy, guns and camping! The Army had recently changed the standard combat infantry rifle from the M-14 to the M-16 (AR-15). However, all of the newer weapons were going to Vietnam, so we trained with the M-14. We were told that if we knew the M-14, we could learn the AR-15 fast enough when we got to 'Nam. Like much of the information provided by the Army, this was partially true. The first day of orientation to the M-14, an instructor held one over his head at the front of the room while rattling off the various specifications of the weapon; weight, barrel length, cartridge size, semi-automatic and automatic firing modes, rate of fire, etc. Then, he grasped the pistol grip portion of the stock and held the rifle in front of him with only his right hand. "Gentlemen, this is not a squirrel gun. This is not a deer gun. This is not a moose gun. This is a people gun. The purpose of this instruction is to prepare you to shoot people."

The first subject was entitled *Know Your Weapon*. We were expected to become familiar with every moving part of the M-14. There weren't that many; seventeen as I recall. A drill instructor reviewed the various components of the rifle and how they worked, while projecting an exploded view on a screen. When we entered the classroom the following day, each desk was covered with an immaculately clean white towel. The instructor had an M-14 on his desk. He took elaborate pains to emphasize the importance of always checking a weapon to ensure it was unloaded before handling it and demonstrated this maneuver. Rifles were then distributed to each of us, and other instructors watched as we checked the breach and magazine for ammunition. Now, things were getting interesting!

The principle instructor, a Staff Sergeant, addressed the group, "You are going to get to know everything about this weapon. You will get to know your weapon better than you know your girlfriend, because you will be sleeping with it for the next year. And, you will need to be able to get it undressed and dressed in the dark... quickly." This was followed by a smile and a wink. "The final exam will be to disassemble and reassemble your rifle in absolute darkness."

There were some groans.

The Sergeant leaned forward on the podium; his look deadly serious. "I will tell you why this is important. I was in a line company in 'Nam. I made a mistake one night that no soldier should ever make. Our Base Camp was semi-permanent, with wooden barracks and tin roofs, surrounded by sandbags. I had been cleaning my rifle and got sleepy, so I left the weapon disassembled under my bunk, figuring I would finish in the morning. In the middle of the night, I awakened to shooting and grenades going off throughout the camp. Before I could move, men started screaming, and there were footsteps running through the barracks. North Vietnamese soldiers (NVA) were coming down the aisle, shooting and bayoneting people in their bunks. I rolled out of the back side of mine and crawled underneath. Fortunately, the closest NVA was busy shooting the guy across the aisle and didn't see me. By the time I got my rifle reassembled, they were gone."

After a long pause, the instructor continued. His countenance was now veiled, but his voice revealed remorse. "Our perimeter had been overrun, and the guys on watch killed. I had been useless in defending our position, or myself... ALWAYS leave your weapon assembled, loaded and within reach, when you are in a war zone!"

. . . .

Over the next few days, we practiced disassembly and reassembly of the M-14's. The instructors emphasized laying out individual parts in exactly the same position every time and in the sequence needed for reassembly. John Merrifield had always emphasized laying out the parts of a tractor in the order of assembly. This would provide prompts, so you didn't forget something in the assembly process, and resulted in the parts being most conveniently located as they were needed. That habit would be even more important now. After several hours of practice, we were instructed to disassemble the weapon, then await further orders.

Without warning, the lights went out. "OK, put 'em back together." came from somewhere in the darkened room.

After practicing weapon reassembly in the dark several times, we were given the news that the final exam would occur the following morning.

On our arrival the next day, each student went to the adjacent armory. A rifle was presented, the breech and magazine checked by both instructor and student, and the serial number checked and recorded. The student then returned to his desk, the customary clean white towel in place, with the assigned weapon.

After everyone was armed, the instructor continued, "You will disassemble your weapons in the dark. When you finish disassembly, raise your hand. An instructor will check your work, and if the weapon is completely disassembled, will tell you to begin reassembly. When you finish this operation, take your assembled weapon to the exit door. An instructor will inspect the rifle again. If correctly assembled, you will have a break outside until the remainder of the class is finished. Anyone who is unable to complete this task will have one additional day to practice with an instructor. The test will then be repeated. If you are still unable to successfully complete the task, you will be pulled out of this Training Company, and start Basic Training over again with the next Brigade." (The Army had some demonic means of encouraging learning.)

The last thing we saw before the room went dark was an instructor holding a stopwatch aloft. I was the second person to present my weapon for inspection at the door. My elapsed time for disassembly and reassembly of the rifle was one minute fifty-eight seconds.

For those readers too young to remember the Vietnam War, four distinct groups of combatants participated in the fighting:

- Members of all branches of the U.S. military served in Vietnam. I will often refer to these Services collectively as "the Army" for simplicity.

- The U.S. was aligned with the South Vietnamese government. We referred to the military forces of that government, collectively, as the ARVN (Army of the Republic of Viet Nam).

- Many South Vietnamese hated their government, a notoriously corrupt series of dictatorships. Some of these citizens formed a clandestine militia called the Viet Cong to fight the South Vietnamese political regime in power at the time. (We referred to them as the VC or Charlie, or by a variety of other names.) The VC engaged primarily in sabotage and ambush attacks against the ARVN and U.S. forces, as well as larger joint operations with the North Vietnamese Army. The VC didn't have official uniforms, and sometimes not even firearms, although as the war continued, they became better equipped. Many of these men and boys were unwilling conscripts, coerced into supporting the insurrection by threats to themselves or their families. A significant number of the VC soldiers were juveniles or children as young as seven or eight. Unfortunately, the child conscripts could kill you just as dead if the circumstances were in their favor.

- The North Vietnamese Army (NVA) sent thousands of troops, via jungle trails, to infiltrate South Vietnam and attack South Vietnamese and U.S. Forces. Most of these soldiers had received formal military training, wore standard military uniforms and engaged in more traditional means of warfare.

— Lock and Load —

Once we had mastered disassembly and assembly of the M-14, we began live fire on a rifle range called the Meter Range. For most of us, this was some serious fun. We practiced different firing positions: lying flat, sitting cross-legged, standing, and learned the preferred method of holding the weapon in each position. The first targets were placed at a distance of fifty yards. After firing a few clips in the various positions, the target distances were increased: one hundred, two hundred, and finally, three hundred yards. The choice of firing positions was also narrowed. We quickly learned the inaccuracy of aiming at distant targets, unless able to brace the barrel of the rifle.

After a surprisingly brief period of practice, we moved to the Record Range where final testing would take place. This was a large field with woods on three sides. The terrain sloped downward slightly from the firing positions to what had been a small creek, about two hundred yards out, then gradually uphill for another two hundred yards. The field was several hundred yards wide, in order to accommodate firing lanes for multiple soldiers at once. Rather than stationary targets, pop-up metal silhouettes painted to look like enemy soldiers in camouflage were scattered throughout each lane. Their distances varied from fifty to three hundred fifty yards. Once a target appeared, the soldier had seven seconds to sight it in and fire. The target would drop out of sight if hit or at the end of the allotted time. A few seconds later, another silhouette would suddenly rise out of the grass.

On this range, we also learned a new firing position. Sections of concrete irrigation tile, thirty-six inches in diameter and five feet deep had been implanted in the ground vertically, to simulate foxholes. We were to stand in these *foxholes*, with our elbows resting on the ground before us, and our non-dominant hand supporting the rifle forestock, somewhat like a tripod. One's standing height was critical. If too tall, you couldn't align the sights on the rifle while keeping your elbows on the ground. If not tall enough, you had to hang from the lip of the tile by your armpits in order to properly position your elbows.

Unfortunately, this suspension system resulted in problems. The axillary nerves pass through the armpits. Compression of these nerves can cause numbness and tingling in the arms and hands within minutes. The proposed solution for this dilemma was several wooden soda crates placed in each foxhole. We were instructed to use the crates as a platform for achieving the proper firing height. Unfortunately, each crate filled most of the diameter of the foxhole, leaving no place to stand while positioning the extra crates on end behind you. To complicate matters further, I could only maneuver the crates with my feet. At my height of 6'2," the tile diameter wouldn't allow me to bend over or crouch down to move them by hand. Standing on a single crate was too high for me, but on bare dirt, even standing tiptoe, my armpits didn't quite clear the edge of the tile. Only the military could have devised this contraption.

. . . .

Everything else about our movements on the Record Range was closely controlled. The Range Officer, located in a tower overlooking the entire field, gave instructions through a loudspeaker. During a firing exercise, an instructor crouched beside each foxhole. On command, a group of trainees marched into position behind individual foxholes. Every order given by the Range Officer was now repeated by the instructors. With the next order, trainees jumped into the foxholes and established a proper firing height (if possible). Very little time was allowed for adjustments. Then, on command, instructors retrieved a loaded clip from an ammo canister and handed it to the trainee. "*Lock and load!*" crackled through the loudspeaker a few seconds later. This meant the trainee should insert the clip into his rifle and load a shell in the chamber. The final orders in the sequence quickly followed, "*Commence firing! Fire at will!*" (Fire at will did not mean an unpopular recruit named Will was located downrange. This command gave the shooter permission to fire

at targets as they appeared, without further orders.) The automatic se-
lector was locked out of our weapons, so the trigger had to be pulled for
each round fired. We were advised to fire only once at each target. Our
supply of ammo equaled the number of targets. If we fired more than
once, we would run out. Any silhouette not scoring a hit was counted
as a miss. The targets appeared randomly at different distances. When
one suddenly popped out of the grass, it was a pretty good simulation
of an enemy soldier arising from a hiding place in the field to shoot at
us.

. . . .

I fired a gun for the first time at the age of seven. For most of us from
farms or with hunting experience, the precautions on the rifle range
seemed excessive, until an instructor explained that this security measure had been adopted after a trainee went nuts one day and started
picking off DI's and other trainees on the range. I'm not sure the story
was true, but it didn't seem far-fetched, considering the state of mind of
some guys in our Company. Again, the practice sessions were surprisingly brief. I had assumed we would spend significant time learning to
shoot accurately; apparently, that wasn't the plan. The goals seemed to
be limited to assembly/disassembly and cleaning of the weapon, plus
the minimum amount of experience loading and firing to allow safe
handling. Whether or not we could hit anything was deferred to a later
stage of training. I suppose this made sense, considering not all of us
would ultimately be assigned to the infantry, however soldiers who
failed to qualify were held back, and made to repeat the training.

The M-14 is a large caliber rifle, equivalent to a .308 civilian big
game rifle. Although I had never fired a large bore rifle, I had plenty of
experience with all sizes of shotguns. I wasn't concerned by the size of
the M-14 or its kick, and I had been shooting pretty accurately in practice. The only thing that worried me was the Range Officer's loudspeaker. I have always had difficulty understanding speech through a
loudspeaker, even when my auditory processing disorder isn't acting

up. Throughout the practice session, the Sergeant assigned to my position repeated each order from the Range Officer, so understanding the amplified voice didn't seem to pose a problem.

We were to fire at fifty targets. A score of thirty-five or above earned qualification as a *Marksman*. Better scores could earn the designation of *Sharpshooter* or *Expert*. An Expert Badge was rewarded with a twenty-four hour pass off-post. I wanted an Expert badge for two reasons. First, after seven weeks at FLW, I wanted to feel some civilian dirt under my feet. Second, I wanted to prove to Uncle Moine that I could shoot. Doing things well enough to please him had always been a struggle for me. As an adolescent, my marksmanship wasn't good enough to earn inclusion in his weekend trips trap shooting at area gun clubs. Admittedly, he set the bar pretty high. He had once achieved a perfect competition score of five hundred clay pigeons hit, without a miss.

. . . .

Since joining the Army, I hadn't thought much about my difficulty understanding speech in stressful situations. There were plenty of people yelling at me, and episodes of auditory processing disorder may have occurred. But in that environment, surrounded by people all performing the same activity, I could just mimic whatever they were doing. Also, the DI's seemed quite familiar with trainees who had difficulty following instructions. If the problem was mechanical, they would grab your arms or legs and put them into the correct position or stand in front of you while physically acting out the proper movements. I suspect a disproportionate number of young men with learning disabilities were getting drafted. In my case, qualification with the M-14 was a painful reminder of the torment my inexplicable handicap could inflict.

On the morning of the test, we were trucked into a staging area, where the day's sequence of events was explained. We were then divided into groups equal to the number of firing lanes available. Those not in the group testing were kept in the staging area before and after their

turn. Some of us speculated that the reason for this was to li
number of targets if another trainee came unhinged. I was in one of
first groups called to the range. Just as the day before, I had difficulty
establishing a proper height. While wrestling with those infernal wood-
en crates, something unintelligible came over the loudspeaker. Although vaguely aware of the instructor beside me pulling an ammo clip
from the box, I didn't hear him say anything. Then came another brief,
garbled noise from the loudspeaker. I was still struggling to get the correct height and assumed my instructor would repeat any order needing
a response. Still, I heard nothing from him.

Unexpectedly, the range erupted in gunfire! I looked around to see
who was firing without an order and realized that *everyone* was firing.
*The orders I had failed to understand were "Lock and load" and "Commence
firing"*! I looked at the Sergeant in a panic. He wiggled the ammo clip in
front of my face. I grabbed it but had difficulty seating the clip in the
weapon. On my second try, it locked in place. I chambered a shell,
kicked all the crates aside, and pulled myself up sufficiently to hang
from the top edge of the tile by my arm pits. Three targets had now appeared and dropped untouched. A fourth appeared at fifty yards as my
elbows finally reached the necessary position. Aiming quickly, the silhouette disappeared before I could squeeze off a shot. Damn, that was
an easy one wasted! Another popped at 200 yards. A shot and a miss.

Now, I was completely rattled.

The instructor beside me calmly remarked, "Forget about what has
already happened. Just settle down and shoot."

A target appeared at 350 yards. I nailed it.

"Now you're talking!" he exclaimed.

I began rocking slightly from side to side, minimizing the pressure
on my axillary nerves. The first four targets had been squandered, and
the next one had evaded my aim, but the reassuring voice of the instructor, when he finally decided to help me, was all I needed.

Of the forty-five targets remaining, I hit forty-three.

ıe *worst* day of Basic Training. Freezing barracks, KP,
e tolerable. *This* was crushing. I *still* couldn't do any-
ospect, it was simply one more example of both the
ory processing disorder, and the power of mentor-
ship. Even now, I don't understand how the difference between negative and positive reinforcement (sometimes as subtle as the tone of a voice) can affect neural pathways in ways which cause profound variations in my performance. However, experiences such as this, and my interactions with John Merrifield, were slowly providing the information I needed to recognize situations likely to be associated with success, and those where I would flounder.

. . . .

An expert badge eluded me that day but produced another souvenir which I still carry. The M-14 rifle uses heavy slugs with a large powder charge. The recoil, or kick, upon firing the weapon is substantial. While suspended from the edge of the tile, part of the pectoral muscle on my right chest became entrapped between the concrete rim and the lower portion of the rifle butt. Forty-six rounds, fired in rapid succession, pulverized a three-centimeter area of the outer few layers of my chest wall, along with the shirt covering it. Fortunately, the Army did not prosecute me for destruction of government property... either the shirt or my chest.

Years later, when my son was little, he was fascinated by my accumulation of scars. He would look me over, pick out a scar, and ask me to tell him the story of its acquisition. The fading, jagged discoloration near my right shoulder, courtesy of that M-14 rifle, was always his favorite.

— A Tapestry of War —

The final two weeks of training were devoted to various field exercises, which served as an introduction to infantry combat operations. These included things like handling and throwing live grenades, exposure to CS gas (a more potent form of tear gas) and other chemical and biological weapons, and practice identifying enemy soldiers in camouflage and estimating their distance. The last two exercises in the series were the Closed Combat Course and the Infiltration Course. The former reminded me of playing war as a kid. We were divided into squads consisting of four or five trainees. A squad would begin moving through a wooded area, littered with obstacles, while firing our weapons at various stationary targets, and providing covering fire for other squad members. Several squads would move forward in parallel. This was a live fire exercise; the purpose being to practice shooting and moving while in close proximity to friendly troops, without hitting them accidentally.

Although this was as close to fun as Basic Training ever got for me, the Infiltration Course was the most memorable. The purpose of this exercise was to imitate advancing on an enemy position, undetected. The fortifications included barbed wire and concertina/razor wire. The experience was enlivened by machine gun fire overhead and explosions nearby, to simulate incoming mortar and artillery rounds. We marched to the course location one afternoon for a brief look and were encouraged to commit the layout to memory. The site was a field, probably one hundred fifty yards in length, sufficiently wide to accommodate several soldiers advancing simultaneously, and barren of any vegetation. A detailed description of the topography and various hazards was provided by instructors.

The point of entry was a typical fortification trench, running the width of the upper terminus of the field. Dirt from the trench formed a protective berm to the front. A half dozen .50 caliber machine gun nests were located above the trench at intervals. Their vertical field of fire was restricted by a steel bar beneath the barrel to keep the gunner from hitting the troops below. The gunners were instructed to hold the barrel against the steel bar and spray fire back and forth across the field, simulating fire from enemy troops defending a position. The instructor calmly added that the elevation of the machine gun rounds would be thirty-six inches above our heads. We were warned several times that under no circumstances should we stand or even sit upright while on the course. This meant almost the entire course would need to be traversed in a low crawl maneuver.

The distinctive element of the low crawl is to keep your butt down, in contrast to how people learn to crawl as infants. Your chest and abdomen maintain contact with the ground, your arms are extended in front of you and flexed at the elbows, legs are splayed at the hips, with the bony protuberances on the inner aspect of your knees and the inner sides of your feet as the main contact points for the lower body. Forward movement requires pushing forward with one knee while pulling forward with the opposite forearm, alternating pairs of extremities as quickly as possible for speed. This maneuver is probably the origin of four-wheel drive. When executed correctly, you look like a lizard skittering across the desert. We had spent hour upon agonizing hour practicing this maneuver and competing in fifty-yard races to improve our speed. Every trainee bore telltale, exquisitely tender, bruises on the inner portions of both knees as a result. By now, we should have all been experts, but some folks continued to have trouble coordinating the combination of movements. They looked more like banana slugs.

. . . . .

Scattered across the terrain were shallow pits, ringed with several layers of sand bags. Within these pits were explosive charges that would be detonated randomly while we traversed the course. If we encountered a low wall of sand bags, it was imperative to crawl around, not over, it. This was emphasized by the story of a recruit who had mistakenly crawled over a sandbag fortification and into a pit containing explosives. He was killed when one of the charges was detonated.

Aside from the explosive bunkers and the machine gun fire overhead, the course included only one other life-threatening hazard, and it intimidated me the most. Southern Missouri is native habitat for rattlesnakes, copperheads and water moccasins; all venomous. The instructor said that during one exercise, a recruit had come face to face with a rattlesnake. The soldier panicked and stood up. He was killed by the raking fire from one of the 50 cal. machine guns. The instructor went on to advise that if we encountered a snake, to back slowly away while saying, "Nice Mr. Snake, nice Mr. Snake". One could then proceed forward at a slightly different angle. A diabolical sense of humor was apparently a requirement for serving as an Infiltration Course instructor.

Near the far end of the course, fields of barbed wire and concertina wire had been deployed along the ground. The barbed wire was mounted on stakes, approximately eighteen inches off the ground. The lanes were too narrow to allow flexing and extending your thighs to provide locomotion in a traditional low crawl. Just barely enough space separated the wire from the ground to allow passage, if you kept your torso flat on the ground and slowly advanced through the obstacle using only your hands and forearms to pull yourself forward while pushing with just your toes.

Once past the barbed wire, there was an open space, followed by rolls of razor wire. Shallow burrows had been carved beneath the loops of wire, just deep enough to allow a person to wriggle past. Drooping loops of wire had to be carefully elevated, to avoid becoming ensnared. In order to traverse this section, one needed to find a burrow, then turn and enter feet first, on your back. Attempts to negotiate these rolls of wire on your belly invariably resulted in uniform or webbing becoming entangled. Disengaging from these pointed shards of sharpened steel was unlikely to be successful while lying face down. Attempting to turn over only worsened your entanglement. The instructors advised that if we became tangled in the wire, to just lie quietly until everyone had completed the course, and the machine guns stopped firing. We were assured someone would return to extricate the victim from the wire, *the following day*. Meanwhile, the hapless recruit could spend the night contemplating his mistakes and hoping a rattlesnake didn't decide to crawl up his pant leg. The penalty for failure in this exercise may sound harsh, but the consequences of making a mistake like this in combat could be far worse.

After negotiating the concertina wire, it was a short crawl to another dirt embankment. The trench on the other side was the finish line. We were advised that this was not a race. The goal was to negotiate the field safely, with deliberate speed and zero errors. Our formal exposure to the course would be late that evening, well after dark. The instructor then added that this would be a moonless night, deliberately chosen, and reminded us to commit as much of the course to memory as possible. For the remainder of the afternoon, there was a good deal of nervous excitement amongst us in anticipation of this adventure.

. . . .

The only part of the course that bothered me was the possibility of encountering a snake. I *hate* snakes, and the only thing worse than a snake, is a snake in the dark. I had grown up prowling the woods, creeks and ponds of Southern Illinois. If one was to be struck by a snake, the face was the most feared location. These bites usually resulted in the worst injuries and were occasionally lethal. I visualized suddenly being face to face with a timber rattler, and kept mentally reviewing this scenario, trying to desensitize myself to the nightmare and fixate on the required response. I *must not* stand up and run!

. . . .

We dined in the field that evening; warm chow from a mess truck instead of canned rations. Plush! About 22:00, we marched back to the Course from our bivouac area, practicing the techniques needed for a night march. Successfully moving a large formation of soldiers in the dark is surprisingly difficult. The course was located miles away from other inhabited areas, and it was pitch black in the Ozark forest. Upon our arrival, outlines of the machine gun emplacements could be faintly seen against the stars. Otherwise, the course was virtually invisible. We formed a single line. A DI checked his roster with a hooded pin light and motioned the first group into the trench, where they took up positions at measured intervals. On command, they crawled over the berm and onto the course. Just then, the field erupted in gunfire. A half-dozen .50 caliber machine guns suddenly breaking a dead silence is indescribable, and a realistic introduction to the unpredictability of a jungle firefight. Every fifth or sixth round was a tracer, trailing a crimson glow as it arced down range. The rate of fire resulted in the tracers looking like brightly colored streamers, slowly waving over the field. The line of trainees was moving quickly now, with no time to look anywhere other than directly to my front. Every hundred twenty seconds, another group was ordered over the embankment. Soon, it was my turn. I scrambled over the berm onto the course and began moving forward tentatively. Within seconds, one of the explosive charges erupted in front of me, followed in quick succession by several more explosions throughout the field. In spite of our afternoon orientation, the size and force of these explosions was startling. Just as my brain was processing this new stimulus, I was showered with dirt falling back to earth from one of the detonations. So, this was what it would be like in Vietnam. I was glad for this exposure beforehand.

As I continued to crawl forward, a white phosphorus flare arced overhead, briefly illuminating the surroundings. For thirty seconds, or so, everything was as bright as day. I quickly noted the layout before me and moved ahead. There was a bunker to my left. As I passed it, another explosion was triggered. Again, dirt rained down. The ground was covered with craters and partially imbedded pieces of railroad ties, simulating a battlefield. A red phosphorus flare went up. I worked my way through craters, around or over obstacles and arrived at the barbed wire sooner than I had expected. I was actually enjoying this, and appreciative for the opportunity to experience unexpected explosions and gunfire.

One of the many advantages of being a farm kid in Basic Training was a wealth of experience with barbed wire. The tips of each barb have a curve to them that punctures clothing and then hangs on. I had learned long ago to stop and slowly work the barb out of whatever it had punctured. The alternative, just yanking on it until it came free, usually resulted in a tear in my shirt or jeans, and a very displeased mother when I returned home that night. I was allotted one new set of blue jeans twice a year, because in that period of time, I had outgrown the old ones. There was no money for supplemental purchases, and torn jeans had not yet become fashionable. (In my mother's opinion, they never would.) In spite of my familiarity with negotiating pointy metal things, the only portion of the course I dreaded was this one. While under the wire, crawling backwards to escape an ill-tempered reptile would be difficult and slow. I really couldn't imagine successful evasion in those circumstances.

I slowly dragged myself forward, feeling for the slightest impedance, indicating I had made contact with a barb. My passage under the wire was uneventful, and devoid of any reptiles. I proceeded forward, anticipating the concertina wire. Another explosive bunker lay to my right. I passed the bunker, located a burrow, turned around, and rolled over on my back. Just then, two more flares, a white and then a red went off, in quick succession. Following their brief illumination, the sky again went dark. The undulating streams of tracer fire provided the only remaining light. In spite of the uninterrupted staccato of the machine guns and occasional explosions, I felt a strangely peaceful aura envelope me. I laid still, immersed in this symphony of sight and sound. A random thought formed. This may be war, but it has its own beauty. The tempo of my brain slowed, and I began to recognize individual elements of the orchestration. I noted the machine gun fire was higher than the thirty-six inches we had been told. Six or seven feet, I would guess; probably a precaution taken after the demise of the unfortunate recruit. A .50 cal. tracer round passing within three feet of you would probably feel like it was in your pocket.

Just then, a deep voice came out of the dark, "You fall asleep over there?" An observer, lying behind the explosive bunker, had noticed my lack of forward progress.

"No, Sir!" I replied. "Just watching the light show."

"Well, better get moving." The tone of his voice was not scolding. I imagine he was thinking the same thing I was.

I scooted under the concertina wire, lifting each sagging loop with my boot, then knee, until able to catch it with one hand, hold it aloft and wriggle my torso past. Soon, I was out from under the wire. I turned around, crawled to the embankment and over it into the trench, which formed a trail below ground level, providing safe passage off of the course. The path was filled with nervous chatter from those who had completed this rite of passage. Everyone was feeling elated. The NCO's directing us back to the staging area seemed to understand and said nothing to dampen our spirits.

. . . .

As I think back on it, the Infiltration Course felt like a movie set piece, and I, an on-set observer. The memories are texturally intense: the feel and smell of the dirt, the chest thump from the explosions, the aerial displays of the flares with their ghostly afterglow, and the continuous rhythm of the tracers weaving each element of the performance into a visual and sonic tapestry of war.

— 4th Platoon —

For most of us, the last two weeks of basic were a big improvement over the first six. Most of the Company had now morphed into at least an acceptable level of strength and stamina. For those of us in good condition at the beginning, the physical fitness tests required for graduation were simply an opportunity to show off. Harassment from the DI's had become more of a game than punishment. The standard penalty for minor infractions earlier in the training cycle, *Drop and give me twenty!* (push-ups), had expanded to *Give me fifty*! but was now effortless. Most of us could do at least seventy-five. The weather had finally warmed up, and we had overcome the initial physical challenges of hypothermia and pneumonia. Squads and platoons were beginning to develop a sense of camaraderie. The last of the field exercises were located in an otherwise isolated area, six to eight miles from our barracks. Typically, we would be trucked to the specified area each morning, in the ubiquitous Army deuce and a half's.

This was the prototypical Army truck, about the size of a small dump truck, and frequently outfitted with a canvas canopy over the bed. Benches installed on either side of the bed were used to convey soldiers, when time and distance made marching impractical. The nickname, deuce and a half, was related to a performance specification that the truck must be capable of carrying two and a half tons of cargo up a sixty percent grade.

Each day, the distance to the training site lengthened. Once the day's entertainment was finished, we might bivouac in the field for the night, or return to the barracks... on foot. These marches, beginning at six miles, were done at time and a half; the Ranger's gait. Our rifles were carried at port arms. In this position, the handgrip under the barrel is grasped with the left hand, and the pistol grip (where the stock meets the breech) with the right hand. The weapon thusly crosses the torso diagonally and is held four inches in front of the chest. Our field equipment weighed about twenty-five pounds. The rifle with sheathed bayonet contributed nearly twelve more. This thirty-seven-pound load was less than half the weight carried by many infantrymen in combat and represented only a road marker on the path to the stamina that would be required in combat.

Although our physical condition had improved considerably, this distance, at this pace, with this load, taxed some trainees beyond their capacity. Every evening, at least one soldier would drop out of the formation from exhaustion. These failures were met with derision from the DI's, and anger from the other members of the laggard's platoon. Any platoon that did not complete the march intact would be sent to the back of the chow line for dinner that evening. I was a member of the 4th Platoon. No one had fallen out of our platoon yet, and we made a pact to maintain that record. If someone felt they were in trouble, they were to notify the soldiers around them. We weren't sure what we would do if this occurred but agreed that we would think of something.

There were only two likely sources of problems. The previous week, we had been allowed to elect *acting* squad leaders from amongst our fellow trainees. These individuals wore armbands, indicating a temporary rank of corporal. One of our acting squad leaders, a twenty-four-year-old attorney serving his stint in the National Guard, was the grand old man of the Company. He was a mentor to many of us and very popular. Unfortunately, he had emphysema. In retrospect, I suspect he had alpha one anti-trypsin deficiency, a genetic condition resulting in the development of obstructive lung disease (COPD) by early adulthood. He should have been exempt from military service, but as I had learned on the day of my induction, the Army wasn't being real picky in February, 1967. Our Corporal insisted he wanted to do his part, just as the rest of us were, and refused to request a medical re-evaluation. In spite of extraordinary effort, he reached his physical limit during one of the evening runs. There was no risk of ridicule if he dropped out. Almost everyone knew he had breathing problems, and he was highly respected. However, in order to retain their appointment, acting squad leaders were required to successfully complete every activity. If he dropped out, CPL Harry would lose his stripes. Our other problem was a recruit who had steadfastly remained overweight throughout the training cycle. He never seemed to work very hard at the physical exercises, complained constantly, and was known to have sneaked out of the Company area to visit a candy machine at the closest enlisted men's club. He was neither liked nor respected.

The perfect storm broke one evening, as we were chugging along a route of about eight miles. For the preceding couple of days, the guys adjacent to Harry in the formation had been asking him to pass his equipment to them while we ran, because he was becoming noticeably cyanotic (skin turning blue) before finishing the marches. Finally, on this day, he could go no further. At the last minute before he passed out, guys on either side grabbed him by the arms and caught his rifle. Now, they had their hands more than full and were in danger of dropping the weapon. I passed word up the line to send the rifle back to me. I am not exceptionally muscular. I have always been clumsy as hell. But I was strong enough, and the pace of one hundred forty steps per minute was in my sweet spot. Right then, I could have run until next week.

The rifle was passed back to me. I found a way to cradle it in my arms between my weapon and my chest. The men in front, managed to link arms with Harry. Initially, they had to drag him because he was barely conscious. Someone else pulled off Harry's pack and slipped an arm through the straps. After a little rest, our acting corporal was able to resume moving his legs, with support from either side. Fourth Platoon kept chugging along. Fortunately, the Drill Instructors were running in a group slightly ahead of the company formation, talking and joking, and didn't notice the *adjustments* to our formation.

Our luck didn't last for long. Soon after the accommodations were made for Harry, our corpulent platoon member began gasping that he couldn't make it any further. I couldn't see him because his position was directly behind me, but the guys on either side of him were of the opinion that he just wasn't trying very hard, as usual. They began threatening him.

One of them was particularly eloquent. "I'm not going to carry your ass, but if you fall out, I will beat you half to death when you get back to the barracks tonight!"

This encouragement worked briefly, but then PVT Corpulent resumed his whining, and actually dropped back a few steps behind the formation. Everyone else in the platoon was galvanized to complete this run successfully. Although talking wasn't allowed while marching or running, the DI's still weren't paying attention. There were frequent encouraging comments from other members of our platoon and offers to take turns carrying the extra gear. People even began trying to motivate PVT Corpulent. I was determined not to lose him. I looked over my shoulder and asked someone to take his rifle. Then I told PVT C. to grab ahold of my pack. He did, and I began pulling him along behind me. The platoon was still intact.

As for me? I would have dragged that son of a bitch all the way to St. Louis, if necessary.

Then, as they say in the Army, our shit got really bad. The Company Commander was rarely present during field exercises. A Second Lieutenant (2LT or Second Louie) designated as the Training Officer (TO), sporadically appeared throughout the day. The Drill Instructors were our only constant companions. From our perspective, the less time the TO was within sight, the better. He was a prick! The DI's seemed almost benevolent by comparison. The only predictable element of the Lieutenant's* surprise visits, aside from his vile temper, was that they reliably ended by about 16:00. It was now past 18:00. To our dismay, the Training Officer suddenly appeared near the head of the column.

"Oh, shit!

I don't remember if anyone actually said it, but we were all thinking it. If he reviewed the entire company, we were screwed!

Slowly, he began working his way back, running alongside each platoon, barking at individuals whose rifle was sagging a little, or row wasn't perfectly straight. Eventually, his attention focused on 4th Platoon. Although we were supposed to be staring straight ahead, I think every eyeball was on the TO.

For a few seconds, his brain didn't seem to process the irregular appearance before him. Then, his head jerked forward, his face reddened, and his eyes blinked rapidly. His jaw seemed to ratchet up and down spasmodically before he sputtered in disbelief, "*What the hell are you doing?!*"

Silence.

He ran to the forward corner of our formation, and began backpedaling, in front of us.

"*What the HELL is going on here?!*"

The Lieutenant's countenance resembled an overly ripe tomato. He was perspiring, the veins were standing out on his forehead, and his facial hue was becoming ever more violaceous.

Finally, someone in front summoned the nerve to speak, "He can't run any further, Sir. He's sick!"

In reply, the junior officer *SCREAMED,* "*Drop that man!*"

The guys in the front row maintained their grip on Harry, as 4th Platoon continued to rumble along.

"*I gave you a direct order! DROP THAT MAN!*" The Training Officer was now apoplectic. Fourth Platoon mutely continued to carry its load.

His bluff called, the Lieutenant clearly didn't know what to do next. His head jerked erratically, as he stared first one way, and then another. He appeared to be coming unhinged.

Then his gaze fixed on the uneven silhouette at the rear of the column. He abandoned the front row and zeroed in on my position.

Ugh! My turn, I thought to myself.

"What are you doing with that weapon?" the TO snarled, not bothering to stipulate *which* weapon we both knew he was talking about. At least, he hadn't seemed to notice the two-hundred-pound man I was dragging behind me.

"Does that weapon belong to the Corporal?"

"Yes, Sir."

"DROP IT! THAT'S A DIRECT ORDER! DROP THAT RIFLE!"

"I do not drop a weapon, Sir." I simply could not think of anything else to say.

"I AM GIVING YOU A DIRECT ORDER! DROP THAT WEAPON!" By this time, the Second Louie's eyes were bugging out like a frog. Sweat was flying off of his face as he ran. His color had changed from violaceous to a deepening purple. He looked as though he was going to have a stroke, and I was beginning to see bars on a cell window at Ft. Leavenworth. A stroke would probably be the only thing to save me.

After a few moments of gasping for air, he started in again, his voice cracking, as he screamed at the top of his lungs, "I GAVE YOU A *DIRECT ORDER!"* (pause)
"YOU ARE DISOBEYING A DIRECT ORDER! DO YOU HEAR ME?!"

I kept running, saying nothing.

And then, at the maximum decibels the squealing little pig could squeeze out, *"I AM GOING TO HAVE YOU COURT-MARTIALED!"*

Shit! Now what to do? I only knew one thing for certain... I was not going to drop that rifle until the military police arrived and took it away from me.

. . . .

At that moment, a staff car appeared about forty feet off to our side. It pulled even with the formation and slowly rolled along at our pace. A rear door opened, and 1LT Baisden alighted at a run.

The Second Lieutenant noticed his boss and ran up to him. *"They are disobeying direct orders! I want them court-martialed!"* The Second Louie reminded me of a tattle-tale girl on the playground in grade school.

Lieutenant Baisden acknowledged his junior officer with a slight nod, as he scanned the trotting company of troops. He fixed on 4th Platoon and began to lope smoothly toward us. I had never seen him run before. He was tall and thin, with the grace and fluidity of a leopard. The TO trotted along, a half-step behind the CO, sputtering that he had given a direct order for the men in the front row to drop a man, and they had refused.

"And *that one* (pointing at me), refused a DIRECT ORDER (he was squealing again) *TO DROP HIS RIFLE!*"

Lieutenant Baisden was now directly in front of Harry, backpedaling effortlessly at our pace. "If this man can't keep up, why won't you drop him?" he asked. His voice was calm, but loud enough for all of us to hear.

The two guys in front, emboldened by the CO's non-confrontational tone, 'fessed up. "If he drops out, he loses his stripes. We like Harry. We want him to be our squad leader. Besides, he has something wrong with his lungs. It isn't his fault that he can't run."

The First Lieutenant, saying nothing, adjusted his trajectory until he was alongside the platoon. He then slowed his pace until the rear of the column caught up to him. He ran backwards and sideways as smoothly and easily as a point guard in the NBA, while we lumbered along at time and a half. He reached my row.

The Training Officer was now literally jumping up and down, like an excited child. *"That's him! That's him! He refused a direct order to drop that rifle! I want him court-martialed!"*

Ignoring the TO, Lieutenant Baisden looked at me, and asked calmly, "Why didn't you drop the rifle?"

I was unsure how to answer the question, but this inquisitor certainly seemed more sympathetic than the last, so I repeated, "I don't drop a weapon, Sir."

He now turned his attention to the trainee still attached to my backpack. "What's going on here?" he asked.

The man behind me said nothing. I was uncertain which one of us was expected to answer, but silence didn't seem an acceptable option. Unsure how best to explain, I ventured the simple truth. "He's tired, Sir. He says he can't make it."

Our CO turned to look at me once again. "And you allowed him to hang onto your pack, and are dragging him along with the platoon? Why?"

I knew my answer to that one. *"No one falls out of the 4th Platoon, Sir!"*

The Company Commander spun suddenly in his tracks and faced the Training Officer. They moved a few steps away from our column. Lieutenant Baisden seemed to be trying to keep his voice down, but we could hear his words clearly. *"You fucking idiot! What do you think we have been trying to teach these men for the last seven weeks! Go get in the staff car!"*

The Second Louie looked like a freshly whipped dog as he trotted off to the brown sedan, which had continued to keep pace with us during this interchange.

LT Baisden fell in beside 4th Platoon once more and ran with us. Then, he dropped back to the row behind me. I couldn't see his face, but his voice crackled with icy contempt. *"Let go of that man!"*

At first, I was unsure of his intended target.

Then he repeated, *"Let go of that man! You don't deserve to be in the 4th Platoon!"*

Unquestionably, *this* was not an order to be ignored. I felt the weight of the soldier behind me slip away and heard a grunt as he stumbled and fell to the ground.

Our Commander yelled back at the whimpering trainee, lying in the road behind us, "From now on, you are in the 5th Platoon!" (There are only four platoons in a company.)

He then picked up his pace, slowly passing the troops in front of us, occasionally offering a comment or compliment to someone.

. . . .

After reaching the front of the column and trotting alongside for a few minutes, he drifted back to my row. "Let me have that rifle, son." His tone sounded almost cordial.

I handed the extra weapon through the column of men to him. He slung the M-14 over his shoulder and adjusted the strap, effortlessly, while increasing his pace, a maneuver none of us would have been able to accomplish on the run. His every action was as smooth and graceful as ours were clumsy and awkward. *An Army Ranger.* So, this was what the best trained and most proficient soldiers on earth looked like in the field.

LT Baisden waved off the DI's accompanying our formation. They fell back and out of sight. He stayed with us until we reached the company area. At the conclusion of each of these runs, we always stopped on a designated line, in front of a podium. The Senior Drill Instructor would then make comments, usually critical, of our performance that day and tell us what was scheduled for the next day. On this particular evening, Baisden stopped us fifty yards short of the podium. He strode back to the 4th Platoon, "4th Platoon! Left, face!"

We turned 90 degrees to our left.

"Forward, march!"

We marched perpendicular to the column until the last of our rows had cleared the columns in front of us.

"Halt!

"Right, face!"

"Forward, march!"

We marched past the other three platoons and took a position at the head of the column. He then led the Company to our usual stopping point. The Drill Sergeants had reappeared and were standing in their positions behind the podium. LT Baisden climbed the steps and addressed the formation. "Many of you are probably unaware of some things that occurred during the march this afternoon. You will undoubtedly hear about them tonight in the barracks. I want to tell you that 4th Platoon exhibited exemplary behavior. They stuck together as a team and helped each other when needed. I am extremely proud of the 4th Platoon, and that is why I wanted them to lead the Company into our compound this evening. I am confident all of you are learning trust and loyalty to one another, and the importance of working as a team. These things will help keep you alive in combat. But, if you have any questions as to how this is done, just look to the 4th Platoon.

Dismissed!"

We were first in the chow line *that* night.

. . . .

Of course, there is a post-script to the above story. Harry did not lose his stripes. In fact, he had met with LT Baisden a few days before this incident. During that meeting, our Corporal identified himself as an attorney and member of the Bar. He then described several episodes during which the training cadre had clearly violated the UCMJ. Harry related the conversation to us later. This was another example of his mentoring. Someone asked how he could be brave enough to criticize the DI's and Training Officer when talking to the Company Commander.

"I made no threats. I identified myself as an attorney and explained that the information provided was meant as a courtesy, because I felt he would want to know. But, I was very clear regarding my familiarity with the UCMJ. I listed the pertinent section and heading for each of the infractions."

"What did he say?"

"He thanked me for the information. By the way he looked and acted, I had a feeling he would act on it."

Lieutenant Baisden's surprise appearance during our run had most likely been prompted by his meeting with Harry. The timing certainly couldn't have been better for me. We were soon to learn that our Commanding Officer was a man of principle and fairness. From that day forward, when we were preparing for the evening run, a staff car would suddenly appear. The driver would inform the SDI that CPL Harry was wanted at Company Headquarters. Harry would get a ride, rather than having to run. And finally, for the remainder of the cycle, PVT Corpulent was never allowed to march with the 4th Platoon again. He marched two paces behind us, by himself.

As with the generic term Sergeant, the same convention is used for officers possessing ranks with more than one grade. In verbal communication, the officer is addressed by the full rank, without distinguishing a subordinate grade. Whether a first or second lieutenant, the individual is addressed as lieutenant. The same is true for Lieutenant Colonels and full Colonels. In verbal communication, they are all referred to as Colonel. Ditto for Generals and Admirals.

— The Combat Medic Badge —

We were increasingly anxious to learn what the Army had in store for us next, and to get on with it. During the last week of training, a buck Sergeant (E-5 rank), twenty-one years old and just back from Vietnam, moved into our barracks for temporary housing. After chow each evening, we would crowd around him to hear stories of his experiences there. Our assumption was that we would all go to Ft. Polk, LA, for further training as infantrymen. The nickname for Ft. Polk was *Tiger Land*, and it was not regarded as a vacation destination. One evening, the visiting Sergeant came into the barracks wearing his dress khakis, with all of his ribbons and medallions attached. Above the ribbons on his left chest, which signified medals awarded, was the Combat Infantry Badge (CIB). This is an image of a Kentucky long rifle in sterling silver, on a blue enamel background, encircled by a silver wreath. It is one of the most beautiful medals in the U.S. Army, and one of the most highly respected. The CIB is awarded to soldiers who have served in combat as infantrymen. We recognized this badge instantly. However, across from the CIB, on his right chest, was another silver medallion, which none of us had ever seen. He explained that the central piece was a field stretcher, used for transporting wounded soldiers. There was a silver wreath surrounding it. He identified the medal as a Combat Medic Badge.

"But you are an infantryman. How could you have won a Combat Medic Badge?" someone asked.

He explained. "We were sweeping an area of jungle, looking for an enemy unit reported to be hiding there. We were ambushed and outnumbered. The firefight lasted for hours. When we finally fought our way out of the trap and regrouped, every medic in the unit was dead or seriously wounded. The platoon leaders retrieved what aid bags they could find, and an officer walked around handing them out, saying, 'You're a medic, and you're a medic...' I was handed one of the aid bags.

It was six weeks before another medic arrived to replace me. Six weeks qualified me for the Combat Medic Badge... and *that* is the worst job you can have in combat."

We knew our orders for Advanced Individual Training (AIT) were to be announced the next day. These would tell us whether we were headed for further training in the infantry, as expected, or if we had lucked out and been assigned to training for something less strenuous and dangerous. There are very few *heroes* remaining by the end of Basic Training during wartime. By then, the reality of one's circumstances has fully soaked in, and individual survival has become most soldier's primary goal.

The Sergeant then observed, "You guys are all worried about getting sent to Ft. Polk. You better just hope you don't get sent to Ft. Sam Houston to Combat Medic School!"

. . . .

The next morning, I received orders to Ft. Sam Houston, for training as a 91A10, Medical Corpsman (aka Combat Medic). That day marks the beginning of my medical career.

During the period of American participation in the Vietnam War, 2,096 U.S. Army medics and Navy corpsmen are known to have died. Fifteen medics and corpsmen were awarded the Congressional Medal of Honor; eight of those awards were posthumous. To my knowledge, the morbidity and mortality rates for medics in Vietnam have never been publicly released by the DOD. By extrapolation from known casualty rates for pilots, it appears that approximately one third of medics serving on MedEvac helicopters perished during those years.

— Graduation —

On graduation day, Lieutenant Baisden offered us two pieces of advice. "First," he said, "Don't ever let anyone call you a boy again. You are men, and you have proven it these past eight weeks. Secondly, always believe in yourself. After the experiences you have just endured, and the way in which you conducted yourselves, believe that you can do anything."

For an adolescent uncertain about his future, this was exactly the type of challenge and validation I had found lacking in college.

The following day, we returned the paraphernalia of Basic Training accumulated over the past eight weeks. In exchange, we received a new pair of boots, just as promised on that first week. We had run more than 500 miles, and the soles, now nearing sixty days of age, looked like well-worn tires. Presentation of our new boots was treated as a minor celebration by the DI's, and we were congratulated individually on the accomplishment.

One of the final items we relinquished was our rifle. Staff Sergeant Rosario was sitting at a table, inspecting and collecting weapons from a line of trainees. When I stepped forward to present the M-14, he looked at my face, but then needed to glance at my name badge to identify me. I had accomplished a goal set during that first week of Basic Training. I had remained invisible to my Platoon Sergeant. It was a small, but significant accomplishment for me. Much of my previous life had seemed to be a series of failures, and on the occasion of my few successes, too often the response was: *You're just lazy!* or *You must have cheated, or If you had tried a little harder, you could have done even better*. Now, I had successfully completed a difficult task, as judged by strangers, and no one was telling me, *But, if you had only...*

The next morning, I left Ft. Leonard Wood for Ft. Sam Houston, TX... At least it would be warm there.

Chapter III.   Ft. Sam Houston

— 91Bravo —

Although the weather had warmed up during the last ten days of Basic Training, orders to replace our woolen winter dress uniforms with summer khakis had not been completed. When we arrived in San Antonio in mid-afternoon on a sunny April day, the temperature was 94°F. We had been told that a military representative would meet us at the train station, and a bus would take us to Ft. Sam Houston. No one responsible for our transportation was at the train station when we arrived, and there was no bus route to Ft. Sam. The only station employee we could locate was Hispanic and indicated he couldn't speak or understand English. (Unbeknownst to us, the relationship between the local Hispanic community and the military personnel stationed in the area at the time was bordering on open warfare. The station attendant almost certainly was fluent in English.) The remainder of the day was spent trying to find our way out of the barrio where the train station was located, and to a military post on the opposite side of a city none of us had ever seen before. In addition to multiple bus rides, the trip required approximately seven miles on foot, in our wool uniforms, while carrying our duffel bags. *What the hell! It's the Army!*

In 1967, soldiers assigned to the Medical Corps all received ten weeks of AIT. Our military job title was Medical Corpsman. Everything in the military has a number, and the number assigned to this Military Occupational Specialty (MOS) was 91A10. Upon completion of training and additional months of experience, one earned the title of Senior Medical Corpsman, MOS 91B20, commonly shortened to 91 Bravo. One of the many uses of acronyms in the Army was to refer to individuals or groups of soldiers by the first three alphanumerics of their MOS. Therefore, infantrymen were more commonly called *grunts*, or *legs*, or *11Bravos* (MOS 11Bravo20). Amongst other soldiers, medics became *docs* or *91Bravos*.

The potential roles of a corpsman were quite varied. In peacetime, or when out of a war zone, the level of responsibility fell somewhere between a medical assistant and that of a licensed vocational nurse. The medic might be assigned to an outpatient clinic, or to work in a hospital, or to a combat unit preparing for deployment. My chagrin at being assigned to this MOS was not related to the dangers described by the visiting Sergeant the night before receiving my orders. I dreaded this job because, as a child, the only thing I hated worse than school was going to the *doctor*!

Many things about the military have changed since I served in 1967-68. I am told that not all soldiers currently undergo infantry Basic Training, as we did. For recent service members who have served as combat medics, my description of AIT may be quite foreign to your experience. From what I can discern, the training has changed dramatically over the past fifty years. Combat Medics have their own MOS now, 68W. You guys even have printed training manuals! The following stories describe our world then, as Vietnam escalated into a major military operation.

We began training during a period of transition in how the Army viewed the role of a medic. At the onset of our course, the previous curriculum was already antiquated. The Army was embarking on an experiment to see whether a generic, nineteen-year-old soldier with no prior medical experience or inclination could be taught to perform a handful of procedures previously reserved only for trained physicians and surgeons... and learn them in a period of time equal to one college quarter of instruction. This goal was prompted by revolutionary and rapidly evolving advancements in life-saving procedures that had emerged within the previous decade. Military medical researchers had quickly applied this new knowledge to insights gained in battlefield care during the latter part of WWII and Korea. In the civilian world, for the first time in history, people whose heart had stopped sometimes returned from the dead with CPR. Proposals were being made to train average citizens to perform this maneuver before transport to a hospital. Military physicians and surgeons already knew a great deal about how soldiers die on the battlefield and realized, in many instances, relatively simple techniques could save lives, if applied soon enough after injury. Why not push the envelope?

These new insights into the physiology of trauma, the possibilities of resuscitation, and the availability of rapid transportation from battlefield to hospital offered tantalizing opportunities. As this lure sparked interest in places like the Armed Forces Institute of Surgical Research, President Johnson ordered the largest deployment of U.S. combat forces since the end of WWII. The experimental hypothesis and the environment necessary for testing it were now both at hand. We became the experimental agent in what would today be called a Phase I/II clinical research trial (with historical controls). Unfortunately, none of this background information was provided to the experimental subjects... us.

The majority of our instructors were medics with combat experience. Many of them had recently returned from Vietnam. The focus of our instruction was heavily weighted towards the role of a corpsman in a combat environment. I must assume that much of the subject material was being reorganized on the fly, because I don't recall ever seeing a bound training manual throughout the course. We were handed mimeographed notes at the beginning of each subject. (A mimeograph was the forerunner of the modern printer/copier machine.) Occasionally, those notes would be replaced with an updated version before we even completed that set of lectures/demonstrations.

If some background information had been provided at the beginning of training, our experience would have been far less traumatic. In the absence of this perspective, we were frequently faced with an unnerving disparity between our capabilities and the impending responsibilities we were expected to assume.

. . . .

The first week of training focused on fundamental information required to work in a medical environment. We had classes on medical terminology, and how to make a hospital bed *the Army way*. As an example of the complete absence of any medical background in our group, one class was devoted to explaining the various occupations to be found in a medical environment: who was who, what they did, and how they interacted. Very few of us had an accurate understanding of the role of physicians vs. surgeons or the responsibilities of nurses, of various therapists, and medical assistants in a hospital setting. We learned to operate a wheelchair, which is more complicated than one might think, and how to measure temperature, pulse, breathing and blood pressure. We learned sterile technique and how microbes spread disease. We studied the vermin that have followed armies since antiquity, and the diseases they carry. In preparation for assisting a surgeon, we watched films showing common surgical procedures, the equipment required, bandages used to cover wounds, and how best to apply them.

During the second and third weeks, the complexity of subjects began to ramp up. There were classes devoted to anatomy, physiology and pharmacology. Some of the material was surprisingly detailed but focused narrowly on conditions we would encounter in the field and procedures we might be called upon to perform. Anatomy of the mouth, throat and neck, and the location of major blood vessels received particular attention. Physiology instruction was limited to the response of various tissues and organs, especially arteries, to injury. The emphasis was on *functional* anatomy and physiology — if a soldier suffered a wound to a specific body area, which structures were likely to be injured, and what associated problems could be anticipated? Did a large artery or vein pass through that neighborhood? What was the result of a puncture wound of the chest wall? How might this affect breathing? Treatment of specific injuries in the field was mentioned, but classes on the associated procedures were mostly deferred until the up-coming weeks.

The technique for performing CPR was our entree to procedures. We spent several hours practicing the various scenarios. We then learned how to use a face mask to assist breathing by practicing on one another. Being the subject of prolonged ventilation by face mask pro-vides remarkable insight into effective technique, as well as the anxiety produced in an awake patient by this procedure. The following after-noon was devoted to endotracheal intubation (inserting a tube through the mouth and into the windpipe) for situations requiring advanced airway support. To our great relief, practice was limited to a manne-quin, rather than intubating each other. In retrospect, we should have been sent to the nearby Brooke Army Medical Center and allowed to intubate real patients in an operating room. Curiously, none of our in-struction was provided by physicians or surgeons, and none of it in the hospital setting. This was probably a function of the rapid advancement in complexity of the course content. Consideration of needed changes in the cadre of instructors and settings simply hadn't caught up.

There were classes on the various types of wounds encountered, how to choose the best site for insertion of an IV, how to identify and control massive bleeding, and the stabilization of shattered bones in order to minimize additional damage. However, little time was spent on injuries to the brain and spinal cord, with the exception of tech-niques for maintaining spinal alignment during transport. A bullet or piece of shrapnel penetrating the skull was usually, but not always, fa-tal. For our purposes, treatment of open head wounds could be deter-mined by one question; *Was the victim still awake?* If so, keep his head elevated as much as possible, cover the wound to minimize contamina-tion, apply pressure to control scalp and facial bleeding, and call the helicopter for evacuation. If the soldier was unconscious, he was usual-ly triaged Code Black, and prioritized last for evacuation... but this would come later.

. . . .

Most classes were accompanied by graphic photos and movies of the subjects discussed. In addition to mastering the information presented, another goal of training was to desensitize this bunch of American teenagers to the gruesome sequelae of warfare. If we were to perform effectively, we needed to become oblivious to the carnage around us. Acquiring these mental blinders was almost as difficult as the technical information presented. A variety of methods were employed for both purposes. The training materials were of good quality, and many of the films were excellent. Most of the senior medical corpsmen who taught at the school were proficient, and almost all had combat experience. However, these advantages did not entirely overcome the facts of our circumstances. We ranged in age from nineteen to twenty-one. We were inner-city punks and farm kids. All of us had graduated from high school, however with three semesters of college, I was one of the most highly educated trainees in our Company. Our aspirations were to become mechanics, carpenters, farmers, or maybe teachers. Not a single one of us had any desire to pursue a career in healthcare, at any level.

In class, we were frequently berated by instructors if they judged us as being insufficiently attentive. A common admonition was the reminder that we might be in combat within three months. As additional encouragement, occasionally a disgruntled instructor would yell, *"If you don't get this shit right, when you get into the field, someone's going to die!"*

More sympathetic instructors would occasionally comment that it wasn't possible to master all the information being presented, followed by the assurance that more experienced medics and surgeons in the Battalion Aid Stations would coach us once we arrived in 'Nam. These well-intentioned efforts belied the stories we were also hearing that the shortage of medics was so acute, we might be the only medic assigned to an entire infantry company in the field. If so, there wouldn't be anyone to ask for help or advice. Although, the fact remained that the results of our errors would be just as grievous. I began to understand why the infantry Sergeant at Ft. Leonard Wood had described the medic as having the worst job on the battlefield. One thing the veteran instructors didn't tell us, if they were aware of it, was that during most of 1966-67, medics in Vietnam were being killed or seriously wounded faster than the school at Ft. Sam Houston could replace them.

. . . .

As our classes in anatomy and the pathophysiology of various injuries became more complicated, many of us suffered a growing sense of anxiety. For most of my classmates, prior education in science was limited to an introductory course in biology during high school. I was working hard to keep up, in spite of the additional experience with anatomy and physiology gained in Mr. Day's advanced biology class, two years before. The complexity and volume of information being thrown at us was overwhelming. I was terrified of the responsibilities we faced, but I found the course material interesting. Also, the familiarity of sitting at a desk, listening to a teacher, and taking notes, all seemed a pleasant diversion from the grim reality awaiting us. Focusing on the science helped me to push from my mind the practical applications of our studies. While others were recoiling from many of the daily subjects and procedures, I was fascinated. Increasingly, my anxiety was overcome by curiosity about the material being presented. During a class on identifying the location of bleeding, it occurred to me that the methods being described were similar to John Merrifield's teaching about evaluating a broken tractor. Now, I was simply studying a more complicated machine. With some sense of irony, I visualized the rat splayed open in the high school laboratory. I had abandoned college in order to get a broader world experience. This certainly wasn't what I had envisioned.

. . . .

Some of the struggling students began asking me for help, and I started coaching them in the evenings. This was my first experience teaching. I quickly noticed a phenomenon known to all teachers. Trying to teach a subject to others exposes the parts that you think you know but have not truly mastered. I focused on these weak spots and soon began to feel more confident in my knowledge of the material. Whether or not I would be able to apply this information in a real situation while under fire, was a question I simply wouldn't allow myself to consider. But, it lurked in the back of my mind, like a cold, grey fog, never far from shore.

Ft. Sam Houston, TX., 4Jun67

— Look What He Did to You —

The medication receiving the most attention in our pharmacology classes was morphine. For field administration, it came in a container resembling a miniature, olive drab tube of toothpaste. Each of these little units contained four milligrams of morphine. A small needle, 5/8" in length, was affixed to the top of the tube. We were instructed to remove the cap, jam the needle into any area of skin overlying intact muscle, and squeeze the tube flat. When other matters were urgent, the injection could be given through clothing, provided the needle still reached below the skin. For someone wounded badly enough to require morphine, the risk of a small abscess from a contaminated needle was the least of his problems.

The instructor, a combat vet, then added, "The manual says that your aid bag is to be stocked with eight morphine ampules for field operations. When you restock at the Battalion Aid Station, there is usually an open box of the ampules available. I would suggest you fill your pockets. If your unit gets hit, eight is never enough, and sometimes morphine will be the only thing you have to offer."

Several things about this conversation raised questions in my mind, and apparently for some of my colleagues, as well. A handful of morphine ampules could easily exceed a lethal dose for one individual. I could imagine diving into the dirt during a fire-fight and being stuck by a bunch of accidentally unsheathed needles, followed by the involuntary injection of the contents from the force of the landing. Maybe our imaginations were running away with us, but it seemed like a realistic risk to me.

One of my classmates raised his hand and described the scenario pretty much as I had imagined.

"We could accidentally receive a lethal dose of morphine if enough of the caps came off of those ampules... couldn't we?"

"They usually don't," was the deadpan answer.

. . . .

In spite of the steady diet of classroom gore, another subject caused even more consternation amongst some of my classmates, and outright panic in others. During a class on precautions required when administering intravenous medications, the instructor nonchalantly mentioned, that later in the week, we would learn to insert intravenous catheters and give intramuscular (IM) injections. He went on to say that inserting IV's would be practiced on a manikin, however for IM injections, we would practice on each other. For most people, very few subjects related to medicine elicit as much anxiety and dread as needles. We were no different. This subject dominated conversation during our breaks up until the day of reckoning. When the dreaded day arrived, we spent several hours reviewing regional anatomy, including the pertinent muscles, the location of a nearby artery, veins and nerves, and why they should be avoided. Sterile technique was practiced. Next came the mechanics of attaching needles to syringes, how to draw up medication, and inspecting the medication for contaminants or signs of decomposition.

The afternoon was devoted to the laboratory session, where we would give each other injections for the first time. The anxiety was palpable. Some people chattered nervously, others were pale and quiet. A few looked as though they were about to vomit or faint. Many of us were busy selecting partners for the exercise, in hopes of at least finding someone with adequate manual dexterity. Our efforts were in vain. After lunch, we were ushered into a large room, accessorized with stainless steel bedside stands. The various supplies needed for injections lay ominously on each stand. The instructor began reading off pairs of names and assigning locations. Special requests for partners were curtly denied. When my name was called, I was paired with one of the clumsiest, most inept people in our company. He was already drenched in sweat, and his face had the unmistakable greenish tinge of nausea. The instructor, who usually completely ignored any evidence of discomfort in the students, was actually quite calming, as he talked my partner through preparing the syringe and needle. However, the tremulous hands and number of items he dropped during preparations were not very reassuring. I had long held a fascination with hypnosis. Desperate, and unable to think of any acceptable alternatives, I decided to attempt self-hypnosis to control my rising panic. I fixated on a distant oak tree visible through the window. I felt my partner squeeze my shoulder, in preparation for the injection. I concentrated as hard as I could on the tree. Something brushed my arm.

Then, I heard my assailant cry out, "Oh, no!"

I struggled to maintain focus on the scene beyond the window.

The instructor's voice sounded distant and hollow, "Don't panic. It's all right. Just aspirate and inject. Now withdraw the needle."

I stared at every leaf on that damn tree!

The senior medic, standing beside me during the procedure, now stepped forward with a grin, "Look what he did to you."

The instructor held the syringe up in front of my face. The needle was bent ninety degrees at the hub. We had been taught to never push a needle into the muscle slowly. The recommended technique was to grasp the target muscle, then propel the needle and syringe with a flick of the wrist, like throwing a dart. This method causes little, if any, pain... but in his excitement, my partner had become a bit too enthusiastic. The flick of his wrist was so forceful that, after the needle sank into my shoulder, it bent at the hub. He then lost his grip. His hand was what had brushed my shoulder after slipping off the syringe.

In spite of this variation in technique, the procedure was completely painless... and the bleeding stopped within ten or fifteen minutes.

I can still see that oak tree in my mind, clear as day, fifty years later.

— Camping —

Our daily experiences fluctuated wildly, from boredom, to misery, to terror. The temperature in San Antonio had continued to rise. Highs were seldom below 100°F during June and early July. The hottest was 115°F. Very few of the classroom buildings were air conditioned, and most were overcrowded. Lectures and labs were broken up by field exercises. These consisted mainly of three activities. None of them were difficult to learn, however their repetition maintained the physical conditioning that would be critical in combat.

The first exercise was the fireman's carry. This consisted of draping another soldier across your shoulders, balancing the load and running without dropping him. The distance covered was forty yards. Partners were rotated to ensure that each of us could successfully complete this carry with the heaviest soldiers in the company. There were some pretty big grunts in those line outfits, and you needed to be able to haul all of them, no matter *your* size. Our speed was monitored, but the priorities were to avoid dropping the patient and to keep moving forward. We were assured that our speed would improve when Charlie was shooting at us. Except for a few absurd physical mismatches, by the end of ten weeks, most of us could carry almost anyone.

In Vietnam, the ubiquitous UH-1D "Huey" helicopter was the mule of military transportation. When configured as an air ambulance, it was also referred to as a MedEvac or Dust-Off. The second of our regular exercises involved four men sprinting sixty yards, while carrying a classmate on a collapsible stretcher. The stretcher and patient were then loaded onto a retired UH-1D chassis. The Huey would accommodate various combinations of stretchers and walking wounded, depending on load factor. These sprints were repeated in series of four to approximate the number of trips required to reach a full load. In the field, when topography permitted, helicopters usually landed at some distance from the troops for safety reasons. If possible, patients to be transported were grouped in one area. Helicopters landing and taking off attracted enemy fire like bugs to a lightbulb, so landing zones (LZ's) were often hot (receiving enemy fire). Because the number of wounded might exceed the existing chopper capacity or loading might need to be aborted due to incoming fire, priority for transport was determined by the medic. Although a stretcher was sometimes included in the field gear carried by each company, rain ponchos were often used as substitutes. When a Dust-off landed, the medic grabbed the forward left corner of the first stretcher or poncho, while three grunts took the other corners. They then ran like hell to the chopper with the medic directing turning and loading. If available, a replacement stretcher would be pulled off the helicopter before running back to the staging area for the next patient.

This round trip was repeated until all patients were on board, or the pilot or Crew Chief indicated the load limit had been reached. We practiced sprinting, loading, securing and off-loading a stretcher and patient like a point guard practices running and shooting, to build endurance and muscle memory. Certain actions needed to be automatic, such as turning the stretcher at the last moment, so the patient was loaded feet first. This allowed the on-board medic easier access to the patient's head while in flight. The Dust-Off's frequently came under heavy fire during loading and take-off. A trip out of the field under these conditions was like a roller coaster ride. Improperly secured patients might cause further injury to themselves or the crew.

An instructor was always standing nearby with a stopwatch. If he thought a group was lagging, he would sing out, "This LZ is hot! Charlie is shooting at you. *You better step it up!*"

Precision execution of maneuvers such as these could clearly impact the chances of survival during our all-expense paid, three-hundred-sixty-five-day trip to the tropics, courtesy of your friendly U.S. Army.

· · · ·

The third, and most hated, exercise was necessitated by the unique characteristics of the war in Vietnam. We fondly referred to this activity as camping. It was always scheduled in late afternoon because, at its conclusion, everyone was too exhausted to sit through additional classes. Our *camping* frivolity began early in the cycle and continued several times per week throughout most of the remaining weeks. The fun always started with a march of at least one mile. The destination was a large, open field, bordered 'on two sides by majestic oak trees providing a tantalizing break from the sun... for the instructors. The middle of the field was as flat as a billiard table, with about as much shade. Parked on this infernal plain sat a row of Army deuce and a half's, shimmering in the afternoon heat. In the bed of each truck were all the materials needed for a mobile Battalion Aid Station, with the tent folded neatly at the rear. The purpose of the exercise was to erect the tent in a fixed amount of time. The truck beds were hot enough to cause second degree burns if touched. We were divided into teams of four. The tent model we used had a footprint of approximately fifteen feet square, one center pole and a height at the sides of about six feet. It weighed approximately four hundred pounds. The canvas had been coated with a water repellant substance that made the tent as slick as a greased pig at San Antonio ambient temperatures. An instructor with a stopwatch observed and evaluated our efforts. At the signal, each team member grabbed a corner of the tent and dragged the beast off the truck. We were required to carry it some distance before beginning assembly. This was to simulate moving well away from the arcing helicopter blades which would be present when this practice became reality.

We received frequent reminders of the unfortunate disparity between the height of the center pole, and the ground clearance of Huey blade tips. The instructors amused themselves with a contest to see who could tell the most gruesome tale of encounters between helicopter blades and inattentive medics.

"Why do you think they call them choppers? *Ha! Ha! Ha!*" was the cheerful summation to many of these stories.

While lugging the tent to the designated site, invariably a corner would slip out of someone's hands. The neat folds would slide open and that portion of the tent would ooze onto the ground. We learned the hard way that the only solution was to stop immediately, before additional folds escaped, lay the entire tent down and refold it... perfectly, before moving on. It was an exercise in both misery and frustration. Once we reached our destination, two people would unfold the tent, while the other two returned to the truck for the center pole and rigging. The floor needed to be staked down securely, and ropes attached to the upper corners of each wall because on a windy day, once the center pole went up, this mass of canvas could serve as a very large sail. After securing the floor and attaching the corner ropes, three team members pulled upward on the ropes, in an effort to create a pocket of open space inside the entrance. The fourth participant fought his way inside, dragging the center pole behind him. He then had to find the grommet in the midpoint of the sagging roof, skewer it with the pointed end of the center pole, and lift the remaining weight of the tent until the center pole was upright. Once this was accomplished, the three guys outside hurried to tie down the upper corners before a gust of wind blew the damn thing down. Since I was relatively tall, I was almost always assigned to the center pole.

Why, you may ask, did I repeatedly agree to the hottest and heaviest job on the crew? *It was the bloody stopwatch!* If we didn't succeed in getting the tent erected and stocked to the instructor's satisfaction in less than twenty minutes, we got to refold and carry everything back to the truck — then start all over again. That fate only befell me once, when someone else was assigned to the center pole. From then on, I grabbed the pole.

Once our canvas playhouse was secure, we unloaded the needed supplies and equipment from the truck. When all was in place, and approved by the observer, we would strike the tent and put everything back on the truck. If the elapsed time was satisfactory, we were done. I don't think I ever performed this exercise when the temperature was less than 105°F. One insufferably hot day, a trainee asked the instructor why we couldn't work in the shade, a short distance away.

His answer, "Where you guys are going, you will need to be acclimated to the heat."

. . . .

In spite of the misery of this exercise, there were practical reasons for the time constraints imposed and frequency of repetitions. These mobile Aid Stations were sometimes positioned only a few miles from an ongoing battle. The choice of sites was dictated by proximity to the action and availability of an LZ. Being close to the battle meant the sites were also close to the enemy. We were told the Aid Stations often attracted mortar fire. Being overrun by a roving patrol of enemy soldiers was another constant threat. And, the location of even large battles rarely remained the same for more than a few days. Consequently, Aid Stations might be moved every twenty-four hours.

A variety of configurations of mobile Aid Stations and Battalion Aid Stations were tried during the war. We were trained for the above scenario, however the location of treatment facilities, staffing, and evacuation patterns varied considerably between units, depending on geography, numbers of wounded, and the logistics of available resources.

Many of the vets amongst the instructors would tell stories and give us unofficial tips of the trade between classes. They reported that in most line companies, a wide variety of weapons were available, often including Winchester 12-gauge pump shotguns, which provided several advantages for medics. We were told the decision to carry a weapon, or participate in firefights, was left to the individual's preference. There was only one conscientious objector in our entire Company. The rest of us were emphatically in favor of being armed and dangerous.

According to the Geneva Convention on rules of warfare adopted at the end of WWII, medical personnel and facilities are designated as non-combatants. As such, they are not to be fired upon by opposing military forces. In return, medics are to remain unarmed. A small caliber pistol is allowed for personal protection. As the war in Vietnam ramped up, casualty rates amongst medics and Dust-off crews were horrendous. The U.S. Military soon learned, through experience and the interrogation of prisoners, that North Vietnam not only refused to acknowledge the Geneva Convention; they were instructing their soldiers to deliberately target troops and helicopters bearing a white cross. (White crosses on helmets, armbands, and vehicles was the agreed upon method for identifying medical personnel in the field.) The North Vietnamese believed that if the medic in a line outfit was killed, this would demoralize the other soldiers, since there would be no one to care for them if they were wounded. We had already heard about the change in non-combatant status for medics, although this wasn't officially acknowledged in the lectures. The only white crosses we encountered during our training appeared on obsolete equipment, such as the Huey chassis used for loading exercises.

— Do Not Puke on My Floor —

Perhaps because of the effects of this wound and its treatment, one injury was deferred until the end of our introductory lessons. However, the day came when the subject could no longer be postponed. One morning, we were sent to an unfamiliar classroom. From the outside, the building looked like the Army version of a movie theater. There were wide double doors in front. Inside was a large, delightfully air-conditioned room, with a projection screen on the far wall. There were double doors on both sides of the room, as well. All windows had been blacked out. The most dramatic alteration from our usual classrooms however, was the seating arrangement. Most rooms were equipped with desks of the classic combination seat and writing surface, reminiscent of high school. They were crammed into the available space, with little room in between. Entrance and exit were slow and laborious. In stark contrast, this room had desks laid out like a checkerboard, with wide spaces on each side, as well as front and back, so that each could be approached easily from any direction. Once we were seated, an instructor entered and stepped to the podium. His demeanor was solemn.

"Some of you will find what you are about to see disturbing. Some of you may become physically ill. Please note the seating arrangement, and the large double doors on either side and to the rear. If you think you are going to vomit, you are free to leave the room until you can regain your composure... but... *Do... Not... Puke... On... My... Floor!*"

With that said, the lights went out. In a few seconds, an old reel to reel projector started up. The room was pitch black, including the screen. The only sound was the clatter of the projector. Then, another sound became increasingly audible. At first, I couldn't place it. But as the volume rose, I recognized ragged, erratic breathing. This went on for several minutes. As my eyes adjusted to the darkness, I thought I could see a small pink area near the middle of the screen; a piece of pastel flotsam in a sea of black. It seemed to move slightly. I stared intently.

Sometimes I thought the darkness was playing tricks on me. The variable depth and rate of breathing continued, with occasional pauses. As we watched, the pauses became longer. I finally concluded that the pink smudge was real... but *what was it?* The slight movement of the patch of color appeared to be in synchrony with the breathing. The camera slowly zoomed in. I could now discern some characteristic ridges. I was looking at the open mouth of a person. The ridges were part of the hard palate. There was a sudden retching sound behind me, and someone bolted for the door. Nothing else was visible on the screen. This was also confusing because, by the position of the mouth, if this was a mouth, it seemed the face surrounding the mouth should also have been visible. It was not.

Over the next few minutes, the breathing pattern became progressively more erratic. One or two more people hurriedly exited the room. Then, the breathing became shallower, and suddenly stopped. Movement of the mouth ceased. The entire film had lasted less than fifteen minutes. Slowly, the reality of what we had seen sank in. *We had just watched a man die.*

The lights came on. The instructor again walked to the front of the room. He paused.

"Gentlemen, today we are going to talk about burns."

The American soldier in the film had suffered 4th degree burns over 98% of his body. He was inadvertently hit by napalm in a strafing run during a combat operation. Only the soles of his feet and his hard palate were spared. The possibility of survival was hopeless, and so, his treatment had been limited to morphine.

After a twenty-minute break, we began the mundane task of learning the formulas to estimate the body surface area of burns, and how to determine the depth of injury. Common errors in burn assessment were described, with drawings and photographs for clarification. Means of identifying airway burns were explained. Airway burns are treacherous, and their initial appearance is often deceiving. Direct contact burns of the mouth are unusual, because the mouth reflexively closes in the presence of flames. The serious injuries are usually caused by the inhalation of superheated air and gases. The mucous membranes of the throat and airways suffer a diffuse injury, like scalded skin. Within an hour or less, swelling of the airways and increased mucous production can result in death from asphyxiation. Early placement of an endotracheal tube or tracheostomy will often allow the patient suffering an otherwise modest severity burn to reach the hospital alive.

Graphs plotting the mortality rate associated with varying severity burns were reviewed. These statistics were then linked to the process of triage of other types of injuries. The importance of accurate triage was stressed. On initial evaluation, burn severity may be underestimated. The clinical course of a burn victim is often protracted and might still result in death. We were cautioned to triage carefully. Soldiers in whom prompt, definitive care could be life-saving should always be evacuated before a burn victim with a low chance of ultimate survival. The conclusion of the discussion was that many burn victims would need to be triaged *code black*. For these soldiers, treatment was limited to morphine, and they were last in line for helicopter evacuation. Always, there was emphasis on limiting further injury for all wounded and preserving the lives of the maximum number of soldiers. Each of us must be constantly on guard not to be distracted by the most severely wounded if their survival was unlikely.

Then it was time for noon break. Not many people ate. Most sat quietly and smoked cigarettes, including some who didn't usually smoke. The thirty minutes allotted for lunch was followed by a class on burn treatment. The time spent on this subject was disconcertingly short. We practiced bandaging and splinting, although the burn dressings carried in our aid bags were inadequate for anything larger than small burns. In the field, our treatment algorithm for large burns was to remove the source of heat, provide morphine, and cover the patient with a plastic sheet or poncho, to reduce fluid loss. We were strongly admonished to avoid putting water on the burn. The ubiquitous water found in rice paddies and streams was grossly contaminated with fecal matter from humans and animals. Using our own canteen water was also discouraged. When in the field, re-supply or return to Base Camp was unpredictable. We were reminded that it was our duty to keep ourselves as hydrated as possible to maintain peak performance in providing aid for others. Most soldiers with anything worse than moderate burns were doomed. Additional practice estimating the extent and severity of burns and potential survivability came next in the afternoon schedule. Then, we role-played the signs and symptoms of airway burns.

The last class of the day twisted the needle completely off the gruesome meter, but by then, we were too numb to react. This class described the unique nature of phosphorus burns, and the treatment methods required. In the field, red and white phosphorus are used in flares and mortar rounds to mark landing zones and troop locations. During the war in Vietnam, white phosphorus (called the benign sounding name, Willie Peter) projectiles were also used as incendiary weapons in grenades, mortar shells and bombs. Pure white phosphorus, in its solid state, is a highly unstable element which bursts into flame when exposed to oxygen. Upon detonation in a projectile, the white phosphorus disperses as granules which ignite either with the explosion or with exposure to the surrounding air. The granules burn at a temperature of 5,000 °F. Upon contact, they stick to the skin and continue burning until completely consumed. In order to extinguish this incendiary, it must be deprived of oxygen. Once ignited, water intensifies the combustion and therefore cannot be used. In the field, the only practical means of controlling a white phosphorus burn is to cut it out. The scalpels we carried were too small for use in removing the amount of tissue required. The only other instrument at our disposal was our bayonet. Practice sessions consisted of forming groups of six. One person acted as the medic, four others pretended to be infantrymen, while the sixth person was the victim. The victim was instructed to either lie on the ground writhing, or run around the area, screaming. He was to resist all attempts to hold him still. The student playing the part of the medic would shout orders for the four grunts to capture and hold the burning soldier to the ground, while the medic imitated cutting the surrounding tissue out of the designated extremity or abdomen with his bayonet.

Mercifully, the Army apparently had not acquired film footage of a white phosphorus burn in progress, however a number of pictures of survivors were displayed. Most had amputated limbs or gaping craters formerly occupied by flesh and bone.

. . . .

The burn series of classes occupied one day during the fourth or fifth week of training. In the preceding weeks, we had looked at photographs and watched movies of men with arms and legs blown off, with gaping wounds in their chest, belly and head, with their faces mangled by bullets or bombs. These pictures were always followed by an instructor's words, "All right, this is what you do about that."

With the exception of white phosphorus, the superficial appearance of most burns is not as gruesome as many other injuries. What tormented us was the futility of available treatment. By comparison, if someone's belly was blown open, you could stuff an ABD pad (a bulky, cotton dressing used to apply pressure to a bleeding site) into the wound, start an IV and try to keep him breathing. The Battalion Surgeons could perform miracles, if the GI reached the operating room alive. On the other hand, when faced with a major burn, the patient was usually completely awake, in horrendous pain, and aside from a few ampules of morphine, there was almost nothing we could do for him.

Until Burn Day, I hadn't been as shocked by the subjects studied as many of my classmates. Having grown up around farmers and men working in heavy industry, trauma was not foreign to me. Farming had one of the highest workplace injury rates of any occupation. Fingers, arms, and legs were occasionally sacrificed to augers, corn pickers, and combines. People could suffocate in wells or silos. The latter even exploded occasionally. Awful things could happen to workers in steel mills, glass works, and munitions factories as well. Some of these hapless victims were the fathers of my schoolmates. However, Burn Day overcame my resilience. I felt as though my head was being held under water, and I was near drowning. The horrific visual images we saw that day, and the feeling of utter powerlessness to improve on the fate of most of these men, remains indescribable. In our mental journey to accommodate the role we were to play in combat, many of us had reached a point of acceptance by using the rationalization, "OK. I can stand anything, provided I can make it better." No such protection was available with burns. In the entirety of the 91Bravo course, nothing approached that day for shock, revulsion, and worse yet, the feeling of helplessness.

As the days passed, small talk became less frequent and the mood more serious. In the barracks, people praying or reading the Bible was not an unusual sight. Only on weekends, when we could escape to the civilian world of San Antonio, did we cut loose. Otherwise, we stumbled on from day to day, struggling to learn as much of the material as we could, and trying not to imagine having to use it. Those not inclined to prayer utilized the protective effect of cynicism, the armor relied upon by soldiers facing the grim prospects of war. The slang term used by all medics for burn victims was *Crispy Critters*.

— Private Kilroy —

In spite of our feelings about the medical training, which varied from strong reservations to outright revulsion, we all worked hard to learn the material. Although many of us still couldn't imagine actually putting into use the things we were learning, we were intensely aware of our impending responsibility for the lives of a combat team. If an instructor felt that students weren't paying proper attention, or not mastering the information sufficiently, he would describe the alternative of failure, with lurid examples. The emotional pressure these episodes produced was sometimes crushing. Occasionally, one of my classmates would break, usually in private. We would walk into the barracks and find someone sitting on his bunk, with head in hands, sobbing. On one occasion, after a very intense class, one of the guys just dropped to the sidewalk and start repeating, "I can't do this! I can't do this!"

These instances were infrequent, but they occurred. And, each time, the uncertain individual got up, went to class the next day, and kept on doing what needed to be done.

In terms of motivation, there was only one exception in our unit. From the beginning of the training cycle, one student (I will call him Kilroy) stated emphatically, to anyone who would listen, that he did not want to be a medic and would not serve as one. Kilroy sat in class but did not participate. When asked a question by an instructor, he invariably answered, "I don't know."

In the military, the term insubordination refers to deliberately failing to comply with a direct order. It is a serious offense. We all thought Kilroy was clearly being insubordinate, and initially assumed he would be carted off to the stockade. When that didn't occur, we imagined our CO was arranging for him to be transferred to infantry AIT. To our surprise, Kilroy remained in 91Bravo School. The instructors began ignoring him, and so did most of us. One day, in a fit of frustration, an instructor exclaimed that if we didn't learn the information being presented and perform competently in a line company, the grunts would just shoot us and hope for a replacement of better quality. We could easily imagine who was at greatest risk of that fate.

— Code Black —

The subject of triage was addressed in either the fifth or sixth week of school and received particular emphasis. This set of classes, like few others, demonstrated the awful responsibility we would be expected to assume in a matter of weeks. Medical triage is the process of evaluating a group of injured individuals and ranking the severity of their injuries for the purpose of determining who should be treated first, in a situation where resources are inadequate to treat everyone at the same time. The instructor, like most of his colleagues, was stern. He began by explaining the definition of triage and its usage in the military. He then leaned forward on the lectern. His eyes blazed, seeming to pick out each student individually, as his head slowly swiveled from one side of the room to the other, like a machine gun firing across a field of advancing enemy.

"You had better pay close attention here! You *absolutely* must understand this concept and be prepared to apply it in the most skillful and dispassionate manner possible. When you are in a firefight and your best pal, crouching next to you in that rice paddy, takes a round to the head, you must be able to crawl away from him to attend to another wounded soldier who is salvageable. If you call in a Dust-Off for soldiers who are either hopelessly injured or could have waited until a safer LZ was established, and that chopper gets blown out of the air by Charlie, you are responsible for the death of that crew. *You had better get it right!"*

Appropriate triage decisions depended upon accurate assessment of the number and severity of injuries a wounded soldier had suffered. We were struggling to master the identification and treatment of various types of injuries when presented one at a time. Now came the reality that both injuries and individuals injured were likely to occur in multiples. The implications of the instructor's words were terrifying, and clearly not exaggerated.

One component of this decision-making produced by far the most anxiety in all of us. In military medicine, Code Black means designating an injured person as unsalvageable. A patient designated as Code Black might not be evacuated until the combat operation had been concluded, and little or no risk remained for helicopters landing at this LZ. The instructor then described loading a helicopter, while another soldier laid there crying for help. You might need to look him in the eye and tell him, *next load*, because you had made the decision that others were more likely to survive. Little imagination was required for us to realize that in the field, designating a soldier as Code Black usually amounted to a death sentence.

An associated topic was not formally addressed at all. We received no instruction in how to counsel seriously wounded soldiers, tell a wounded soldier he was going to die, or comfort those who had already come to that conclusion on their own. Even the most experienced instructors seemed ill at ease discussing these situations, although most had faced them. One instructor suggested we not form close friendships with other members of our combat team because we might need to assign them Code Black at a later time.

The guys in infantry AIT were being pushed to their physical limits. We were being pushed to our intellectual and psychological limits. All we could do was to focus solely on getting through the day we were facing, while forcing ourselves to ignore the implications of what we were learning, and what would come next.

— LOD: Yes! —

In spite of the disturbing subject material and psychological pressure, training was not without moments of humor. These were probably accentuated by our circumstances. The topic of one class, squeezed in between the otherwise steady diet of blood, guts and gore, was devoted to completion of the intake form required for any soldier needing treatment at a medical facility. If assigned to a clinic or hospital Emergency Room, we would be responsible for completing this document. The subject promised to be stupefyingly dull. As the instructor droned his way down the page, line by line, I noticed an item he had skipped. In the upper right corner of the form was the following:

LOD: Yes_____ No_____

I returned to the task of trying to stay awake, as our teacher described each item in excruciating detail: name, rank, serial number, assigned unit, chief complaint, vital signs, etc. etc. Finally, he reached the bottom of the page.

After pausing for a moment, he said, "You may notice an item in the far upper right corner of the page: LOD. As you know, members of the military are regarded as government property. There are military regulations, which prohibit damage to, or destruction of, military property. If you work in a clinic, you will occasionally see some fool who has done something really stupid, resulting in bodily injury to him or herself. If this injury has rendered the soldier unfit for duty in his/her assigned job, this is a violation of Army regulations. This act may be punishable by Article 15 (the military version of a traffic ticket) or court martial."

He continued, "LOD stands for 'Line of Duty.' Based on the soldier's explanation of what caused his illness or injury, and your examination, you are expected to provide your opinion as to whether this constitutes something that occurred in the line of duty:

- Injury in the performance of his military occupation, this is LOD - *yes.*
- Illness from an unavoidable disease process, LOD - *yes.*
- Injury due to an unpreventable accident, LOD - *yes.*

However, if the soldier was acting irresponsibly, or engaging in a prohibited activity and was hurt badly enough to affect the performance of his military job, this is LOD - *no.*"

Following another pause, "It is your responsibility to provide an opinion. This part of the form must be completed for every patient presenting for treatment. If a doctor is on duty, you may discuss questionable cases with him. The doctor may also overrule your opinion. If the determination is made that this injury or illness constitutes LOD - no, you must write the facts of the incident and the reasons for your conclusion on the back of the Intake Form. A copy of this form will be forwarded to the soldier's unit commander, who will decide how to proceed."

He went on to give various examples of appropriate *LOD - yes* vs *LOD - no* decisions. The discussion prompted numerous questions, and the instructor had to quiet the room several times. This was unusual. Almost everything in our classes was regarded as serious and most of the subject material sufficiently intimidating to discourage questions. The instructors did not tolerate talking or sleeping, and laughter was rare. But, at this point, many of us were thinking of the same questionable circumstance.

Finally, someone got up the nerve to ask, "What about the clap?"

There was some scattered snickering.

The instructor waited for silence with a deadpan expression, "*Line of Duty – yes.*"

Upon hearing this answer, many of the students could not suppress a laugh.

The instructor remained motionless until we became quiet, then... with absolutely no visible sign of emotion, he said, "It is the opinion of the United States Army that a soldier who won't fuck, won't fight."

The room erupted in gales of laughter. The instructor's countenance never varied from a look of absolute aplomb throughout the entire exchange.

— Trach —

The last two weeks of the 91Bravo course were devoted to practicing and solidifying our mastery of the material already covered, and an introduction to several advanced procedures.

Injuries to the lung frequently occur in combat. These wounds can cause collections of either air or blood to form between the lung and chest wall, causing the lung to collapse. Death can result within minutes or hours. A half day laboratory session was devoted to methods of treating these problems, temporarily, until the soldier could be evacuated to a hospital. The first technique (thoracentesis) involved passing a needle between the ribs into a pressurized pocket of air that had been produced by a punctured lung. This procedure could be performed very quickly and might allow the lung to re-expand. The next class covered a similar technique involving the insertion of a tube (chest tube), approximately the diameter of a man's middle finger, into the same anatomical location. The chest tube allowed for drainage of blood or higher volumes of leaking air.

The subject of the last procedural class was an operation called a tracheostomy (*trach* in medical slang). The trachea, or windpipe, is a relatively flexible tube composed of semi-circular rings of cartilage imbedded in connective tissue. The inner lining of this tube is a mucous membrane which provides moisture for the incoming air. The trachea serves as the air passage connecting the rear of the mouth and nose to the lungs. The vocal cords are located at the top of this structure, just above the *Adam's apple*. The lower end of the trachea extends into the middle of the chest behind the midportion of the sternum, or breast bone, where it divides into the mainstem bronchi, which connect to each lung. The design of the trachea allows for bending, twisting, and elastic expansion and recoil while resisting the mechanical forces which might cause collapse, like a kinked garden hose. It is one of the engineering marvels of nature. In thin people, the trachea can usually be felt by gently pressing on the skin in the midline of the neck.

The purpose of inserting a tracheostomy tube was to provide an airway and an attachment for mechanical ventilation in a patient who couldn't breathe adequately on his own. Alternatively, it provided a bypass from the normal upper air passage through the mouth, nose, and throat, in the event of obstruction resulting from some injury. The procedure is not overwhelmingly complex as surgical procedures go... when performed on the ideal patient, under the proper circumstances, by someone with the proper training. Our circumstances did not include any of these necessities.

The surgical approach we were taught consisted of using a scalpel to make a two-inch, vertical incision in the neck through the skin and tissue overlying the trachea. The edges of the incision and underlying interstitial tissue (that's the pink, mushy stuff that all looks alike when it is cut and bleeding) could then be pulled apart to expose a portion of the trachea... provided the incision was in the correct place and the blood could be mopped away fast enough. In most people, palpating the trachea and finding the exact middle of the neck
can only be determined with certainty if the person's neck is extended away from the shoulders, and their head tilted backwards. In an acutely injured patient, there are many reasons why this maneuver is more difficult and dangerous than it sounds.

Once the incision was made, and extended through the interstitial tissue, if the trachea still wasn't visible, you could excavate the trench a little deeper, using needle-nosed forceps to spread the deeper tissue apart. It was best not to use the scalpel though... if the trachea couldn't be positively identified. On either side and slightly behind it are the carotid arteries; the major source of blood flow to the brain. Oh, and next to them are the jugular veins. By the way, in the same neighborhood are the phrenic nerves, which stimulate the diaphragm to contract, controlling breathing. If you accidentally cut any of those things, you are going to be in deep do-do... but, never mind. *The trachea will be right there in front of you, and everything will be fine.*

Unless, of course, a sliver of shrapnel had penetrated the soldier's chest wall and lung, along with the pieces that had hit his lower face, causing extensive bleeding and difficulty breathing; the reasons you embarked on the tracheostomy in the first place. If the unidentified shrapnel in his chest had resulted in an anterior tension pneumothorax, it would be pushing the right lung posteriorly and downward in the chest cavity, dragging his trachea in the same direction, to the right and farther back in his neck. If that was the case, you weren't *gonna* find that puppy, and get a tube into it, until you vented his right chest with a needle thoracentesis. But, that sliver of shrapnel *wasn't much bigger than a needle*. It hadn't caused any external bleeding that you could see, and your patient couldn't tell you there was something wrong with his right chest, even if he could feel it, because part of his tongue had been blown away, he couldn't breathe, and he couldn't talk. But, right then, as they say in the South, he was fixin' to die. *No pressure. That trachea must be there somewhere!*

The instructor hadn't bothered to mention anything related to that possible scenario. *Well, never mind.*

Once the trachea was located, you were to look for one of the rings of cartilage. They form ridges in the outer wall that are usually easy to see. Now, you could use the scalpel again. Make two incisions in the form of an X diagonally across the front side of the ring chosen.

Not too deep, or you will cut the trachea in half.

Then grasp the upper edge of one of those incisions with another needle nose forceps (a skin hook would have been easier to use but wasn't included in the field surgical kits I saw). Tugging upwards on that forceps in the direction of the face should cause the intersection of the X incisions to open, although some trimming with surgical scissors was often needed to enlarge the opening sufficiently to insert the tracheostomy tube.

But, don't take too long making it pretty!

As soon as a hole is opened in the trachea, part of each breath leaks in and out of that hole, usually accompanied by blood from the incisions. This combination of liquid and gas reliably causes intense coughing... if the patient has survived long enough to get to this point in the operation.

The tracheostomy tubes available to us were made of stainless steel. They were about three and a half inches long, curved, and slightly smaller in diameter than a man's little finger. The exterior end of the tube had a fitting of larger diameter designed to connect to an Ambu bag, if assistance with breathing was needed. Once the tube had been successfully inserted into the trachea, with the curve pointed toward the chest, a piece of cloth tape was tied to a flange just below the adaptor, passed around the back of the patient's neck, and tied once again to the flange on the other side of the tube in order to hold the tube in place.

Easy, peasy... right?

Oh, I forgot to mention anesthesia... There wasn't any. Our only alternative was morphine, however if too much morphine was given, the soldier might stop breathing before the tracheostomy could be successfully completed. Our instructor's suggestion was to have two or three grunts hold the patient down, while we performed this delicate operation. We could all imagine how that would work out.

. . . .

In spite of the implausibility of success under the conditions we were likely to face, when one of my classmates fell asleep during the presentation, the instructor slammed his fist on the lectern, and reminded us of the possibility that someone might die because we weren't paying attention. By now, that guilt-loaded missile had been fired too often.

The instructor was a medic who admitted never having performed a tracheostomy. He was neither knowledgeable nor imaginative. He read from a handout with crudely drawn pictures of the proper sequence of maneuvers, while operating a slide projector showing the same crude drawings.

I suspect this class had been added to the curriculum recently. Most of the instructional slides and movies used in other classes were professionally prepared and of good to excellent quality. The material provided for this class looked like it had been thrown together the night before. Of all the procedures taught, this one begged for a laboratory session with manikins or mock-ups on which to practice. These sessions had been invaluable in learning other procedures; providing an opportunity to become familiar with the instruments required, and the sequence of steps to be followed. Even when the mock up was only a vague representation of human anatomy (we used oranges to practice giving intramuscular injections), mechanical skills are mastered primarily through repetition. The practice session after the tracheostomy presentation consisted of forming small groups around tables on which several of the hand-drawn pictures were displayed. We then took turns describing the individual steps required for the procedure and their proper order.

If the class had begun with an explanation that its purpose was to familiarize us with a procedure that could be potentially life-saving, but would require additional training and experience to master, the information presented would have been useful. Unquestionably, the class should have been taught by a surgeon experienced in treating combat injuries and performing tracheostomies. Surgeons with those qualifications were available at the Brooke Army Hospital nearby. Unfortunately, the instruction and expectations, as presented to us, were absurdly unrealistic. The impression given was that we would be expected to perform a tracheostomy in the field, if necessary. We were left to struggle with the knowledge that this procedure might be life-saving, but realistically, was well beyond the level of knowledge, skill, and experience we possessed. In fact, tracheostomy tubes weren't even included in the field surgical kit we used for training, nor was an Ambu bag or other apparatus to assist the patient with breathing after the tracheostomy tube was in place.

During the first nine weeks of the 91Bravo course, with each new challenge, all of us (with the one noted exception) had accepted the task and done our best to learn the information or master the procedure. The tracheostomy class was simply over the top for everyone. In the entirety of our training, I don't think our group was ever as discouraged and disgusted as at the conclusion of that afternoon.

.   .   .   .

In retrospect, the choice of instructors for the class may have been a result of the rapidity with which the goals of our training were evolving. Several days later, when several of my classmates described our frustration with the class on tracheostomy, another instructor taught us an alternative means of establishing an air passage through the neck using large bore needles. Although the method he described has significant limitations, and is inferior to a properly placed tracheostomy tube, the possibility that we could successfully perform the needle puncture method in the field was infinitely greater.

The mortality data from WWII and Korea had shown that, of soldiers who died from combat wounds before reaching a hospital, uncontrolled bleeding and compromised breathing were the two most frequent causes which might be affected by improved battlefield care. Therefore, the skill set we were expected to master was heavily weighted toward those two problems. However, the knowledge and technical prowess required to salvage a greater percentage of these soldiers meant the level of complexity in the medical corpsman training program must rapidly escalate. In early 1967, most of the 91Bravo course was a grand experiment, and we were laboratory rats; running an experimental wheel like hamsters, carrying heavier and heavier packs of knowledge and technical skills. In order to answer the questions posed by the planners, some of the hamsters would need to be run to the point of exhaustion. In our class, no one fell off the wheel, not even the rat with the shakiest start.

— Orders —

Before graduation, each student had to pass a series of tests on the material presented during the ten-week course. Many of my classmates were quite anxious about these exams. Over the last few weeks, as the coursework increased in complexity, more and more of them began asking me questions about our daily assignments. Several of our instructors had noticed my interest in some of the classes, and a few of the students mentioned that I was helping them study at night. In preparation for the exams, a group of instructors appointed me as a tutor. For the last week of school, I was allowed use of a classroom and a portion of the teaching materials during the evening for any students wanting review sessions.

Some of the guys joked that if they didn't pass, at least they wouldn't be going to 'Nam quite so soon. However, the lowly status of trainees made most of us long to complete this phase of our Army lives, no matter what lay ahead. A rumor spread that there was such a shortage of medics in Vietnam nobody was going to flunk the exams.

Exams came and went, and the rumor was confirmed. Everyone graduated, including Kilroy. A graduation ceremony, which I barely remember, was held on Thursday of our last week. The following day, we gathered under a cluster of large oak trees near the barracks. Orders for each of us were read aloud. Almost half of the company received orders to Vietnam. Most of the remainder went to Battalions and Divisions in Korea preparing to replace units scheduled to rotate out of Vietnam within the next few weeks or months. Consequently, nearly the entire company would be headed for 'Nam soon. A handful of graduates were going on to specialized schools, such as radiology or physical therapy. These soldiers had enlisted for an additional year, in exchange for guarantees of receiving this training. And finally, eight graduates received no orders at all. Waiting as approximately two hundred-fifty names and destinations were announced, one by one, was agonizing.

The process took more than two hours. Names were read in alphabetical order with the exception of soldiers without orders, who weren't announced until the end. *Turner, James, US56******* was the very last name read. I had not received a unit assignment.

. . . .

Before we were dismissed, a Sergeant read the section from the UCMJ which described the punishment for not reporting at the designated time and place for deployment to a war zone. The punishment was death by firing squad. Those of us who did not receive orders were instructed to appear at the Orderly Room at 07:00 hours the following morning.

— You Lucky SOB —

The military, especially in wartime, is in constant motion. When the Army relied partially on draftees, this movement was even more complicated. Hundreds of thousands of people, with varying qualifications and lengths of enlistment, needed to be matched to upcoming vacancies at military installations throughout the world. Eligibility for leave (vacation) before transfer had to be calculated and accommodated, and transportation arranged. Even in 1967, a computer was used to assist with this process, but vastly more human input was required then than now. Occasionally, orders, and people, were lost in the process. When this occurred, a sequence of corrective actions was initiated. When a soldier failed to receive anticipated reassignment orders, clerical staff in the soldier's current unit were expected to notify the Personnel Office at The Pentagon immediately. All military assignments originated in a group of offices located in this building and housing one of the few mainframe computers in existence in 1967. Twenty-four hours were allowed to identify the error and reissue the orders. Time was short, because the Training Company had to get these excess soldiers out of their barracks, in order to accommodate the next class of trainees scheduled to arrive within a few days. If the Personnel Office was unsuccessful at correcting the snafu, the soldier was transferred to a unit called Holding Company. This was the military version of purgatory.

Soldiers remained in Holding Company for the time required to repeat the process of linking them with the never-ending and ever-changing upcoming needs of the military. This matchmaking might take weeks. In the interim, the orphans of Holding Company were used as a day labor pool for the most onerous tasks on the Post. KP was a frequent employer.

For those who had received orders, two weeks of leave was the next thing on their agenda before having to report to the site of embarkation for transfer overseas. That evening, the guys with orders were busy packing for home. No matter where their next military destination, they were going home first! There was a lot of excitement and laughter. The lonesome eight without orders felt like high school kids who hadn't been invited to the dance. The worst part was, after weeks of misery and abuse in Holding Company, we would probably be sent to 'Nam anyway. The torture was simply prolonged. Every one of us eight lacking orders would have gladly traded our position with any of the guys being sent to Vietnam, just to avoid Holding Company.

The next morning, the lonesome eight reported to the Orderly Room. The Sergeant in charge had a nasty reputation. He was an angry black man, surly to all the trainees, but especially to those of us with lighter complexions. If *he* was to be responsible for our upcoming weekend, it would not be enjoyable. The Sergeant was waiting for us with a glare. Our morning began with a tirade directed at the trainee who had entered the room thirty seconds after 07:00. Following this rant, the Sergeant *slowly*... agonizingly... repeated the description of the process which would determine our fate. Next, a stack of orders was carefully retrieved from a desk drawer, painstakingly arranged directly in front of him, with the corners of each document slowly aligned... perfectly. Every action was performed with measured deliberation... and obvious relish at our discomfiture.

After clearing his throat and pausing ceremoniously, he began reading the orders. The name of the first prisoner was announced, followed by a brief silence... "*Holding Company!*"

Then, another period of silence... allowing the unfortunate man to contemplate the sentence just delivered.

A second name was read, followed by the same pause... "*Holding Company!*"

This dirge continued on through seven names. No orders for permanent duty stations had been located for any of them. All had been condemned to Holding Company.

Once the seventh name and destination had been announced, the Sergeant paused even longer. Then... his stare swiveled toward me. After one more pregnant silence, he said with a snarl, "And Turner, *you lucky son of a bitch...* you are going to The Pentagon."

. . . .

It felt like I had just won the lottery. I had no idea what a medic would be required to do at The Pentagon, but I was pretty sure it beat the hell out of any immediate alternatives.

The Sergeant returned his attention to my seven not so lucky comrades. In a monotone, he described the restrictions and expectations associated with assignment to Holding Company, before suddenly bellowing, "*UNDERSTOOD?*"

This query was followed by, "*DISMISSED! ...except for you, Turner.*"

The other soldiers filed dejectedly out of the Orderly Room, tracked like a searchlight by the Sergeant's glare of contempt.

Once the door had closed, the Sergeant leaned on his desk, and his gaze turned back to me. His voice softened slightly, "I don't know if you realize how lucky you are."

Exercising a considerable bluff, I replied, "Yes, Sergeant, I believe I do."

He continued, "At The Pentagon, you are going to be surrounded by the most powerful people in the Army. You may even have the chance to become friends with one or two of them. If you know which side of the bread your butter is on, you will never have to put up with another son-of-a-bitch like me for the rest of your Army career.

DISMISSED!"

. . . .

The next morning, I was on the first airplane ride of my life, headed for home.

The Pentagon, Washington, D.C.

Chapter IV. The Pentagon

— A Weekend Pass —

I reported to the U.S. Army Dispensary, The Pentagon on 4 Aug 1967 at 16:00 hours. This was a Friday afternoon. My interpretation of the orders was that I needed to be there by midnight. A medic was at the front desk. I approached with orders in hand, "Private Turner reporting for duty."

His look was quizzical as he slowly took the envelope. After scanning the three pages of military blather, his gaze shifted back at me. "What the hell are you doing here now?"

I assumed he was going to berate me for not appearing for work at 07:00 that morning, so I replied that the orders stipulated to report by midnight.

"I know what the orders say. I'm just wondering why you showed up now. This place operates Monday through Friday, 8:00a to 5:00p, except for the poor son of a bitch... that would be me... who happens to be on call. There is nothing for you to do until Monday morning."

I was surprised at his use of civilian time. We had never been allowed this during training.

His tone softened, "You just got out of AIT, didn't you?"

I answered in the affirmative.

"You're in the real Army now. The rules are quite a bit different. I will get you a bus pass. You can go stow your gear in the barracks. We are billeted at Ft. Myer, VA. Just be back here by 08:00 on Monday."

"Where is the bus stop? How do I get back here? Which barracks am I assigned to?" I tried not to sound frantic.

For the past twenty weeks, I had been told what to do during almost every waking moment. While in Basic Training, we weren't allowed to leave the company area unescorted, except to go to Sick Call. During AIT, a pass signed by the CO was required to leave the grounds of the Fort. The time allowed, where we could and couldn't go, and how far away from the Fort we could stray were all stipulated. It was amazing how quickly my fiercely independent and inquisitive nature had returned to the tethered condition of early childhood.

My new colleague and advisor patiently replied, "The bus stop is outside the door you just entered and to the right. You take the same bus back here on Monday morning. Just remember the Ft. Myer/Pentagon route. We all stay in Train Barracks. It is six stories tall. You can't miss it."

Although I still had a dozen questions, it seemed best not to try his patience any further. I thanked him for his help, hoisted my duffel bag, and headed out the door. The bus stop was easily found, and a military coach with Ft. Myer on the marquee soon arrived. The trip seemed about six or seven miles, but the route was labyrinthine. Walking to work would be out of the question. He was right about Train Barracks, too. It was the tallest thing within sight and looked like an apartment building rather than a barracks. The entrance consisted of sets of large double doors which opened onto a lobby. Army life has changed considerably in the past fifty years, but in 1967, the terms lobby and barracks were mutually exclusive.

A soldier in uniform was sitting at a desk to one side. My duffel identified me as a new arrival, so I handed him my orders without further explanation. He checked a roster, found a vacancy in the section occupied by our company, and disappeared into a small room behind the desk. He soon returned with a key and a meal pass. After explaining that my room was on the fourth floor, he pointed in one direction toward the building elevator, and then another, indicating the location of our assigned mess hall. I felt like I was checking into a hotel.

I took the elevator to my new home. What a strange feeling that was. The room contained four beds with small nightstands beside them. Although there was no space for additional furniture, individual closets containing drawers and space for hangers lined the inner wall. The opposite wall was dominated by a large picture window. This was palatial by Army standards!

. . . .

Ft. Myer nearly encircles Arlington National Cemetery. Train Barracks was just a parking lot away from the border separating the two. The window in my room looked out over the cemetery. If one could ignore the purpose of the cemetery, it was a beautiful view. None of my new roommates were at home, it now being early Friday evening. After unpacking my duffel bag, I headed outside to explore. The cemetery perimeter was marked by a low, stone wall. Walking alongside it, I tried to imagine who built it, and when. This had been the home of Robert E. Lee before the Civil War; a plantation belonging to his wife, the great granddaughter of George Washington. Had this wall been built by slaves before the war began, or constructed as part of the defenses erected by Union soldiers when the plantation was seized after Virginia's secession from the Union? Or was it simply an ornamental facade, erected decades later. Whatever its origins, the appearance was timeless; a stone boundary between the living and dead, wandering through the woods and hills as far as one could see.

The visitor's center, Kennedy gravesite and Custis-Lee Mansion were on the opposite side of the cemetery and not visible from this vantage point. *My view* was of thousands of white tombstones dotting the manicured carpet of green grass, interrupted only by fingers of hardwood forest shading the rolling Virginia landscape.

After following the wall a few hundred yards, I turned back to explore the street in front of our barracks. This thoroughfare transected the Fort. To the left was the bus stop and our mess hall. Walking a few more blocks in that direction revealed nothing else of interest to me. I reversed course; now heading north. Just past Train Barracks was an aged, three-story brick building. Wally Draper had stoked my interest in history back in high school. Now, my antennae went up. A placard identified the building as "Home of the 3d Infantry." The building was a remnant of the original Fort, but its majority tenant was considerably older. Formed in 1784, the 3d Infantry Regiment remains the oldest continuously active infantry unit in the U.S. Army, and the most visible. Its members guard the Tomb of the Unknown Soldier and provide the military escort for the President at official functions. Wally had been dead-on right when he taught us that an awareness of history could make everyday scenes and events so much more interesting. My new neighborhood was a gold mine!

A short distance ahead, the traffic lanes separated just enough to embrace a guard shack between them. An MP was checking the identity of incoming vehicles. Beyond this obstacle, the road curved down a hill into dense woods and disappeared. Its path beckoned. I stopped when parallel with the guard shack... remaining motionless, fixated on what might lie ahead. The guard finally spoke, asking if he could help me. I replied that I was just curious about what was down the road.

"D.C.," he answered.

I continued to peer in that direction.

"Well, if you're so curious, why don't you go down there?" he asked.

"I just got here, and I don't have a pass," I replied.

"You're fresh out of training, aren't you?"

"Yes."

"Have you got a military ID card?"

"Yes, I do."

"Well then, you can go anywhere you want. You're in the real Army now."

This just kept getting better and better.

He continued, "If you walk down that road, you will come to an intersection. Turn to the right. This will take you to the nearest bridge over the Potomac and into the city... but, it is farther than it looks."

. . . .

Sundown was approaching as I started down the winding road through the woods. After walking less than a mile, the vista widened. Trees gave way to grass on my left. Directly before me, the ground sloped gently downward to the Potomac River. Beyond, the Lincoln Monument, Washington Monument, and Capitol were visible in the distance. I was mesmerized. Pictures of this scene and these buildings from former school books and calendars were like part of a family album. Now, they were right in front of me. As I gazed upon this magnificent vista, the sun began to set to my left. I turned to watch. The Iwo Jima Memorial, with the sun's last rays gleaming through clefts in the sculpture, leapt out of the trees. At first startled by its seeming nearness, I stood transfixed as daylight faded, and the sky slowly darkened. Shrouded lights came on, illuminating the statue from below. The hair on my arms stood straight up. My chest tightened. Here was the generation before mine at war. This was why I had decided it was time to take my turn.

What I had seen in just the past hour was powerful corroboration for my dissatisfaction with college and yearning to see the world. Before joining the Army, my travels had been limited to Illinois, Missouri, and Kentucky. Now, the country boy had come to town.

I soon discovered it was two and a half miles from my barracks to the Lincoln Monument, and another two miles to the Capitol at the far end of Capitol Mall. Over the next forty-eight hours, I walked more than twenty miles.

— Don't Unpack —

My first day of work began with forms to complete and procurement of a building ID badge. A questionnaire for a security clearance was filled out, followed by an interview. Most of the interview related to ethnic heritage: how many generations had the family been American citizens, did family members continue to correspond with or visit friends or family in the country of origin? An additional series of questions of particular interest focused on the presence of any previous social or legal indiscretions, either personal or family. In particular, anything that might be regarded as embarrassing, and a potential tool for blackmail by an agent of a foreign government. During our orientation at Ft. Leonard Wood, the importance of information security, and the possibility of being approached by a foreign spy, had been described in one of the classes. Now, the subject seemed a lot more realistic. Hot damn!

Later that day, I noticed something to drive the point home. When I was a young child, the telephone system was little different from that originally installed when service became available to the mass public around 1900. To make and receive calls, connections were made manually by an *operator* at a central switchboard. In rural areas, a single telephone line, running along a country road, might serve to connect as many as seven homes to the central switchboard. This configuration was referred to as a "party line." Each home was assigned a number from one to seven. For incoming calls, the operator routed the call to the appropriate line, and then generated a ring tone, from one to seven rings, to indicate which home was the intended recipient. However, the phone rang in each of the residences, so everyone knew who was getting a call, and since the line was open, the neighbors sharing that line could listen in on the conversation via their handset. This was a common form of entertainment for many rural folks, and the origin of much gossip, as well as humor.

In the mid-1950's, the rotary dial telephone was introduced, which allowed automated switching, and wiped out the jobs of thousands of local telephone operators. The appearance of the new phones for home use was also quite different. The standard model was a black, plastic box with a rotary dial wheel mounted on the sloping front side and a cradle for the receiver on the flattened top portion at the rear. The receiver was shaped like a curved cabinet handle with an earpiece at one end and the microphone for transmitting your voice at the other. The receiver was attached to the base by a cord. By lifting the receiver, a switch was opened, providing a connection to the system for receiving or initiating a call.

In the flat portion of the cradle of every Pentagon telephone was a sticker which became visible when you lifted the receiver. The sticker contained a drawing of the hammer and sickle symbol as seen on the Soviet flag. A telephone line was also depicted, draped across the sickle, with the hammer poised in mid-air just above. Printed above the drawing were the words, *BE CAREFUL!* and underneath, *You may have a Party line!*

. . . . .

Following completion of the paperwork and security clearance interview, I met with Sergeant Major (SGM) Gilbert. He served as the administrative boss for all enlisted personnel assigned to the Dispensary. Although a kindly appearing man, his first words to me were, "Don't bother to unpack. You will be in Vietnam within 90 to 120 days."

After just three days at this post, and three hours on the job, I could already understand the reason for his admonition. This was a plush assignment. Everyone I had met that morning was pleasant, friendly and helpful. Ft. Myer was luxurious, compared to my training stations, and Washington, D.C. lay just across the river. The Sergeant at Ft. Sam had been right. I was a lucky son of a bitch. But my luck wasn't going to last forever. Becoming too comfortable in this environment would only make transitioning to Vietnam that much more difficult. The Army hadn't drafted me with the intent of providing a cushy job in a vacation destination. The Army had drafted me as cannon fodder, with the intention of getting me killed, if necessary. It would be unwise to forget this was a *temporary* assignment.

The Sergeant Major went on to explain some of the ground rules and expectations for this unit. Emergency medical services were maintained 24/7, consisting of a team of one physician and two medics. The team rotated every twenty-four hours, which meant staying overnight in the Dispensary. However, on-call days only averaged about one per month. We had very few responsibilities extraneous to the Dispensary; the only exception being a requirement to "stand guard" at the barracks approximately once per year, which meant sitting at the desk in the lobby. Most important, there was no KP.

Then, the tone of my new boss became more serious, "We are responsible for the medical care of the highest-ranking members of the U.S. military and some of the most powerful civilians on earth. This is the best assignment you will ever have in the Army, no matter how long you stay in the Service. The Colonel (our Commanding Officer) is a very reasonable man. As long as *the Brass* are happy, he is happy. But, if the Brass aren't happy, it must be fixed immediately. If you are the reason one of *the Brass* isn't happy, you will be in Vietnam before you have time to pack your toothbrush.

"Oh, and one other thing. Your experience with people of superior rank has so far consisted of sergeants, lieutenants and an occasional captain. Being around an officer probably makes you nervous, doesn't it?"

I readily admitted that it did.

"Get over it. Here, we are surrounded by colonels, generals, and ranking civilian members of the government. You will be required to interact with them on a daily basis. Show them the proper respect, but keep in mind, they put their pants on one leg at a time, just like we do."

The orientation was clearly coming to an end. The Sergeant Major leaned back in his chair, "Most of the medics are assigned to one clinic or doctor and stay in that assignment during their entire tour here. Since we don't expect you to be with us for very long, I am going to move you around a bit. People are always coming and going in the Army. We have medics leaving positions all the time, and sometimes their replacements haven't arrived. So, I would like to use you to fill those vacancies, wherever they may occur. You may be changing assignments every few weeks, but the advantage is you will get a wider experience as a corpsman. I hope that is alright with you."

I stuttered for a moment, in disbelief, then managed to get out, "That will be fine, Sergeant Major. I like learning new things."

"Good. Your first assignment will be the Shot Clinic."

. . . .

I left his office, still trying to process what had just occurred. One of the highest-ranking enlisted men in the U.S. Army had given me an assignment, and then asked if it was all right with me. This was certainly a different kind of Army than I had experienced up until now.

— The United States Army Dispensary —
The Pentagon

A Medical Dispensary is Army terminology for a facility loosely equivalent to a civilian multi-specialty clinic. The medical staff of The Pentagon Dispensary included eight physicians, practicing a variety of specialties, a general surgeon, part-time ear, nose, and throat (ENT) surgeon, and the Commanding Officer. Other services included a podiatrist, an optometrist, a pharmacy with six or seven pharmacists, and a large physical therapy clinic supervised by a licensed physical therapist. The support staff included two Medical Service Corps officers (the military equivalent of a hospital administrator), approximately sixty medics, several nurses and a small secretarial staff. There was a fully equipped operating room for ambulatory surgery and surgical emergencies, and a resuscitation room for medical emergencies. Our mission was to provide routine medical care for the military personnel who worked in the building, and emergency care for any occupant or visitor in need.

On normal weekdays, building occupancy was approximately 35,000 people. Our patient population equaled a small city, under one roof. Wisely, significant attention had been directed towards emergency care. The officer corps stationed here was remarkably top-heavy, including the largest collection of generals and admirals anywhere on the globe. These men were typically forty to sixty-five years of age (promotion of the first woman to the rank of brigadier general occurred while I was stationed here) and possessed every possible risk factor for atherosclerosis, heart attack, and stroke. Although the building was only three and a half miles from the closest major civilian hospital, very few hospitals in 1967 had designated Emergency Departments or medical staff readily available to care for patients arriving with emergencies. Civilian vehicles designed specifically as ambulances were not available, and there was no communication system to identify the location of medical emergencies or coordinate transportation of these patients to the nearest appropriate hospital. Walter Reed Army Hospital was twenty miles away but required a driving time of almost one hour in daily traffic. Consequently, The Pentagon had one of the most sophisticated emergency medical response systems in the world. The Dispensary was the operational center of that system.

A four-digit number, dialed from any telephone in the building, linked directly to a dedicated line at the Dispensary front desk. This bright, red phone was answered by a clerk during the day or one of the two medics on-call at night. Anyone responsible for answering the red phone was trained to first ask three questions of any caller:

1. The room number closest to the patient?
2. Was the patient awake?
3. If not, was the patient breathing?

Once the location of the incident had been established, negative or inconclusive replies to either of the latter questions prompted a *Code Red* announcement overhead in the Dispensary. If the patient was reported to be awake, additional questions determined potentially unstable conditions. Any suspicion that the patient was a medical or surgical emergency would also prompt a *Code Red* announcement. Otherwise, a dispatcher was notified, and one of the standard transport vehicles would bring the patient to the Dispensary for evaluation. If the situation was deemed a *Code Red*, the senior medic for the day immediately grabbed a large bag of medical supplies kept behind the front desk. He then ran to the scene of the emergency. The junior medic followed with a gurney. Upon arrival at the scene, the medics performed an initial evaluation, followed by the equivalent of advanced cardiac life support procedures, if necessary. The patient was then transported back to the Dispensary by gurney, if further evaluation or treatment was required. Most calls, as is true of EMS calls today, were not life-threatening problems, once evaluated.

The doctor stayed in the Dispensary, unless requested to come to the scene by the senior medic. The rationale for this incremental response? The docs were too slow. They were about ten years older than the medics, and the sedentary life of medical school and residency had taken its toll. Besides, the doctor would be in much better condition to use his skills in the case of a true emergency if he hadn't just completed a brisk jog across the building and back. During on-call nights, the junior ranking medic slept on a cot behind the front desk, in order to be within reach of the Red Phone. The physician and senior medic staked out the most comfortable exam tables available as their guest quarters.

In responding to an emergency, speed, endurance, and familiarity with the building layout were of paramount importance. The Pentagon contained 6.6 million square feet of floor space on seven levels, connected by seventeen and a half miles of corridors. Under ideal conditions, it was physically possible to reach the most distant room in just over five minutes, at a run. This elapsed time had recently taken on new significance. The concept of the five-minute limitation for brain recovery from cardiac arrest had been recognized only a few years before. To our advantage, the pentagonal shape of the building expedited travel between offices, and the room numbering system was infinitely logical. The factors working against us included the massive floor space, the warren of individual offices, and the volume of foot traffic in hallways during weekdays. Out of necessity, there were also a few locations that violated the room numbering system. This aberrancy soon led to one of the most interesting assignments of my life.

Because of the developments mentioned above, the 1960's was an incredibly exciting time to be contemplating a career in health care. Considering my proclivity for excitement and adventure, these possibilities weren't lost on me.

The Immunization Clinic, or "Shot Clinic," as everyone called it, was located near the entrance to the Dispensary because of the volume of traffic at this location. In 1967, permanent U.S. military installations existed on every continent except Antarctica. On any given day, soldiers and sailors were literally traversing the globe. Immunization requirements varied by region and changed frequently, due to new outbreaks of infectious disease. When a soldier or officer stationed at The Pentagon received orders for overseas travel, they came to see us. Military mail was slow and unreliable, so when traveling, Service members always carried their medical records with them. Everyone learned to guard those records closely. If lost, the entire basic series of immunizations might need to be repeated and prescriptions couldn't be refilled until physician appointments were scheduled at the new location, provided there *was* a physician at the new location.

A civilian R.N. was assigned to the Shot Clinic. When a patient arrived, she would review the orders and medical records, then consult a manual containing the immunizations needed for each geographic area. Appropriate syringes would be filled, and I would administer the shots. The immunization schedules were kept in a ring binder because the requirements changed so frequently. The Shot Clinic provided immunizations for 27,000 service members working in the building, plus several thousand people at another office complex called Main Navy. Some days, we were quite busy. From day one, the nurse began educating me on the ways of the building, coached me on nuances that were important when interacting with the big-wigs, and described her encounters with many of the interesting people she had met. The information she provided was both invaluable in learning to navigate this very unusual workplace, and fascinating for a kid who had never been in the presence of anyone more important than a local politician. She was a delight to work with and such an unexpected change from the snarling Sergeants who had ruled my world for the past six months. I felt like I had landed on a different planet. That feeling was about to be reinforced dramatically.

At noon, on my first day, the nurse hailed another medic with, "Why don't you show Turner where the cafeteria is."

I hadn't even thought about lunch, or where to find it. The bus from Ft. Myer had stopped in a covered area on the ground floor of the building. The largest set of steps I have ever seen in my life connected the bus stop with an enormous hallway on the second floor. The Dispensary was literally at the top of those steps at one end of that hallway. I hadn't ventured any further.

The medic introduced himself. "This your first day at The Pentagon?"

"Yep."

As we walked through the Dispensary doors, leading into the largest office building on earth, he said, "You're not going to believe this."

. . . .

Many Pentagon employees picked up a habit unique to the building. They learned the fascinating trivia associated with the place and quoted these statistics to listeners whenever given the opportunity. These facts were sure to amaze almost any audience. My lunch companion was a proud member of this group of de facto tour guides. The area outside the front door of the Dispensary was actually one of the five sides of the outermost ring of the building. It was known as the Concourse and served as Main Street for the building. Stretched along its 920-foot length were facing rows of civilian style shops which offered a cornucopia of goods and services. The shops were separated by a promenade approximately fifty feet wide. This was the first indoor shopping mall I had ever seen, and one of the first ever built. My companion began his oratory.

The stores arrayed before us offered anything a traveler might need, in addition to catering to the special needs of military personnel. Some Service members who served on inspection teams or were attached to the State Department or Diplomatic Corps traveled constantly. Since their assignments could be in civilian environments, some of these personnel wore civilian clothing at work. Consequently, there were stores selling civilian clothing and shoes. A military clothing store also specialized in alterations to accommodate new rank or unit patches. A cobbler's shop repaired shoes and sold accessories. Everything was designed for speed. Clothing could be purchased, and alterations completed within one day. Shoes could be repaired in the same time frame. A drycleaner could process uniforms or civilian clothing within a few hours, if necessary. There was a civilian pharmacy with a large selection of sundries, a bank, credit union, post office, bookstore, barber shop, camera shop, travel agency, Western Union telegraph office, and a radio station. Service members could fly into Washington, take a taxi or staff car to The Pentagon, give reports and briefings to their superiors, restock personal items on the Mall, and leave for their next destination overseas, without ever having to venture outside the building. Candy and jewelry stores, as well as a florist, provided wampum if the traveler was spending a few days at home. The Concourse offered all the goods and services a world traveler might need, and with amazing efficiency.

The architecture and infrastructure section of my guided tour came next. Everything about this place was on a scale that belied common dimensions. The building consisted of five concentric pentagonal rings. Each of the five sides forming the outer ring is 200 feet longer than the U.S. Capitol. There are five stories above ground, plus a mezzanine and basement below grade. The Dispensary was located on the second floor, E (outer) ring, at the southern end of the Concourse. The segment located on the first floor, below the Concourse, actually had a multi-lane road running through it with additional space for vehicles awaiting passengers. This served as a bus/taxi stop and meeting point for government staff cars and limousines. On average, 8,000 people visited the building for work related business each weekday. Civilian and military buses made 900 daily stops to accommodate the flow of workers and visitors. A massive set of steps and row of escalators connected the transportation tunnel and Concourse.

My guide steered us left, across the mall, and onto a ramp leading to the first floor. It looked to be about the width of a highway off-ramp. This being the lunch hour, the ramp was filled from curb to curb. Pedestrians shared the road with bicycles and a variety of motorized vehicles about one third the size of their normal counterparts. These included delivery trucks, mail trucks, and something that resembled a smaller version of a San Francisco cable car. The latter conveyance transported people unable to walk the distances required to negotiate the building. The curbs which lined these ramps and hallways, and looked so out of place to me, prevented the vehicles from scraping the walls. As we dodged people, trucks, and buses, the medic continued a stream of facts, figures, and anecdotes. The five concentric rings were connected by intersecting corridors, like wagon spokes. We were headed for the A ring, approximately one eighth mile away, on one of these corridors. This particular thoroughfare was almost the width of a two-lane neighborhood street. Ramps between floors allowed vertical travel for vehicles, and efficient pedestrian traffic as well. The building footprint covered twenty-nine acres. The innermost (A) ring encircled a five-acre open air park. Maximum occupancy of forty thousand people had been anticipated when the project was designed.

As we walked along this corridor, the visual landscape so violated usual proportions as to be disorienting. I felt like I had nibbled one of Alice in Wonderland's mushrooms. My mentor went on to explain that the building had its own post office and mail delivery system, both for security reasons and because building employees generated 128,000 pieces of mail per day. He also mentioned the possibility that we might see a fire truck during our trek to the cafeteria. A fire department, with miniaturized trucks and specialized techniques and equipment traveled through the hallways to fight fires, since traditional fire equipment and methods were inadequate for a structure nearly a quarter mile wide. An ambulance had been considered, but the idea discarded because the density of pedestrian traffic made motorized travel too slow in emergencies.

During our hike to the center of the building, I suddenly realized this informative chatter had a purpose other than tourist trivia. Within a few weeks, I would be on call for the first time and expected to navigate this leviathan alone in the case of an emergency. Without the information he had provided so far, I wouldn't have been able to find my way to lunch, let alone to a medical emergency. I needed to start exploring, fast!

Over our meal, he continued to expound on the remarkable characteristics of this very unusual place. One of the facts I remember from that conversation concerned telephones. The building had its own telephone system, completely independent of Ma Bell, and isolated from the public system, except through special connections which were monitored by the snoops of the Defense Intelligence Agency. This network included one hundred thousand miles of telephone wire... enough to encircle the globe four times at the equator.

. . . .

As I became familiar with the building over the ensuing months, I too joined this trivia club, and loved to shock and amaze people in letters home with arcane but amazing building facts and statistics. However, for the entirety of my seventeen months working there, the answer to one question eluded me. I am a compulsive reader of historical plaques. I have learned some fascinating things about otherwise nondescript-appearing locations by scrutinizing the information provided on small bronze plates screwed to ancient walls. Soon after I began frequenting The Pentagon cafeteria, I noticed a plaque near the entrance. The marker proclaimed this to be The Lewis Keseberg Memorial Cafeteria. I was unfamiliar with the name. Over the course of my tour of duty, I queried a number of people but was never able to learn what deed had gained Mr. Keseberg this honor. A few years ago, I noticed a news item describing a remodeling project being performed on The Pentagon cafete-

d alteration of the entrance, which required modi-
g walls. According to the article, a worker had re-
ıe beside the doors and asked his supervisor what
ıpervisor contacted someone in the project chain of
of building archives could not locate any directives
autho.... g ming of this cafeteria. Fortunately, someone who
shared my curiosity took up the hunt. He discovered that Lewis
Keseberg was a member of the Donner Party and later admitted to can-
nibalism during their disastrous entrapment in the Sierras over the winter of 1846-47.

I must admit deep admiration for the prankster who affixed this
plaque to the cafeteria entrance and perpetuated the joke for so many
years in a building that prides itself on internal security.

— War Stories —

Under any circumstances, life in the military is nomadic. But during wartime, the environment seemed to be in constant motion. Medics were leaving for Vietnam or other assignments or leaving the Army altogether. New people were arriving, some just back from 'Nam. For most of us, this was a first experience being surrounded by people who shared no common background. These weren't cousins or school mates or even from the same geographic areas of the country. When the staff psychiatrist mentioned he had grown up in northern Louisiana and Arkansas, he and I joked that we were *homies*, because no one else assigned to the Dispensary had roots anywhere in the lower Mississippi River Valley. Because of this lack of shared history, casual conversation often revolved around our experiences in the military. The stories most sought out were the tales of guys coming back from the war. During the autumn of 1967, three medics in our unit had survived remarkable combat experiences.

. . . .

One of them, a SP5, was a few years older than me. He was pretty quiet. I never learned much about him personally, other than he was quite proud to have served in the First Infantry Division, a.k.a. The Big Red One (this nick-name referred to the unit patch worn on uniforms). His outfit was assigned to the lower Mekong Delta. This large, swampy area was densely forested, with rice paddies interspersed. Motorized ground travel was almost impossible. The Delta provided ideal shelter for guerrillas and was infested with Viet Cong like termites in an old house. Amongst the American forces, the area had a reputation for technically difficult operations and deadly ambushes.

One day, when a bunch of us were having lunch together, the conversation turned to armament, a popular topic. People were discussing the various choices of weapons being carried by medics. The SP5 spoke up. "I carried a shotgun."

"Where did you get a shotgun?" someone asked.

"Our Battalion Commander was a big fan. He arranged to have a bunch of them shipped from the U.S."

"What was it?" someone else questioned.

"A 12-gauge Winchester pump with a 20-inch barrel. Automatics were tried, but they jammed in the mud. The Winchesters were very reliable. With the plug out and one in the chamber, you could load five shells. They were fairly light, and with a little practice, you could pump it as fast as a semi-automatic."

There were some scattered comments about the pros and cons of this particular weapon. I was able to add that I had inherited a previous version of this shotgun from my grandfather, and it had been working flawlessly for seventy years.

The SP5 continued, "We were on a search and destroy mission. We got ambushed and overrun. I was on my knees, working on a wounded grunt, when one of our guys yelled, 'Doc, right!' I looked as I stood up. There was a VC running toward me with a rifle and fixed bayonet. He wasn't more than 15-20 feet away. He must have been out of ammo because he could have shot me point blank from where he was. I turned, pulled up the Winchester and fired from the hip. He was so close that when the shot hit him, he just disappeared into a cloud of pink. Soon after, the other VC disappeared back into the bush. We started searching the bodies to make sure they were dead and not holding a grenade. Some of us walked over to the guy I had shot. He was no more than twelve or fourteen years old. The shotgun blast had hit him in the abdomen and nearly blown him in half.

The grunts started whooping and hollering and yelling to the other guys, 'Hey, Doc's a killer!'

I was leaning against a tree, puking."

Some of the VC and NVA would feign death after a battle. When an unsuspecting soldier came within range, they would shoot him, even knowing they would be riddled by bullets from other soldiers. If dying on the battlefield, the VC were also trained to clutch a grenade, pull the pin, and roll into a position where their chest was compressing the hand holding the grenade, thereby keeping the handle in place. If an unsuspecting G.I. moved the body at a later time, the handle would release, and the grenade would explode.

Another of our medics wore the combat unit patch of the 101st Airborne Division. I don't know where he was assigned in the Dispensary or what he did. He came and went very quietly and didn't fraternize much with others in our unit. Someone told me his story before I met the guy. My informant said he had been in Carpenter's Company, then added, "But, don't ask him about it. He's still pretty fucked up over it."

In 1966, during a firefight in the Central Highlands, a Company of the 101st Airborne was surrounded and overwhelmed by a much larger force of enemy soldiers. The Airborne position was overrun, resulting in hand to hand fighting. The Americans were hopelessly outnumbered. The Company Commander, CPT William Carpenter, called in an airstrike with napalm on his own men's position. The incident received widespread press attention at the time, and the Captain's decision was publicly credited with saving his unit from annihilation, however many men were lost, and many suffered grievous injuries. Later, different versions of the story, and opinions regarding the choices made, were not all in agreement. Whatever the truth is, the results were horrific.

The third guy was anything but quiet. He was animated and funny as hell, but he had a vibe about him that anyone with street sense could read. This was not a dude to be messed with. Johnson had served in the First Air Cavalry. The designation "Air" was new to the unit name, and their role in combat was a new concept for the Army. The infantry traditionally *travels on its feet*, and the cavalry, historically, were *horse soldiers*. The First Air Cav had traded horses for helicopters. The Cav was inserted into hotspots by air, in hopes of trapping the VC before they could melt back into the jungle. During 1966-67, they saw a lot of action and developed a bit of cache. Some of their members had a reputation for being flamboyant. Johnson certainly matched the description. He had stayed in 'Nam for twenty-seven months, instead of the requisite twelve, and was wounded five times. He said the Army had forced him to come home when he did, although he would have preferred to stay longer. He told stories about firefights like kids tell stories about cowboys and Indians, but few doubted his veracity. He was simply a warrior who reveled in war. I have known guys who liked to fight and would start a fight out of boredom. Johnson wasn't like that. He never displayed any belligerence around us and was always friendly. However, twice on the streets of D.C., thugs attempting to rob him quickly learned they had picked the wrong mark. At work, Johnson was cheerful and easygoing. The tales he told were self-effacing, and most of them hilarious.

He was twenty-two years old when I met him, 6'0" tall, 185 pounds, and looked like a professional boxer. His only obvious physical flaw concerned his back. One of his wounds occurred when an incoming shell exploded behind him. His back was riddled with shrapnel. After multiple surgeries to remove fragments, the surgeons decided he would just have to carry the rest. They predicted that many of the smaller pieces would work their way to the surface over time.

"They don't bother me much, but I can't sleep on my back." he said. "I get a new set of uniform blouses (shirts) every few months because the shrapnel protruding through my skin cuts 'em up," he added, with a grin. "The Army is going to be paying for this wound for a long time."

"Damn! Do you ever have more of the stuff taken out?" was the next question.

Johnson's face broke into a conspiratorial smile. "Yeah. The Old Lady makes me go see the surgeon every six months. She says the stuff sticking out cuts her fingertips when we're doin' it."

During another of our frequent stories about armament, someone asked Johnson what he carried in the field, anticipating the answer would be entertaining.

"Well, I carried an M-16 with two bandoliers. I kept a .45 auto on my belt, and a .38 special that a friend sent to me, in a leg holster. I had a Bowie knife in a sheath on my other leg."

Somebody said, "Damn! Did you have any room for medical supplies?"

"Oh, yeah. I carried two aid bags and four bottles of plasma." (Twice the assigned number of each.)

"Jesus, you must have weighed three hundred pounds!" someone else interjected.

"Well, when I finished outfitting for the field, I probably did. After loading my gear, I would hang as many grenades on the webbing as I could stand up with, usually six or eight."

By now, almost everyone in the room was laughing at the mental image of Johnson and his cargo.

His face took on a glow and a smile as he relived his glory days in 'Nam. Then, he grinned and added, "We were on patrol one time and got hit. Man, there was shit flying everywhere! We couldn't even tell what direction it was coming from.

One of the guys started screaming, 'I'm hit! I'm hit!'

I yelled over at him to hang on, and I would be right there.

He hollered back, 'No, no! I'm all right. Stay away from me, you fucking ammo dump!'"

Johnson just kept chuckling as the rest of us roared with laughter.

. . . .

Johnson, old buddy, I hope you have stayed sharp and quicker on the draw than your adversaries. My guess is, you are giving the V.A. fits. And man, would I love to watch you go through an airport scanner!

— The Demonstration —

After six weeks on the job, I was beginning to settle into this interesting, if temporary, phase of my military tour of duty, as well as the eccentricities of a most unusual workplace. Although we were very small cogs in an enormous wheel, there was a common identity amongst many of the rank and file employees, whether military or civilian. Considerable pride was felt in being associated with one of the most famous buildings, and organizations, on Earth. Our day-to-day jobs might be limited to the sifting and storage of minutiae or serving the needs of the legion of higher-ranking building inhabitants, but a position near the bottom of the food chain didn't keep us from being interested in the larger perspective, and the events shaped by the power brokers with offices on the fifth floor. This institutional curiosity was fed by an extensive, and surprisingly accurate, informal network of information. New rumors spread through the building faster than a satellite could circumnavigate the globe. For an organization obsessed with confidentiality, one would think this robust rumor mill would have been cause for alarm. I know personally that surveillance of personnel was routinely performed. However, the internal leaks seemed to be accepted as an inescapable facet of managing this volume of information by this large a number of people housed in one place. What was emphasized, was that stories were never to leave the building. In my limited experience, this proviso was honored conscientiously.

When I arrived, one of the hottest topics orbiting the unofficial information cloud related to an anti-war demonstration scheduled for late October. The training phase of military service isn't conducive to keeping abreast of events in the civilian world. When I had entered the Army just six months before, young men in Southern Illinois wore their hair short, and their politics leaned conservative. A few of the adults in the generation before us were beginning to express reservations about U.S. involvement in a skirmish on the other side of the world, now beginning to cost the lives of American soldiers. However, the consensus was, "If Uncle Sam called, you went." Long-haired hippies were a phenomenon limited to San Francisco and East Coast college campuses. Civilian news of current events had not been readily available while we were in training, nor had most of us noticed its absence. Our thoughts were consumed, first by adjusting to life in the military, and then the mass of information and its implications thrown at us during Combat Medic School. Our news sources had been the instructors. They provided pretty accurate information regarding the realities in the field, but the evolving civilian reaction to this deepening quagmire was not included in their reporting. Nor were the profound changes occurring in American society as our civilian baby-boomer brethren came of age. When I reached The Pentagon, I had no idea anti-war sentiment was rapidly expanding beyond the East and West Coasts, or that well-attended anti-war demonstrations were now occurring in most large U.S. cities. I was soon brought up to speed on events in *the real world*.

In April of 1967, a group calling themselves, The National Mobilization Committee to End the War in Vietnam, (affectionately known as The Mobe) proposed a mass demonstration in Washington, D.C. on October 21st. A surprisingly large number of groups had signed on. Organizers were now predicting the crowd might reach hundreds of thousands. An original goal of inclusiveness soon proved unwieldy, as a diverse cross-section of society, from Black Panthers to church ladies, indicated their interest in participating. Some of the more confrontational organizations also announced an intent to march from the Lincoln Monument to The Pentagon, as part of the protest. This excursion then morphed into a goal of surrounding the building and "shutting down the war machine". Initially, the military had not taken the demonstration very seriously, but as the projected size of the crowd increased, and the intent of encircling the building became known, the possibility of a *hippie attack* had sent the Brass into a frenzy.

Contributing to their anxiety was a confidential report from under-cover FBI informants that a radical splinter group was plotting to gain access to the building and detonate one or more explosive devices. This was no idle threat. A member of the group was known to have technical expertise in bomb-making. The individual had been under constant surveillance for some time, but less than four months before "D-Day"... the agents lost him. The FBI attempted to keep this information confidential, not wanting to admit to other agencies or the public that they had been outwitted by some "dope smoking hippie." Of course, this fumble was simply too good a story to keep quiet, and the FBI had too many enemies in other branches of the government. The news circulated throughout The Pentagon almost immediately. A monumental cat-fight quickly erupted between the multitude of civilian and military agencies with overlapping responsibilities for security.

In preparation for the approaching cataclysm, one of the few items readily agreed upon was the role of The Pentagon Dispensary. We were tasked with treating any injured military personnel, as well as anyone else with a life-threatening emergency. Word soon circulated in the Dispensary that a team was being formed. The upcoming demonstration looked like history in the making to me. With my insatiable curiosity and fondness for history, I promptly volunteered. We were told to anticipate having to stay in the building for three or more days. This dampened the enthusiasm of most of my colleagues. To further reduce the number of contestants, none of the guys recently returned from Vietnam were asked to participate, and none volunteered. In spite of my lowly rank and meager experience, I made the team.

We began preparing almost immediately. Our first meeting, con-ducted by SGM Gilbert, was surprisingly candid, and focused almost entirely on the political and tactical military issues, rather than the medical. He reminded us that we were stationed in a political town, and therefore, conduct must be adjusted accordingly. This assignment would require political sensitivities well beyond anything we had previously experienced. Planning for the event also involved many uncertainties. He then described the, as yet, confidential information about the bomb plot, and missing bomber. *Now*, he had our attention.

Next, the Sergeant Major described the plan for defending the building. We needed this information in order to allocate medical resources and prepare for contingencies, however I was surprised at the detail he provided. The preparations were impressive. The building would be encircled by a line of military policemen and infantry veterans. Additional infantry troops and U.S. Marshal's would be clustered between the line and the building. Strike teams of 82ndnd Airborne troops would be located on the first floor E ring corridor. They would respond to any incidents which seemed to threaten building incursion. Meanwhile, on the roof, teams of snipers would be looking for the bomber, or anyone else with firearms or weapons capable of launching explosives. If the bomber was identified, undercover FBI agents were responsible for taking him into custody. If things really got out of hand, several .50 caliber machine gun nests would cover the main entrances. At this point in the briefing, several of the volunteers were becoming uneasy. This sounded more like preparations for an attack on a Base Camp in Vietnam.

One of the guys spoke up. "What about the tunnel? If the demonstrators get in there, they can come up the steps and be at our front door within seconds!"

The Boss smiled knowingly. "The tunnel will be adequately defended," was all he said.

Now came the political instructions. In spite of the physical risk, strict limitations were being placed on the military response. Soldiers on the perimeter would be armed with M-14's however, no rifles would be loaded, and no ammunition would be available outside the building. Although previous demonstrations that summer had included physical assaults on police officers with fists, rocks and bottles, we were under strict orders not to respond in kind. *No soldier,* and that included us, was to display any aggression towards a demonstrator, even if attacked. Neither could the soldiers on the line advance on any demonstrators, except in support of a U.S. Marshal. In the event demonstrators attacked soldiers, only the U.S. Marshals had permission to cross the line and attempt to subdue the attackers. In this scenario, the line of troops would then balloon outward to encircle the perpetrators and protect the Marshal(s), while the offenders were pushed, pulled or dragged back behind the line and into the building for arrest.

The Sergeant Major went on to explain. The *White House people* were fearful of any physical confrontations between soldiers and civilians. No one wanted newspaper pictures of a soldier clubbing a college kid with the butt of his rifle. One incident such as this could result in a public relations nightmare. An example was given, and attributed to President Johnson, of the political effect such an image would have if it appeared as a newspaper headline. Strict discipline was to be maintained at all times. Civilian and military personnel would receive their orders through a remarkably truncated chain of command consisting of parallel branches of military and civilian authority. Only six links in the chain separated us from the President of the United States. Approximately ten people had decision-making authority. All of that small group, including the President, would be on duty during the weekend, and watching us very closely. As for us medics, just as in combat, our responsibilities were to go wherever there was an injured soldier, provide initial evaluation and treatment, then transport to the Dispensary if necessary. In defending ourselves, we were under the same limitations as the other soldiers. We were not to display aggression towards a demonstrator, under any circumstances.

At the conclusion of his remarks, SGM Gilbert again repeated the importance of avoiding any aggressive actions, and the source of the admonition. His summary statement was in the most serious tone I had yet heard him use. "If any of you are uncertain whether you can tolerate a demonstrator punching you in the face and withstand the temptation to punch him back, tell me now, and you will be excused from this duty."

There were some muffled comments around the room, but no one raised his hand.

He then added a final comment. "Monday morning, if a picture of any of you striking a demonstrator shows up on the front page of the New York Times, God help you!"

. . . .

During our second meeting, we began preparations for D-Day. Our marching orders were to regard this event as a siege, and plan accordingly. We catalogued the potential types of injuries, and the possible numbers. Most of these calculations involved pure speculation. No one had any idea how many demonstrators would actually appear at the Lincoln Monument, how many of those would cross the river to The Pentagon, how many would be violent, and if any would be armed. We simply pulled numbers out of the air, based on field experience in Vietnam, to determine the amount and types of supplies to be stockpiled. For the medics, additional tutelage on the care of wounded soldiers was superfluous. At its worst, conditions were unlikely to be as adverse as the combat operations for which we had trained. The Dispensary surgeon did hold some evening classes on trauma care for the physicians, much to their annoyance. Aside from the politics, adjustments for this particular situation were pretty straightforward... we thought.

The meeting once again veered into political exigencies. Field care, unless presenting a life-threatening injury, should be avoided. Injured soldiers were to be retrieved and brought within the walls of the building as quickly as possible. This would minimize risk to the medics, and photo ops for the press. The injured would then be transported to the Dispensary for treatment. The Sergeant Major reiterated that we were unlikely to need to attend anyone beyond the troop line, since they were prohibited from advancing.

He then brought up the question of injured demonstrators. "If an arrested demonstrator is behind the troop line, and is seriously injured, you will provide treatment. If the wounds are not serious, let the Marshals decide about diverting to the Dispensary or a local Emergency Room before incarceration. Several local hospitals have agreed to accept those patients. If a demonstrator is outside the line of troops, we have no official responsibility for them. However, incidents may arise where a demonstrator in the crowd appears to be seriously injured. In that situation, you are free to exercise your own judgment on whether or not to provide aid. Just remember, if you are outside the line, and get jumped by a bunch of demonstrators, the troops are not allowed to advance to retrieve you. The Marshals may come to your aid, if they aren't too busy with other problems, but basically, you are on your own.

Over the course of history, wars have been started with far less planning than went into the government's preparations for this demonstration.

In the days leading up to the demonstration, all Commands[2] located within The Pentagon were notified that only critical need personnel would be permitted inside the building on the weekend of Oct. 21-22. All cars were to be removed from the surrounding parking lots, no later than Friday evening, Oct. 20. Any cars remaining, would be towed. The government had already learned that vandalized or burning vehicles are favorite targets for news photographers. On Thursday afternoon, SGM Gilbert and the Executive Officer, LTC Kilmer, made rounds in the Dispensary. They met with each member of the team to answer last minute questions, and I think, to assure themselves they had chosen the

---

[2] *In the military, the term Command refers to an administrative unit comprised of members from multiple Services and/or civilians who are responsible for a large administrative task, usually affecting multiple Service lines or geographic areas. All members of the Command are directed by a single uniformed officer.*

right people. Comments included one of the Sergeant Major's frequent admonitions, "Bring your toothbrush!"

We were also advised to pack in any favorite snacks, as all cafeterias and restaurants within the building, as well as all stores on the Concourse, would be closed.

Late Friday afternoon, we headed out for an early dinner before the cafeterias shut down. Boxes of field rations had been delivered that afternoon and were now stacked along a hallway wall. Returning from dinner, our next task was to secure sleeping quarters. Enlisted men rarely pulled rank on each other in our unit. Usually, we treated one another simply as coworkers. This weekend was different.

The SP5's claimed the most comfortable exam tables available. The shiny new single stripe on my sleeve, earned earlier that month, didn't get me very far in the game of musical beds. By early evening, the officers were holed up in the conference room/library, several card games had been organized, a few groups of medics sat talking, while others disappeared into offices to write letters or read. Just like nights on call, by the middle of the evening, everyone was getting bored.

Some of us took off to walk the building corridors, just to pass time. Everything about The Pentagon is massive in scale, including the human population. Normally, the smallest number of people physically present within the building was 12,000, which occurred on midnight shift Sunday nights. Now, there were probably no more than four thousand people in the entire 6.6 million square feet of space. It felt like a ghost town. We walked for miles without seeing another person. Eventually, we returned to our office and hallway homesteads and tried to get some sleep.

· · · ·

Saturday morning was a beautiful autumn day in the Capitol (although the government had been praying for rain). We arose from our exam tables and cots. A few people tried the C-rations for breakfast, but scrambled eggs, canned during the two previous wars and now sporting a slick, green patina, just weren't very popular. The wiser amongst us grabbed the chocolate bars out of the K-rations. Everyone else settled for the chips and candy bars squirreled away in preparation. We divided into teams and quickly devised a schedule to keep the Dispensary continuously manned, provide the capability to respond to more than one location simultaneously, and allow for four-hour blocks of sleep.

As the morning wore on, the lack of outside information became maddening. Since the Dispensary was located on the outer side of the E ring, a few offices had windows facing the surrounding grounds and parking lots. Unfortunately, we were on the southeast corner, facing away from the Capitol Mall. There was nothing to be seen from this angle but an occasional police car. Even on the side of the building facing the Mall, visibility was obstructed by thick tree cover near the reflecting pool and entrance to the Lincoln Memorial, where all the action was occurring.

Live television coverage did not yet exist. "Up to the minute" reporting could only be done via radio, and we couldn't just turn on a radio to catch the news anyway. The Pentagon was electronically isolated for security reasons. Rooftop antennas were hardwired to a handful of highly selective locations within the building. All other incoming (and outgoing) radio and television signals were blocked by the concrete walls and deliberate electronic jamming. Our only source of information about the events unfolding just a few miles away was a clandestine portable radio, with its antenna wired to a window frame on the outer wall of the building. Finally, reports began trickling in via our radio. The crowd was described as orderly, with government sources estimating attendance of 10-50,000, and some independent observers reporting much larger numbers.

By noon, everyone was bored. One of the few enlisted women in our company was a secretary who had previously worked upstairs in the office of the Joint Chiefs of Staff. I didn't know her well, but had discovered in conversation that she had a taste for adventure, as did I. There was no identified need for a secretary that weekend, but she had managed to talk her way onto the team. At some point early Saturday afternoon, she found me.

"Hey! Do you want to go see what's going on?"

"What do you have in mind?"

"Just go look out the windows," she added coyly.

I knew from previous exploration that most of the offices on the side of the building affording a view of the city were in controlled access areas. I pointed this out.

She smiled and said, "I know a way. Do you want to go, or not?"

I and one co-conspirator took off across the building with the secretary in the lead. She began climbing the ramps to the fifth floor. By then, I knew where she was headed.

"We can't go up there! Those offices belong to the Big Guys." I also knew there weren't any windows in the hallway facing the desired direction. In order to see anything outside, we would need to enter one of the offices.

She smiled again, "Yes, we can."

At that point, my anxiety was beginning to overcome my curiosity. The offices of the most powerful men in the U.S. military are clustered on one corridor, on the top floor of The Pentagon: the Secretary of Defense, the civilian Secretaries of each Service branch and their Under-Secretaries, and the military Chiefs of each Service. Wall coverings in most corridors of The Pentagon were limited to an occasional picture or poster, affixed to the exposed concrete of the building superstructure. At best, these surfaces were adorned with paint in various shades of battleship gray. Our proposed destination, which I came to call *Admiral's Row*, was unique to the building. The walls were paneled in mahogany. Beside the doorways leading into offices of the major players, were large, professional, framed portraits of the occupant. In the center of this very impressive hallway, on the side facing the city, was a conference room and suite of offices for the workings of the Joint Chiefs of Staff. It was no surprise that these offices enjoyed an excellent view of the major monuments, with the Capitol visible in the distance. This was the Rodeo Drive of Pentagon real estate.

I had already discovered this hallway while updating the corridor map used by the medics on call, so I was familiar with the layout. We soon rounded one of the corners joining the segments of the outer ring. Before us lay nine hundred feet of mahogany paneled splendor. The hall was devoid of any other traffic, and every sound we made echoed loudly. The other medic and I looked at each other uncertainly, then fell in behind our *point man*, the secretary. I don't think we would have been on higher alert if this had been a suspected Viet Cong village. After covering about three hundred feet, she stopped, tested a door quietly, then opened it quickly and stepped inside. My buddy and I remained standing, frozen, in the hall.

"Oh, come on in. There's nobody here!" she exhorted, with a tone that implied we were being wimps.

Wimp or not, I had no interest in tangling with a four-star general or admiral. I still remembered quite vividly what the Sergeant Major had said during my orientation to the Dispensary, "If *the Brass* aren't happy..."

Well, at least the entrance about to be violated didn't have a picture beside the door. We gathered our courage and stepped meekly across the portal. Once inside, she closed the door and quickly led us through a maze of small offices. Finally, arriving at a large, ornate, noticeably different door than the rest. She opened it confidently and led us inside.

We were in the conference room of the Joint Chiefs of Staff!

The room was all wood, brass, and plush green carpet, with a beautiful conference table in the center, and a spectacular chandelier overhead. Facing northeast were windows with panoramic views of the city.

My compatriot blurted out, "Oh, shit! We shouldn't be in here!"

Our fearless, female leader replied, "Look, none of *the Brass* are going to be around. There is no way any of them want to get trapped in the building for the weekend. The cleaning crew won't be here until Sunday night. No one is going to be up here!"

Everything she said seemed painfully obvious. We tried to calm down and turned our attention to the view. The Lincoln Memorial was approximately two and a half miles in the distance. The Capitol Mall remained mostly obscured by trees, even at this elevation, but we could see Memorial Bridge, which spanned the Potomac River from near the Lincoln Memorial to the Virginia side. As our vision adjusted to the distance, we could see people on the bridge. It was packed with demonstrators, from guard rail to guard rail and from one end to the other! Nearest us, people were streaming off the bridge and onto the road leading to The Pentagon. On the far side, a mass of protesters, formed a human traffic jam, awaited their chance to cross. This bridge, including pedestrian walkways, was eight lanes wide and almost half a mile long. A few years before, I had been in a crowd of over 50,000 people at a Beatles concert. That crowd now seemed small by comparison. As the enormity of the human tsunami cascading off the bridge slowly registered on each of us, someone quietly said, "Holy crap!"

. . . .

After watching the spectacle for a few minutes, we headed back to the Dispensary to report. As we exited the door onto the hallway and turned to leave the forbidden ground, several officers, and at least one person in civilian clothing, appeared from a nearby doorway. They turned and *headed straight towards us*! I didn't want to risk making eye contact, but a sideways glance confirmed the outsized gold trim and insignia of Flag Officers. We walked on in dread, with our heads down, waiting for the challenge, "What are you doing up here?"

Just as the two groups passed each other, a voice came from the gaggle of Brass, "Is everything squared away with the medical preparations?"

I replied, with as much confidence as I could muster, "We're ready to go, Sir!"

"Good! Good!" came the response, echoing down the hall behind them, as both groups hurried in opposite directions. (Thank God for the free pass afforded to people in medical smocks almost anywhere.)

It was not until I was doing some fact-checking for this book that I learned the probable identity of the group of men we encountered. Our female leader of the reconnaissance mission couldn't have been more wrong about her prediction of vacancy on Admiral's Row. While reading The Pentagon, A History by Steve Vogel, I learned the officers and civilians supervising the response to the demonstration, including Secretary of Defense Robert McNamara, were in the building on that morning. The demonstrators had failed to completely encircle the building, and therefore, the civilian and military officials were able to come and go relatively unimpeded. Sec. McNamara's description of the sight (recounted in Mr. Vogel's book, p. 366) and the emotion elicited, was very similar to what we experienced from approximately the same viewing position. I can't confirm he was the civilian with the group of generals we encountered, but there aren't many possible alternatives.

Back at the Dispensary, we geared up for the onslaught. Last minute adjustments to our plan needed to be made. During morning reconnaissance, some of the guys had noticed non-coms and marshals using walkie-talkies outside the building. We realized these guys weren't familiar with the communication eccentricities of the building, and probably wouldn't know how to communicate with the Dispensary if they needed medical assistance. Our plan was quickly modified. The mobile response teams would continually circle the building, checking with officers on the perimeter at each doorway, in order to identify injured patients. On our first pass, we stopped at each troop encampment, both inside and outside the building, to advise them how to access our emergency phone number from an interior phone, and the futility of trying to reach us by walkie-talkie.

By then, protesters had arrived and were yelling and waving banners. Some of the crowd was pretty hostile, but the majority were peaceful and considerate. This was my first significant interaction with college students since I had become a soldier. Their day-to-day life was as far removed from mine as if we lived in different countries. My reaction felt similar to suddenly meeting someone as an adult who you were close to as a child. Much had changed in the intervening time.

By 3:00 p.m., things started to heat up. At first, the forward line of troops experienced a few in-coming projectiles. The ordnance was typical of college demonstrations; eggs and rotting vegetables. Interestingly, I observed other demonstrators admonishing the people who were throwing things, and sometimes successfully interrupting them. Then a larger group began a barrage which included beer and wine bottles, as well as an occasional rock. Some of the soldiers suffered bruises and abrasions to their faces and their fingers, which were unprotected as they held their rifles. A few of these men were pulled off the line for treatment. One soldier was hit with a flag pole, swung by a demonstrator. That trooper suffered a fractured facial bone and abrasions. Over the next hour, several attempts were made to rush the line of troops. Each assault was successfully repelled. Our mobile teams transported injured soldiers back to the Dispensary. As I recall, a demonstrator with a broken arm was brought in by the Marshals.

Although assaults on the line were keeping the defenders in those areas quite busy, violent demonstrators represented a very small percentage of the total group. In areas away from the Mall and River entrances, the scene was in stark contrast. Protesters began singing peace songs. Flower garlands were placed around the necks of some of the troops, and single flowers were placed in the muzzles of rifles. Some demonstrators tried to convince soldiers to leave the line of troops and join the protest. A variety of inducements were offered; a bottle of wine, a joint or just the opportunity to protest their own plight. One girl, with flowers in her hair and wearing a loose dress, had a more compelling argument. She walked up to the line in several places and raised the hem of her dress to her neck. (I'm sure her purpose was to convince the soldiers she was unarmed.) She then offered a weekend pass to any soldier who would abandon his post. No one in uniform accepted her offer... I later searched for her in vain.

At 5:00 p.m., one of the most potentially serious breaches occurred. A little-used set of French doors which opened from the E-ring onto the building exterior had apparently been overlooked in planning the defense. The troop line outside this access point was only one person deep and had not been bolstered. Suddenly, a small group of determined protesters rushed the line and broke through. They quickly reached the doors, which inexplicably were unlocked, and began surging into the building. Fortune soon turned on them.

．　．　．　．

During our planning sessions, we had been told a unit of the 82nd Airborne Division, freshly returned from Vietnam, would provide the muscle in the event an assault on the building occurred and was going badly. We were *not* informed of the alarm this proposal had elicited amongst the planners from the West Wing. The politicians feared these troops, with recent combat experience, would be the least likely to resist the temptation to return violence with violence, if attacked. The debate continued until the night of Oct. 20th. At the last minute, the 82nd was flown into Andrews Air Force Base; a few minutes away from the building. Some of the troops were deployed to the E-ring where they could, hopefully, remain out of sight.

The leaders of the phalanx of demonstrators burst into a hallway filled with part of this group of paratroopers, now sleeping after their night in transit. The uninvited visitors were quickly introduced to the unforgiving butt of an M-16 rifle stock. Having satisfied their curiosity about Pentagon hospitality, the invading demonstrators couldn't seem to leave fast enough. The incursion lasted no more than a few minutes.

. . . .

Near sunset, the energy of the protest ebbed, almost as suddenly as it had flowed earlier in the afternoon. As both daylight and warmth faded, the majority of demonstrators turned their attention to food and shelter. Small groups split off from the demonstration and began walking down various roads leading away from the building. Surface areas of parking lots and grass once again became visible. They were strewn with trash. This image seemed so foreign to me that it has remained imbedded in my memory since. On any other day, not so much as a cigarette butt ever hit the ground on Pentagon property. Some of the remaining demonstrators picked up trash to use as fuel for bonfires. By dark, the area looked more like a state park campground during spring break.

Field kitchens had been set up for the troops in the building's central park. The mood of most of the soldiers was increasingly jovial, and stories from the day's events circulated quickly. The military detachment had protected the building successfully, and injuries suffered were no worse than anyone had seen on field maneuvers in Basic Training and AIT. I don't mean to imply everything was sweetness and light. Many of the soldiers expressed either anger towards, or a feeling of betrayal by, the demonstrators. Some still hoped they would have the opportunity to "crack heads" tomorrow, and the potential for harm to the building remained. This was no time to let down our guard. Much mischief occurs under the cover of darkness, and the spectre of a homemade bomb still loomed. However, the anticipatory nightmares shared by military and civilian planners had not come to pass. I spent most of the evening roaming the halls and protected area outside the walls, listening to the stories being told by the soldiers and marveling at what I was seeing. Excepting one isolated incident, Saturday night remained pretty quiet.

Sunday morning promised another glorious fall day. Thousands of protesters joined those who had remained on the building grounds overnight, but this combined group was only a fraction of the crowd seen on Saturday. The aura of the crowd also seemed quite different. I don't recall any violence directed against the soldiers that second day. The demonstration seemed to have spent its venom. Even the words were less hateful. Troops and government officials were visibly more relaxed. Individual encounters between protesters and soldiers were as often playful as they were antagonistic. In the Dispensary, people were bored and looking for something to do. On Saturday morning, we had noticed the upper terminus of the stairs to the bus tunnel was lightly guarded. Only a handful of MP's were present at the top of this massive stairway. Although their positions suggested they weren't allowing anyone to traverse the steps, the number of MP's present was insufficient to contain much of a crowd coming from the other direction. Some of us had gathered in the open area near the front desk.

A question arose, "Hey, I wonder what the Sergeant Major meant when he said the tunnel would be adequately defended? There sure aren't many guards over there now." After a brief period of speculation, he added, "I'm going to go find out."

Someone else replied, "I don't think they are letting anyone go down the steps."

The first soldier's facial expression said, "Watch me!" as he got to his feet.

We positioned ourselves to observe the fun. As usual, a medical smock and purposeful gait got him past the MP's without so much as a challenge. He disappeared down the steps. In no more than a minute, he came bounding back up the stairs, laughing. He trotted over to the Dispensary steps where we had gathered.

"You won't believe it!" he exclaimed. "There is an entire column of APC's[3] down there with fifties (.50 caliber machine guns) mounted on top. And, sitting next to them is a medium tank!"

We burst into laughter. As usual, Sergeant Major Gilbert had his facts straight.

I spent most of the morning out roaming the halls, trying to see whatever I could. I was getting cabin fever... even in a cabin as large as this one. By then, the team framework had loosened, and the Boss instructed us to simply keep a sufficient number of medics in the Dispensary to attend to any unexpected needs. I circled back to home base just often enough to confirm that I hadn't gone AWOL, and to rest my feet. Early in the afternoon, I made an appearance, and was just hanging out when an unidentified civilian and two MP's appeared at the Dispensary front doors. The civilian reported a rumor circulating amongst the demonstrators that someone in the crowd had a broken leg but was afraid to seek medical treatment. If the story was true, the person would probably have been injured the afternoon before. An untreated leg fracture, even of the lower leg, can result in life-threatening complications. If the injury was to the upper leg bone, the femur, the patient was probably in shock and at significant risk of dying. Our informant asked if any of us were willing to go into the crowd to look for the person. (In retrospect, I suspect the unidentified civilian making the request was a staffer for the Under-Secretary of the Army.)

Two of us quickly volunteered. I had been dying for an opportunity to get farther outside. Having already witnessed the mood of the crowd that morning, I really wasn't concerned about a bunch of demonstrators attacking me. Nevertheless, we were warned that once across the troop line, we were on our own. We chose a location with a scattered number

---

[3] *APC stands for armored personnel carrier. Their appearance is similar to a small tank minus a turret and cannon on top. They were used to transport groups of soldiers while providing protection from small arms fire. The explosive power of IEDs in recent wars has rendered that model of APC obsolete.*

of demonstrators, none of whom were acting aggressively, and plunged into enemy territory. As we passed through the line of soldiers, some asked where we were going, some laughed, and some called out, "You'll be sorry!"

The day before, demonstrators had been shoulder-to-shoulder in most places. Now, there were only small clumps of people talking, interspersed with individuals just wandering aimlessly about the large areas of open space. We found a benevolent appearing group and approached them. After excusing ourselves for interrupting their conversation, we asked if they could help us. Their looks were a mixture of shock and incredulity. We explained our purpose and reassured them we had no intention of getting the person into trouble and were only concerned about his or her welfare. (That was, unfortunately, a half-truth. We did not know the identity of the civilian in the Dispensary. He might have been an FBI or Defense Intelligence Agency {DIA} agent, using us to ferret out someone they were seeking to arrest.)

Our audience denied knowledge of the rumor but immediately offered their help. They fanned out to pass the word to others. We were wearing white medical smocks, which stood out brightly amongst the tie-dyed T-shirts. With a laugh, everyone agreed to direct anyone with information to the patch of white amongst them. For the next ninety minutes, we attempted to systematically survey the occupied portion of the grounds outside the building. People were unfailingly polite, even friendly, when they learned our purpose. Quite a few thanked us for our concern. We stayed longer than was *really* necessary for the mission assigned. The variety of people we saw and met was fascinating. By the time we returned to the Dispensary, some of our associates were predicting we had either been kidnapped or killed.

The rest of the day was uneventful. I don't remember staying overnight on Sunday. I believe most of us were sent back to the barracks. At midnight, the one hundred fifty diehards refusing to leave government property were arrested by the Capitol Police... for trespassing. The event permit had expired. The troops packed up, transport vehicles re-appeared in the parking lots, and shortly thereafter no evidence of a combat military or police presence remained. Clean-up crews worked all night. At 07:00 on Monday morning, as the mass of employees began to arrive, the last of the graffiti was being scrubbed from the walls. It was business as usual at the world's largest office building.

This story represents events I personally witnessed, information provided in military briefings I attended, or descriptions I heard from people I regard as reliable sources. It is not meant to be a thorough recounting of this episode in American history, nor the many individual dramas played out over that week-end. However, I do disagree with some of the information and opinions published both during and after the demonstration concluded. I suspect the crowd size was significantly under-reported in official pronouncements. Conversely, the level of violence ascribed to the demonstrators was certainly exaggerated in several reports. More importantly, I believe the impact of the demonstration on the attitude of elected officials in Washington, D.C. was far greater than has generally been credited. I think the Founding Fathers were probably smiling that weekend. Almost two centuries later, the Bill of Rights they had fought to create was still functioning as intended.

— Fix It! —

After a few weeks in the Shot Clinic, I was moved to the Eye, Ear, Nose, and Throat (EENT) clinic. The enlisted man assigned to this office was a lifer (the nickname bestowed upon career enlisted personnel by those of us who were counting the days until our required military service was complete). SP6 Moon, Moonie to everyone who knew him, had been in the military since I was in grade school. He liked what he did, was good at it, and was popular with everyone. A family member with health problems, had prompted Moonie to arrange an extended leave in order to help out at home. I was transferred into the clinic a month ahead of his departure, so he could teach me the basics of the job. Primarily, this entailed fitting glasses, simple repairs, and serving as the assistant to the ENT surgeon when he did minor procedures. I hadn't been lying when I told SGM Gilbert that I liked learning new things. What Moonie taught me was interesting and unlike anything I had learned before.

As I became acclimated to my new surroundings that autumn, one of the senior medics befriended me. He was several years older than most of us, a round, baby-faced, fat man with porcelain white skin and pink cheeks. He looked like the antithesis of a U.S. Army fighting machine, but everything about this guy was a contradiction. Some of the medics said he had a Ph.D. in psychology, which he confirmed. Others said his degree was from a mail order college, which he also admitted. Whatever the quality of his education, he was unmistakably bright, and regarded as one of the best medics in the Dispensary. His Pillsbury Doughboy appearance was also misleading. He had a fifth-degree black belt in karate, which appeared very real when he began teaching me sparring techniques some weeks later.

One day, he mentioned the Colonel had given him a very time-consuming special assignment. I asked if he could tell me anything about it.

He actually giggled, as he confided, "Listen to this! A few weeks before you arrived, we had a Code Red one night. The caller said that he was in the War Room. There was some confusion as to the location and specific room number, but directions to the general area were finally provided. The medics got as far as the area described but couldn't find the room. It did not appear to exist. After some minutes of searching, they called back to the Dispensary for instructions. Of course, the physician had no clue, so he called the AOD (Administrative Officer of the Day) for help. Eventually, a guy in civilian clothes showed up and led them through a labyrinth of concealments to the appropriate entrance, which was guarded by two Marines. The medic's ID badges did not indicate a sufficiently exalted security clearance, and the Marines would not let them pass. Although their civilian guide turned out to be the chief of building security, even he had difficulty convincing the Marines that he possessed the authority to override their orders. Several phone calls were required. When the medics finally arrived in the War Room, they found a four-star general lying dead on a conference table. A group of very discomfited flag officers and civilians were milling about, staying as far away from the corpse as possible. Elapsed time from call received to arrival—forty-five minutes. One of the medics later said, 'Man, that guy was approaching room temperature by the time we got to him.'"

The War Room is a highly secure area underneath The Pentagon. Reportedly, it is ninety feet below ground, encased in concrete, and able to withstand a direct nuclear strike on the building above. A communications link, separate from the main building system, allows people in the room to direct world-wide military operations in the event The Pentagon itself is damaged beyond operability. High level meetings were sometimes held there because of the mapping and communications capability, as well as the security afforded. The movie, "Dr. Strangelove," starring Peter Sellers, features a scene representing the

War Room. Although the movie used a Hollywood set, my friend's description of the actual space was quite similar.

The story circulating in the Dispensary later was that the morning after this event, our Commanding Officer received a telephone call from one of the members of the Joint Chiefs of Staff. The conversation reportedly went like this:

"Colonel, are you aware of the incident that occurred last night?"

"Yes, Sir."

"Fix it!" was all the Four Star said before hanging up.

SP5 Jones went on to say that within a day or two, he had been called into the Colonel's office and assigned the task of devising a solution to these conflicting needs for prompt medical care and military security.

My curiosity was growing like a fish following bait.

"So, is there a committee trying to figure this out, or is it just you and Colonel Di, or is Lieutenant Colonel (LTC) Kilmer involved?"

"No. It's just me. I haven't met with the Colonel since he gave me the assignment, and I wasn't given any contacts in other Commands."

"Man! That sounds like the most interesting job on earth."

"Do you want it?" he responded.

"They wouldn't give a job like that to me! I'm twenty years old and a Private E-2."

"They will if I tell them to," was all he said.

I had no confidence in the declarative prediction of my new friend, but I couldn't get this conundrum out of my mind. It represented a very interesting puzzle. The longer I thought, the more complexities came to mind. This physical and regulatory maze was several orders of magnitude more complicated than anything I had ever imagined.

A few days later, Jones and I were walking down a hallway in the Dispensary when Colonel Di (the nickname used by virtually everyone in the Dispensary for our CO) suddenly appeared in the distance. When he spied my companion, the Colonel headed straight for us. Until then, I had only caught glimpses of our CO. Now, we were face to face. He possessed a perfect appearance and persona for the position he occupied. Nearly six feet tall, he had avoided the centripetal obesity that befalls many men of his age. Although not trim, he remained an impressive figure in uniform, always impeccably groomed, and possessing a demeanor of reserved command.

"Jones! How is the project coming along?" The Colonel stared intently at my companion without even a glance towards me.

"It presents some very thorny issues, Sir, and is going to take some time, but we are making progress."

I was learning that no matter what the truth was, it was best to report progress was being made when an officer inquired about a project. Otherwise, he or she was likely to try to help... which almost always made the job more complicated.

"Good, good!" the Colonel replied.

"But, you know, Colonel, my enlistment is up next month. I will be leaving the Army on November 18th," my friend added.

The Colonel's smile faded, replaced by a look bordering on terror. "You can't leave, Jones! You can't! This problem must be resolved!"

"But, I *am* leaving, Sir," Jones replied gently. "November 18 is my last day."

"*What will we do?*" cried the Colonel, and actually looked as if he might burst into tears.

"Don't worry about a thing," Jones said. "I have been training Turner here to take my place. He already knows almost everything I have learned about the issues we are facing. When I leave, he will take over."

The Colonel's countenance and posture visibly relaxed. "Can he do it?" (still without giving me even a sideways glance).

"I'm sure he can, Sir. Don't worry about a thing."

Colonel Di now turned and looked at me for the first time. He stared first at my name badge, then surveyed my face, as men characteristically do when assessing a new male in their territory. *Then, he stuck out his hand!*

I was paralyzed. Colonels do *not* shake hands with privates. After an awkward pause, I regained enough composure to shake the Colonel's hand.

"If you need anything, come see me," he said tersely, then turned and resumed his brisk stride down the hallway.

As we watched the Colonel disappear around a corner, Jones deadpanned, "I told you so."

. . . .

Holy crap! I had the job! But, now what? I had just been handed this amazing opportunity. What if I screwed it up, like most of the other things I had attempted before entering the Army?

For the remainder of the day, I literally could not sit still for more than a few minutes. I paced. My mind raced. I imagined a multitude of potential problems that might arise. Finding a solution to this problem was really important. I assumed at least one of the Joint Chiefs of Staff would be reviewing whatever plan we devised. I was overcome with uncertainty. *Why* did I ever say that this sounded like an interesting job? When the Colonel reached to shake hands, *why* hadn't I dropped to my knees, genuflected, and pleaded, "I'm not worthy!" How could a twenty-year old private with less than three months experience in the building possibly sort out this mess without screwing it up? One of the things I would come to love about the Army was that, in spite of a universe of rules and regulations, most superiors learned to avoid micromanaging. You were given a job to do and pretty much left to your own devices to accomplish the task. However, I did not yet have the experience and confidence to relish this degree of independence. In less than a month, I would be on my own with this mission.

I finally calmed down enough to sit and reflect. As an adolescent, whenever I tried to imagine life in the military, Uncle Red was my usual reference point. Most of my uncles told tales about their military experience, but Red's stories were the most entertaining and memorable. Now, my mind wandered to my red-headed mentor. As a child, his given name, Jesse Ralph, soon succumbed to his flaming red hair and animated personality, and he was known as Red to everyone except his mother for the rest of his life. He began his career in the Navy as an enlisted man, but shortly after the attack on Pearl Harbor, was awarded a commission as an officer and assigned to supervise new submarine crews during their first war patrol. It occurred to me that he had morphed from the enlisted ranks to officer in the time required for a signature, and suddenly had responsibility for overseeing the decisions and actions of submarine commanders, all of whom outranked him, and overruling them, if necessary. Throughout WWII, whenever he took a new sub and crew to sea, 110 men were relying on Red's skill and judgement for their lives.

The challenge I faced was *nothing* by comparison. Hopefully, I wouldn't create a security breach allowing a bomber or spy inside the building. Otherwise, the worst I could do would be to humiliate myself. I imagined being in the living room at Red's home, explaining my new assignment to him. He would sit there grinning, with that twinkle in his eye. And, I knew what he would say.

"Hell, Jim! Just bluff and do the best you can. That will be good enough!"

The next day, I cornered SP5 Jones. "We have a lot of work to do before you leave!"

. . . .

In fact, Jones had made very little progress. His efforts to gain information or locate people who might be able to help devise acceptable solutions had been uniformly rebuffed. Each individual he approached stonewalled, claiming to know nothing about subjects that were well within their responsibilities. These responses confirmed our assumption this project wasn't going to be easy, but the complexities of the competing demands were exactly what had attracted my interest. We reviewed the War Room Code Red event step by step, trying to identify each individual component that had contributed to the conundrum. Like peeling an onion, every identified problem and proposed solution revealed other problems, almost all of which were related to security or to the many administrative fiefdoms existing within the building. I had always been interested in how things work, both in nature and society. In the next six weeks, I would get an expedited course in social psychology and organizational behavior, courtesy of the world's largest organization under one roof.

There were three fundamental issues affecting our ability to reach critically ill patients in the shortest time possible. The most obvious was camouflaged access points to secure areas. In retrospect, we couldn't really expect large hallway signs announcing, *War Room > This Way*. The need for discretion was obvious. This led to corollary questions. Were there other locations with hidden entrances and, if so, how many?

A second problem was access. Once we found a location, there was little for us to contribute if we weren't allowed inside. Both Jones and I had experienced Code Red calls during which we turned down a minor hallway at a gallop and suddenly were confronted by a door blocking the passage, with armed guards who threatened to shoot if we advanced farther. In both of these incidents, an unexpected solution appeared, which is probably best left unexplained for the sake of ongoing building security. Unfortunately, the method that had worked for us couldn't be relied upon for all similar problems in the future.

These physical obstructions also illustrated a third issue. How many building thoroughfares were now blocked by doors and walls erected as *tenant improvements* after the original construction? Serendipitously, Jones and I had both stumbled upon the same guarded doorway. Jones knew the building better than anyone else in the Dispensary, but during his year of deployment, he had traveled only a fraction of the seventeen miles of corridors. Where were the other barricades?

These barriers affected more than just the offices located within their perimeter. The building design and room numbering system was so logical and efficient that one could mentally visualize the hallway map with a little practice. In our case, that map had acquired a few enhancements. When a Code Red call was received, the medics located the room number spatially in their mind, then plotted the most efficient route to the location, based on their previous travels within the building. There weren't many geographic shortcuts, however, the redundancy of some of the ramps and nearby stairwells provided means to circumvent areas of congestion during peak travel times. In order to achieve a scene arrival time approaching five minutes in this gargantuan concrete maze, every possible efficiency was required. If a medic plotted a course to a distant location, but encountered a barrier en route, he would need to retrace his steps to the last intersecting corridor and devise an alternate path from there. The time wasted might push the five-minute goal out of reach and doom an otherwise salvageable patient. We took this challenge very seriously. Response times were monitored and reviewed by the medics and SGM Gilbert. Speed and appropriate on-scene performance were a point of pride for almost all of us.

There was another motivator for our performance. As a generality, soldiers tend to work hard when necessary, and play hard when possible. Some of that play occasionally runs afoul of either military or civilian regulations. SGM Gilbert had said during my orientation that as long as we kept *the Brass* happy, the colonel was a protective and benevolent CO. That was not a hollow statement. As long as the infractions weren't too serious, Colonel Di would reliably arrange for the reports of, and punishment for, minor skirmishes with the MP's and civilian authorities to somehow evaporate. All of us had experience with

Commanding Officers who weren't so generous. This insurance policy was rare and highly valued by its beneficiaries.

. . . .

I now assumed responsibility for dreaming up ways to acquire the needed information and solve the security problems. Jones became my consultant and sounding board, as well as partner in brain-storming sessions. In addition to the straightforward issues of maintaining security, we would probably face objections from Commands who interpreted our efforts as an infringement upon their turf. In this building, that list would be a long one. We hoped Colonel Di had a sufficient cadre of political allies to overcome the objections but, realistically, this would likely require the clout of the Joint Chiefs. I decided to test the Colonel's offer of assistance. A meeting was requested and granted promptly. The help provided was more tangential than I had hoped. His advice actually led me to a mysterious room in the basement, and the attention of two Defense Intelligence Agency spooks, who followed me for several days. (Regrettably, the details of that encounter must also be omitted for security reasons.)

With that adventure behind me, Jones and I admitted defeat. We divvied up the remaining unexplored corridors and ran the entire building, a few segments at a time, noting obstructions or any features which varied from the standard layout. At least, we now had an accurate list of barriers and their locations. Even if we couldn't solve the access problem without intercession from a higher authority, half a loaf was better than none. Jones discharge date was upon us, and I now had at least *something* of value to report to Colonel Di. On Nov 18, Jones cheerily wished me luck and literally skipped down the hall and out of the Army. It was my baby now.

I organized our collective notes and reviewed them one more time, looking for any clues we might have missed. I found none but did uncover an additional significant problem. We now had an accurate map of the building corridors with alterations annotated. Obviously, people in other agencies, whose priority was security, would insist this information be highly restricted. A proposal to distribute our new and improved maps to sixty enlisted men would almost certainly raise objections. I could see their point. The thought of one of these maps being left at a table in the cafeteria, or worse yet, a copy being returned to building security from some local bar or restaurant after a weekend of revelry, kept me awake at night. This was the sort of unintended consequence that had terrified me when I first contemplated the assignment.

I spent the next week trying to craft an acceptable solution. Unless successful, this could be a deal breaker for even our partial solution. After several failed attempts, I settled upon an auxiliary document of my own creation. It would be physically distinct from the current map and describe the locations of obstructions in a shorthand that wouldn't make sense to a casual reader. The listings would be hierarchical, in order to mimic the method used to choose our route to a call. With a little more tinkering, I was pretty happy with my new pirate's map. I also decided to propose distributing them only to the senior medics. An alternative plan, limiting availability to two copies of the map, which the medic could retrieve when a Code Red occurred, was considered and discarded. My pirate's map certainly wasn't as simple to interpret as the existing map. It would require practice and repetitive use by the medics in order to be useful.

There was nothing further I could accomplish without assistance. I carefully organized my notes, gathered my nerve, and went to see the Colonel. After quickly reviewing the original problem, I described the issues we had identified in our efforts to solve it. Then, I outlined the proposed solution.

The Colonel's look was impassive throughout my presentation. When I finished, he thanked me for the hard work and said my recommendations would be forwarded up the chain of command.

. . . .

A few weeks later, I was called into Colonel Di's office. He was more somber than usual. My plan had been rejected. Apparently, the proposal to create a more accurate map for the medics had been greeted with alarm by the folks in the security hierarchy. *No surprise there.* The Colonel emphatically ordered me not to create such a map, and to destroy all preliminary examples already in existence. Any related notes and documents were also to be destroyed. Basically, any written record of the past six weeks of work should cease to exist.

He went on to say the proposed number of medics who would need enhanced security clearances was unacceptably high, and out of the question.

After a pause to allow this news to sink in, he continued. "This is what we are going to do. Your file is being submitted for review for an elevation in security clearance. Is there any reason to think that you won't pass this examination?"

"No, Sir."

"You know that friends and family members will be contacted and interviewed. You are not to discuss this matter with them at any time."

"Yes, Sir."

"Good. If a call occurs in an unusually secure area, the medics will notify you to respond to the location."

This wasn't sounding good at all!

"But Sir, that will mean I must stay in the building 24/7. That doesn't seem very practical." (For reasons I won't further elaborate, I now had visions of sitting in some windowless office with the chief of building security, eating crackers, playing cards, and slowly going insane.)

The Colonel thought for a minute. "Well no, we wouldn't expect you to stay in the building all the time. Just stay close. No long weekend trips out of town, that sort of thing. We will try to find a two-way radio for you."

Ah! An escape plan was now materializing. Because of the location of the building, the access roads, and the limitations of wireless communication in those days, if I was allowed out of the building and not restricted to a military post, for all practical purposes, I was off the grid. Any more questions risked further deliberation, which might not end in my favor. This time, my brain pressed the fail-safe response button. "I will do my best, Sir!"

"Thank you, Turner.

Dismissed!"

．　．　．　．

For a long time, the outcome of this project puzzled me. The Joint Chiefs had apparently accepted a very unworkable solution for a problem with serious consequences to themselves. Why? I think I finally figured it out. From almost the day I joined the Army, both commissioned and non-commissioned officers had been quite blunt in reinforcing the idea that soldiers are expendable. It occurred to me, after reviewing the ideas I had proposed, and the associated risks to building security, the four-stars had concluded they too were expendable and chose not to accept those risks for their personal benefit.

In retrospect, the degree of importance SP5 Jones and I attached to our efforts was undoubtedly inflated by naivete. Realistically, our role was similar to that of undergraduate research assistants who provide background information for a professor or, in our case, Colonel Di. However, I don't think our impression of both the importance and the sensitivity of the project was exaggerated. Of more significance to me, personally, I was now a respected member of a military team with considerable medical responsibility, and I was beginning to acknowledge the attitude of my superiors that I could perform satisfactorily in any job they assigned. I still didn't grasp the importance of mentoring for people like me. I only knew I was quite comfortable working for SGM Gilbert and COL DiLorenzo. This budding self-confidence was like a new suit of clothes. It had a different feel and didn't always seem like a very good fit. I kept expecting the clothier to tell me to take it off and put it back on the rack, but the longer I wore it, the better I liked it.

There was another, unanticipated result of this project. Our Sergeant Major came to view me as the de facto medic in charge of the Emergency Response Team (the official chief of the team was the Dispensary cardiologist, Dr. Fletcher.) For the remainder of my time at The Pentagon, I was responsible for orienting newly arrived medics, organizing our continuing education classes with Dr. Fletcher, and helping to present them. I was also first in line for new projects. None of the other guys wanted to do this stuff, so there was little envy aroused amongst my colleagues. As for me, I liked to learn new things.

. . . .

Of course, there is a post-script, I never received the two-way radio, and I most certainly never inquired about it. I was never given a new ID Badge, or informed what level security clearance I had been granted. I was never called to the scene of a Code Red in an exceptionally secure area, per the plan outlined by Colonel Di. During the remainder of my tour, one other medic encountered a guarded entrance while on a Code Red call. The same surreal solution occurred on that occasion, just as SP5 Jones and I had experienced.

"What the hell! It's the Army!"

— Another Job —

Not long after SP5 Jones introduced me to the Emergency Medical Response Team project and briefings for the upcoming anti-war demonstration had begun, SGM Gilbert called me into his office. "Turner, I have another job for you, if you are interested. We have a team of medics who occasionally go to the White House for outdoor events. Their responsibility is to provide medical care for the spectators, if any of them fall ill. You do not have responsibility for the President or any other officials present. The White House has their own team for those people. Are you interested?"

Hell, yes! Who wouldn't want to go to the White House and stand around for the afternoon? I promptly agreed to the new assignment.

He went on, "Four guys are on the team, and two go for each event, so this duty probably won't come up very often. I will send you with SP4 Smith the first time. He has been on the team the longest, and can orient you on how to enter the grounds, where to go, where to stand, etc. I only have one thing to add, and I can't stress this strongly enough. If the President suddenly appears ill, or slumps to the ground, *DO NOT APPROACH HIM!*

"When the President is outdoors at the White House, teams of snipers are positioned on the roof. During events, he may be quite close to civilians in the crowd, and to you, for that matter. If he goes down, the security detail doesn't know if he has been attacked by someone in the crowd, or by whom. Under those circumstances, the snipers are instructed to shoot anyone not on their approved list who moves toward him... You won't be on their list. Don't worry about trying to keep other people away. The Secret Service is responsible for crowd control, not us. Just make sure you stay away. You know how those security guys play. If they start shooting, you will be dead before you hit the ground, and they'll check your ID later."

. . . .

After a brief pause to let that information soak in, the Sergeant Major added, nonchalantly, "By the way, I received this letter in the mail a few days ago. I thought you would be interested in it. I made a copy for you. Of course, the original will be placed in your file."

He casually passed a letter across the desk.

I had absolutely no idea what this was about. Just as in childhood, my antennae immediately went up, scanning for any sign that I was in trouble. Had I been caught on some surveillance camera violating one of the thousands of building rules? Had some VIP written a letter, either complimenting or condemning me, for something I had said or done? Had some of the other medics dreamed up a prank to pull on me and convinced our boss to assist in the ruse? As usual, SGM Gilbert's expression was uninterpretable. He must have been one hell of a poker player.

I gingerly turned the proffered letter to face me. The letterhead was imprinted, *Headquarters U.S. Army Medical Training Center, Ft. Sam Houston, Texas*. The text of the letter began:

Pvt. Turner:
I would like to commend you for having been selected as a Graduate with Honors… blah, blah, blah…"

I was struggling to pay attention long enough to get to the punch line and keep an eye on the Sergeant Major at the same time. My gaze captured another sentence.

"In a company of 518 trainees, you earned a score of 926 points out of a possible 1,000."

This was followed by several lines of standard nice going blather, which I skimmed over. The letter was signed by the commanding officer of the Medical Training Center.

I looked up at SGM Gilbert. *Now,* he was smiling.

"Congratulations, Turner. That was exceptional work."

. . . .

Well, I'll be damned... I left his office and wandered down the hall in a daze. I liked lots of action, but things had been coming at me pretty fast over the last few months. What was more confusing than the rapidity of events was the results were consistently positive. I had managed to get through Basic Training without screwing anything up, except the final exam on the rifle range. Even then, my score was acceptable, although disappointing. I had served as a tutor to other students at Ft. Sam. After two months in Washington, D.C., I was already part of the support team preparing for an unprecedented demonstration, and now, an opportunity to go to the White House. I had never experienced a string of luck such as this!

Interestingly, I still remember my reaction to the composite score reported in the letter. I was irritated that it wasn't higher. Even though Mom was literally a thousand miles away, in my mind, she was still looking over my shoulder, saying, "If you had only tried a little harder, you could have done better."

. . . .

The outdoor ceremonies we attended at the White House were usually prompted by visits of foreign Heads of State or their ministers. On these occasions, pre-screened civilian spectators were allowed to attend on request. To ensure a positive experience for the guest and the press, as well as to maintain security, anyone suspected of potentially causing a disturbance was excluded. This screening sometimes resulted in the number of eligible spectators being quite small. In order to assure a robust welcome for the visitor, the crowd was augmented by rank and file government employees from offices throughout the city. A roster of people who had been screened and cleared for this duty was maintained by the White House. When needed, an appropriate number of these individuals would be summoned from their usual jobs, like ordering extras for a movie set. Each spectator was provided with a small flag as they entered the grounds. Half of the flags issued were American and half were the flags of the visitor's home country. Spectators were encouraged to wave their flags often and enthusiastically. When you see one of these ceremonies on your nightly news broadcast, that is how they work.

Two of our team members weren't particularly interested in the duty, so I went on almost all White House details from then on. A staff car from The Pentagon would drop us at a side entrance to the grounds located behind the Executive Office Building. At this point, our ID's were checked against the daily roster of expected personnel. Once cleared, we would pass through a wrought iron pedestrian gate and walk up a driveway to our destination. The ceremonies were usually held on the South Portico with the crowd standing on the lawn below. After remarks by the President and visitor, the dignitaries would sometimes descend to the South Lawn to review a color guard of troops. Occasionally, they also circled past the visitors, who were cordoned off with decorative ropes. At the time, there was a large coniferous tree in that area, standing about sixty feet from the White House. The limbs were long and droopy, with heavy foliage extending to the ground, but conveniently spaced to allow us to stand in close to the trunk without much difficulty. Once the ceremony began, we were instructed to step in amongst the tree's branches, so as not to appear in photographs or news footage of the ceremony. We could find breaks in the clusters of needles allowing us to see the crowd, while remaining unnoticed.

Over the next fifteen months, I attended five of these ceremonies. Not a single spectator became ill during that time, but I did have a few interesting, and unexpected, experiences.

On one of my first trips, I signed in, passed through the pedestrian entrance, and began walking up the driveway. I soon heard the larger iron gates reserved for vehicles groan, as they opened behind me. Then came the crunch of gravel under the tires of an approaching car. Military courtesy dictates that a soldier in uniform must salute the passing vehicle of a flag officer or, of course, the President. I had no idea who was in the car, but the probability that he or she outranked me was beyond calculation. As the vehicle approached, I stepped off the road and onto the curb, then turned to face the driveway. Out of the corner of my eye, I could see an enormous limousine gliding up the drive. I came to the position of attention and saluted. The rear passenger window of the limo silently lowered, interrupting the solid black exterior. As the car passed, a smiling face appeared at the window and waved to me, like I was a familiar neighbor. It was Dean Rusk, the Secretary of State.

A few years before, I had been a farm kid, spending much of the summer alone in the fields surrounding Greenville, Illinois. On many of those days, the closest I got to another mammal was a ground hog or deer at the edge of the field. Now, one of the most powerful men on earth had passed no more than six feet in front of me. Even more amazing, he had smiled and waved.

When I was a child and Uncle Red came home on shore leave, he would tell us fantastic stories of places he had been and people he met along the way. Red was fond of saying, "If you are half bright and show a little initiative, there is no limit to where you can go in the Navy!"

I now realized he had not been exaggerating. I was going to follow his advice. Before leaving for Vietnam, I intended to capitalize on my good fortune, and enjoy every new adventure of living that came my way.

— Merry Christmas, Soldier —

Assignment to temporary duty stations addressed several logistical problems for the military. They served as a source of short-term manpower for unexpected needs, allowed time for the Personnel Section at The Pentagon to correct the original error, and provided a destination for the *homeless* individuals dropping off the end of the training station conveyor belt without the expected orders.

However, the emphasis of these assignments was on *temporary*. They typically lasted for ninety to one hundred twenty days, followed by another transfer to the soldier's intended long-term destination. When I arrived at The Pentagon in August 1967, the first thing SGM Gilbert had said to me was, "Don't bother to unpack."

The next few months passed quickly. My departure for the tropics was anticipated in November or December, but Thanksgiving came and went with no news. Now the days began to crawl by. December 4th marked one hundred twenty days since my arrival at The Pentagon. I felt as though in suspended animation. Adjustment to this unique and very unexpected assignment had proceeded smoothly, and the opportunities provided so far were simply amazing. I needed to frequently remind myself that my vacation in this wartime oasis was finite, and the arrival of one piece of paper would snatch me from civilian-style comfort to combat misery as irrevocably as a pedestrian being hit by a bus.

I sometimes tried to imagine where my name might be on the electronic assembly line that matching a trained medic with a combat unit in need of a replacement. Once the order was created and printed by the assignment center, it would go to the building post office — along with the other 128,000 pieces of mail sent that day. The notification would be delivered to COL DiLorenzo and SGM Gilbert first. Then I would be called into the Sergeant Major's office to receive the news. Every weekday morning, as I rode the bus from the barracks to work, anticipation swelled in my chest until it seemed like I couldn't breathe. After about three p.m., the tension would begin to dissipate, as the chances became progressively less likely any news would arrive that day. The next morning, the suspense would begin all over again.

Military personnel moves are complicated, multi-step processes. Ideally, another soldier must be transferred into the unit to assume the duties of the person leaving, travel needs to be arranged — and for soldiers being sent to a war zone, two weeks' leave was usually granted before shipping out. I calculated and recalculated the number of days this sequence of events might require, trying to keep a moving estimate of the potential dates for a leave, and whether or not they would coincide with Christmas. The three weeks following Thanksgiving seemed interminable. If I was destined to depart before the holidays, the timing now seemed increasingly awkward. Either I wasn't going to get leave before going to 'Nam, or I wouldn't receive orders until January.

. . . .

When the third Monday, December 18th, came and went without any news, I headed for the Sergeant Major's office. He had been on the lookout, too, and provided the opinion that it was now very unlikely I would receive orders for arrival in Vietnam before January.

Hesitantly, I suggested, "Well, if I'm going to 'Nam in January, it sure would be nice to go home for Christmas."

The casualty rate for medics was a closely guarded secret from the public, but common knowledge around the building... because it was a *big* problem. I had been told the Training Center at Ft. Sam Houston wasn't graduating enough new medics to keep up with current losses. I knew the Sergeant Major was well aware of these statistics. However, I had another motive for the request. Up until then, I had managed to spend every Christmas of my life with Grandma Darnell. When I joined the Army, I had assumed this Christmas tradition would come to an end. Now, there was a sliver of hope we might be able to extend it at least one more year. She would be eighty-five in January, and the cold reality was that neither of us could be certain we would be around for Christmas 1968.

. . . .

My boss leaned back in his chair and stared pensively into space. "We aren't usually very busy around here during the holidays. See if you can hitch a ride home for Christmas through New Year's. We won't count it against your leave."

I had already checked with other guys in our company. No one knew of *anyone* who was driving to the St. Louis area. I worried about trying to find a ride with a stranger. If something happened causing me to be stranded at home, and I wasn't back on duty when my orders to report to a war zone arrived, the consequences could be draconian. Commercial transportation seemed the only prudent alternative. I was twenty years old. I had never bought a ticket for a bus, train or plane in my life. The Army provided all the commercial travel I had ever done. I asked one of the more experienced guys in our unit. He explained that a travel office in the building arranged and purchased tickets for military personnel.

I called the number. A polite but very harried-sounding woman answered the phone. I asked if she could make reservations for me on the requisite dates.

"You want plane tickets *now*? For *Christmas*? Everything has been sold out for weeks! Why didn't you call earlier?" She sounded incredulous.

I explained my predicament. Her tone changed. "I will try. I won't promise you anything. I don't know of *any* available tickets going to St. Louis, but I will try."

She didn't sound at all encouraging. After a pause, she asked, "What's your phone number?"

I recited the number at the Dispensary front desk and hung up. In my naiveté, I hadn't realized travel would be such an insurmountable issue. My initial elation from the sergeant major's holiday largesse now evaporated. I turned my attention to the next patient and tried to put the holidays out of my mind.

. . . .

A few hours later, the front desk alerted me to an incoming call. It was the travel agent. This time, her voice was warm and pleasant.

"There is a Congressman who is really mad at me right now. I bumped him off his flight to get you a ticket. I told him you were an ambassador. *Merry Christmas, soldier!*"

— *Doc* **Brown** —

By the end of January 1968, I was beginning to allow myself a little cautious optimism about the future. My orders to Vietnam had still not arrived, and the seven hundred thirty-one days of Army internment was nearly half over. If I received orders now, factoring in fourteen days of leave plus travel time, my tour would be less than one year. Every day I remained at The Pentagon, I was chewing up one more day of availability as a target for some VC sniper.

Moonie had returned to the EENT clinic, and I had migrated to Physical Therapy. In terms of floor space, this was the largest clinic in the dispensary. Wounds and other physical injuries were common amongst service members and provided a large and varied supply of patients needing our services. My new boss, Major Hartmann, was one of the most popular officers in the Dispensary, and a very good teacher. This was my first experience with the chronic phase of wound care. I was still unwilling to admit even a faint hope of becoming a physician, but I found everything about medicine interesting, including the role of physical therapy.

This was also my first experience providing services to individual patients requiring more than a few minutes of interaction. Giving immunizations and fitting eye glasses were perfunctory tasks that usually involved very little conversation. The physical therapy treatments typically lasted fifteen to twenty minutes. Although most of the patients were field grade (major, lieutenant colonel, or colonel) or flag officers, and we had been instructed not to initiate casual conversation with them, many would ask questions and offer comments of their own accord. These interactions typically began with: where are you from, what are your plans after the Service, any particular goals or aspirations, or sometimes an enquiry about family; the sort of casual conversation a coming-of-age young man might have with an older, more experienced individual in a civilian setting. As these conversations continued to occur, several of the officers mentioned that their current duties were quite stressful, and they found the opportunity to have an informal chat with someone who understood their day to day environment but wasn't in their chain of command, with its attendant restrictions, pleasant and relaxing. Although some of them asked fairly detailed questions about my background, I was not at liberty, per military custom, to ask similar questions about theirs, or about their particular roles in the massive organization we both served.

I quickly learned two things from these conversations. First, exceptionally high rank comes with enormous responsibilities, and second, most of these men possessed remarkable capabilities, commensurate with their rank. This may seem like a foregone conclusion to some, but in 1967, most of us who had been drafted thought the Army represented the antithesis of intelligence and rational thought.

Three of my patients stood out in particular. One was a Vice Admiral who sat on a very influential threat assessment committee. Another was a Colonel on educational leave to earn his Ph.D. in history and political science at Georgetown University. When I expressed surprise that the Army would support this level of education for a career officer, he explained; the DOD maintained a task force trying to understand the cultural background and motivation of the various factions who were driving events in Southeast Asia, as well as in other areas of the world. I loved hearing the nuggets these men occasionally shared about debates going on upstairs. None of them revealed any deep, dark secrets, but most people enjoy explaining an engrossing subject to an interested student, and I certainly provided the interest. With practice, I learned to ask carefully worded questions which could increase my understanding of a topic without intentionally soliciting information the officers were not able to reveal. If I mentioned something I had seen or heard on the news related to our conversation of the day, the response was often a quick smile, followed by, "The truth is not always what it appears to be in public." Their facial expression would then dissolve into a bemused stare which seemed to dare me to read between the lines and deduce the next move in this political chess game. During our conversations, they provided few, if any, facts about specific events or conversations, but they introduced me to the methods of analysis used by governments to choose a path in international relations. This was the kind of education I had been missing in college, and I found it fascinating. Not that I had any desire to become either a politician or a career military officer. I simply had an insatiable curiosity about how the world works.

The third of this triumvirate of patients was introduced to me as Dr. Brown. He always wore a suit to his appointments, and I assumed he was a physician from another facility. He wasn't very talkative but was polite and never failed to thank me after each treatment. One morning, I was feeling particularly cheerful about my current circumstances and extraordinary good luck. Dr. Brown was my first patient of the day. Although I was on time, he had arrived before me, as was his habit, and was sitting on the exam table with suit jacket, shirt, and tie hanging neatly on the coat rack in the corner. His back was turned to me. As I walked around the table to face him, I slapped him on the back, and said, "How ya' doin' Doc!"

He startled visibly and regarded me with an unusual expression. The look on his face wasn't exactly disapproving, but something told me he wasn't accustomed to this degree of familiarity. I was now at a loss for words and proceeded with the prescribed treatment in silence. There certainly wasn't any small talk between us that morning.

Once his treatment was completed, and he had dressed, I managed to squeak out, "Have a good day," as he left the room.

His reply was an unemotional, "Thank you."

. . . .

As the morning wore on, a creeping anxiety overtook me. By lunchtime, it had evolved into full blown panic. Who was this guy? I was now pretty convinced he wasn't a physician, as I had previously surmised.

Cripes! He was probably some admiral or general. I might as well head for the barracks and pack my toothbrush, as the Sergeant Major was fond of saying. I didn't want to ask MAJ Hartmann about the patient's identity, for fear of giving away my indiscretion.

By the next day, I had managed to partially overcome my terror. Whoever Dr. Brown was, I would just have to rely on my luck, which had been in such abundance recently, to get me out of this jam. His next appointment was almost a week away. Maybe he would have forgotten about the incident by then.... Not likely!

. . . .

A few days later, I decided to scout Admiral's Row on the fifth floor, in hopes of ruling out the possibility this Doc was a really big cheese. During lunch break, I made my ascent into the political stratosphere. Turning down the elite corridor, I tried not to look like a tourist, while at the same time examining the framed portraits for a familiar face.

On my infrequent previous visits to this neighborhood, I had exercised my compulsion for reading plaques, while attempting to connect names to faces. It seemed worthwhile to learn the who's who of the building, what they did, and where their offices were located. Besides, it was useful to be aware of how powerful the man or woman standing next to you in the elevator (or sitting on your exam table) might be. As I cruised the boulevard of stars on this particular day, a familiar face suddenly peered at me from one of the portraits. It stopped me in my tracks. Good god! It was him. There was no doubt about it. Slowly, my gaze ventured down the ornate molding to the brass plaque at its base, inscribed with the name and organizational title of the subject:

Harold Brown, Ph.D. Secretary, U.S. Air Force.

Holy shit! I was DEAD! I stared at the picture, and suddenly realized I did not want to meet him coming out of this office. I scurried to the nearest set of steps and down to an altitude more appropriate for my lowly rank. The remainder of the week was agony. I imagined a thousand possible scenarios occurring at his next appointment, if not before. None of them were pleasant. Every day I expected to be called into SGM Gilbert's office and presented with orders banishing me to Southeast Asia.

His admonition from six months before kept echoing in my head, "If *the Brass* ain't happy, and you are the cause..."

I had since learned this was no idle threat. Several months after my arrival, one of the Dispensary physicians had been interrupted while taking a nap on the operating table, as Colonel Di conducted a tour for some visiting dignitaries. The following day, the guilty doctor was spotted briefly, looking exceedingly glum as he cleaned out the desk in his office. Within seventy-two hours of the incident, the somnolent surgeon received orders for Vietnam.

Even worse than the prospective unpleasant change in locale, I was mortified. This would cause embarrassment for MAJ Hartmann, who I liked very much, for COL DiLorenzo, who had been very good to me, and for SGM Gilbert, who was the best NCO I had ever met. The other medics, many of whom already regarded me as somewhat of a golden boy in the eyes of the Colonel and Sergeant Major, would no doubt have some cutting observations about how Golden Boy was doing now. Maybe the Boss would just get it over with quickly, hand me the travel orders, and let me slink away as quietly as possible.

Monday morning finally arrived. Walking down the Dispensary corridor to the Physical Therapy clinic, I felt as though I was approaching court, with the date of my execution about to be announced. I paused before opening the door to settle my nerves, then stepped inside. MAJ Hartmann wasn't anywhere to be seen. I quickly removed my jacket and headed for the treatment room. As usual, Dr. Brown had arrived before me. He was sitting on the exam table, in his usual attire and facing the opposite wall. I made as wide a passage around *the Secretary* as this small room permitted, took a breath, and faced him.

"Dr. Brown, I need to apologize for my behavior last week. I should never have slapped you on the back. I meant no disrespect, Sir. In truth, I had assumed you were a physician. In the Medical Corps, the officers tend to be quite informal with us enlisted men, but I should never have made an assumption about your occupation. I apologize for my behavior and want to assure you I did not intend for my actions to be disrespectful."

His face broke into a smile, "Oh, that's alright. It did startle me, though. There aren't many people around here who have the nerve to slap me on the back."

The incident was never mentioned again, and I certainly never again slapped him, or anyone else at The Pentagon, who I didn't know personally, on the back.

Dr. Brown, a physicist by training, later served as U.S. Secretary of Defense from 1977 until 1981.

This incident is a good example of a characteristic shared by many of us atypicals to suddenly do or say, without forethought or intention, something that violates the expected decorum of the situation in the minds of normal individuals. The utterances and tics of people with the label Tourette's Syndrome probably represent the far end of the spectrum of this phenomenon, but I have observed many of us not tagged with that label are also prone to these untimely words and deeds. Often, we aren't even aware of the rule of etiquette we have violated at the time of the transgression. As a child, I came to dread the awkward silence that sometimes followed what I thought was a perfectly innocent comment or action. If not then, I would certainly hear about my error later... from my parents. Unfortunately, I have neither outgrown, nor learned how to avoid, these self-inflicted wounds. I wonder if Ben Franklin was knowingly describing atypicals with his observation, "It is difficult to say the right thing at the right time. But, it is far more difficult to leave unsaid the wrong thing at the tempting moment."

— Derm Clinic —

Once a trained physical therapy technician arrived, I was no longer needed in that clinic. It was time for another move. By then, I was getting relatively busy with the responsibilities of the Emergency Medical Response Team and White House duty, plus I seemed to be *the go-to guy* for the Sergeant Major and Colonel when new projects came up. That suited me just fine. Everything I had done so far was interesting and some of it unusual. The Top Kick decided to put me in a clinic less dependent upon my continuous presence. I was assigned to work for the staff dermatologist, Dr. Elliott Rustad. Until then, I had known who he was but never interacted with him personally. On my first day, his greeting was cordial. He had a warm smile and very pleasant voice. The first thing he said after I introduced myself, was to insist that I call him Elliott unless a patient was present. His informality was reassuring. Apparently, I had been gifted with another of the Sergeant Major's many acts of kindness.

Our clinic consisted of two small offices, each of which opened onto one of the central hallways in the Dispensary. Elliott's office barely accommodated a desk and chair, one additional chair for a visitor, and a bookcase. Next door was the procedure room. Its dimensions were approximately ten by fourteen feet, oriented perpendicular to the hallway. An exam table consumed most of the real estate, and was positioned diagonally, on the long axis of the room. This arrangement allowed just enough space for the doctor to stand on either side of the table while performing procedures. An overhead operating room light, mounted on a floor pedestal, occupied the far corner of the room at the head of the exam table. At the near end, the door opened just beyond the foot of the table. At a little past ninety degrees in its opening arc, the door cleared the exam table by no more than twelve inches. If one opened the door further, its travel was soon interrupted by a hall tree, wedged into the corner behind the door. With the door open sufficiently to encounter that obstacle, just enough clearance remained for an adult to squeeze past the foot of the exam table, in order to reach the far side. The coat rack, which seemed absurdly superfluous on initial inspection, was indispensable for patients needing to undress for examination. There were no changing rooms in the Dispensary, with the exception of the surgical suite. And because the building had been constructed entirely of concrete, doors between adjacent offices were not easily added. In spite of this architectural eccentricity, we were expressly forbidden asking a patient to travel one of the hallways to the nearest bathroom in order to change into an exam gown. Apparently, the visual of a four-star flag officer paddling down a public hallway, attempting to hold a surgical gown closed over his backside with one hand, while carrying his shoes in the other and uniform draped over his arm, was a non-starter for *the Brass*.

The remaining wall of the procedure room was lined from back to front with a hamper for soiled surgical drapes, a supply cabinet, and a small desk and chair. A straight-backed patient chair was squeezed into the space between the desk and the wall adjoining the hall. The room was so constricted that the knees of anyone sitting in the patient's chair blocked the office door from opening. Before arriving at The Pentagon a few months before, I had been in mortal fear of accidentally brushing the sleeve of even a low-ranking officer in a crowded corridor. Now, I was greeting patients at the procedure room door and preparing them for examination or treatment, in a space only marginally larger than an elevator carriage... and fully furnished. Most of these patients were field grade officers but visits by generals and admirals were common. There could be a lieutenant general (three stars) sitting in my office, and if I needed to leave the room to retrieve an unexpected item or notify Dr. Rustad of the patient's arrival, I first had to ask the General to get up from the chair he was occupying and go stand in the corner by the hall tree, so I could open the door. Upon my return, I would crack the door open a few inches, cautiously. If knees were visible, I then had to ask the officer to get up once again and move to a far corner of the room, so I could re-enter. Only the military could have devised a set-up like this and expected it to serve as a work space rather than a storage closet.

Considering that we were inhabiting the largest office building on earth, the paucity of space allotted to us seemed odd. Apparently, building planners had decided that on-site medical services were a necessity but not a priority. Fortunately, no matter how high their rank, most of the patients responded to these inconveniences with good humor.

. . . .

Several things stood out about Dr. Rustad. First, he was blazingly smart. One of the brightest people I had ever met. Second, although he was not a large man, what he lacked in size, he more than made up for in speed. He was a human dynamo. When doing procedures, I learned to take refuge in the only available corner of the procedure room large enough to squeeze into. Otherwise, I could not get out of his way fast enough. Third, he had a wicked sense of humor.

Dr. Rustad had been drafted upon the completion of his residency, and before he was eligible to sit for the dermatology specialty board exam. He was not pleased with this untimely interruption in his career. The exam in dermatology is rigorous, one of the most difficult of all specialty examinations in medicine. Our patient population was a steady stream of *scratch and itch* stuff, so it presented no intellectual challenge for him, but interfered greatly with his ferocious pace of review and preparation for the board exam.

On that first day of orientation, he said, "OK. Here is what we are going to do. For the next month, I am going to teach you everything I can about Dermatology. From then on, you are going to see patients, and I am going to study. Dermatology is ninety percent visual recognition. You should be able to learn that portion of it pretty quickly."

The next few weeks were a crash course. As my knowledge and experience improved, I became increasingly adept at maximizing the use of his time. I would see each patient first, record the history of the skin problem, and help the patient expose or position the area needing to be examined. Then I would write a note in the chart describing the findings and plan, according to the standard format for medical records. With additional experience, Elliott insisted that I write out the necessary prescriptions as well. Once all this was completed, I would go next door to his office, describe the history and physical findings, and the treatment I thought appropriate. With that information, Elliott could see the patient, confirm the information I had gathered, and sign the record and prescriptions, if he agreed with my diagnosis and plan. If not, he could make appropriate corrections. This method mimicked the way medical students are taught by attending physicians. I made sure corrections weren't needed very often. If I was unsure about a diagnosis or treatment, I delayed committing anything to paper until he told me what to write.

Sometimes, he would ask me to read questions to him from a study guide for his exam. He then practiced answering each question (part of the exam was oral). After honing his answer, he would explain the simpler parts of the medical basis for the question to me. His knowledge of medicine seemed encyclopedic. I was beginning to understand what a wide variety of tasks physicians perform in their day to day practice of medicine, and how different the roles of various medical specialists might be.

I had initially rejoiced at my assignment to The Pentagon because of what I was postponing. It seemed to me that getting thrown to the wolves in a line company after a few months of experience was far better than landing in the same place, with the same overwhelming responsibilities, straight out of 91Bravo school. This was why the Sergeant Major had moved me from one clinic to another during my first six months. Although we inhabited a vastly different environment than the jungle, everything in medicine has some connection to the entire body of knowledge used to keep a human alive and healthy for as long as possible. It's all useful, if you pay attention.

. . . .

As an adolescent, I despaired of ever finding a job in which I could be successful and happy. Amongst the many things that concerned me had always been my susceptibility to boredom. I did not like doing the same thing all day, every day. And, if forced into this routine, I was already painfully aware that trouble usually resulted. There was another aspect of choosing a career that disturbed me, although my perception wasn't entirely accurate due to my inexperience. It seemed jobs could usually be separated into two groups: those focused on thinking vs doing. In general, I preferred doing, but I was learning that without the stimulus of some thinking and decision-making, the most exciting of action jobs could become mundane.

I couldn't explain what drove my interests, but what I was learning about medicine and the real-world tasks of applying that knowledge to patients was a siren's song. I began to realize I actually looked forward to coming to work every morning. These were the sorts of things I could enjoy doing as a career. From my perspective, there was only one thing standing in my way — ability. Fortunately, Dr. Rustad, and the other doctors who had taken an interest in me, had a different perspective.

— The Project —

Our days on call for the Emergency Medical Response Team averaged about one per month and spanned twenty-four hours, beginning at 08:00. Two medics and one physician had to be present within the building at all times. During normal business hours, we performed our usual assigned duties, and responded to any emergencies. After 17:00, everyone else went home or to the barracks, while we hunkered down for a night in the building. Although we didn't maintain an after-hours walk-in clinic, the large, swinging doors at the Dispensary entrance weren't locked, and someone would occasionally stop by with a medical problem. Unless it was urgent, the person was directed to return the next morning. We were there only for emergencies. Neither was there an expectation to remain awake all night, since we had to perform our usual duties the following day. Consequently, there weren't many all-night card games either, except on weekends.

In spite of the huge number of employees and visitors in the building, most offices had a single entrance and exit, for security reasons. When I first saw them, I thought the choice of doors for the Dispensary was decidedly odd. They were exceptionally wide, covered in dark green leather, and each had a porthole large enough to see someone directly on the other side. Both doors swung freely, back and forth, were as wide as a department store entrance, and reminded me of a Wild West saloon. After my first experience returning to the Dispensary with a patient on a gurney, I better understood the design choices. Each door was sufficiently wide to allow passage of a gurney while accommodating continued foot traffic through its mate. Considering the volume of traffic, this feature minimized the inevitable slowdown if people needed to back up, rather than just move laterally, as we came barreling through with a stretcher and patient under CPR. I never did hear a rationale for the leather upholstery which covered the doors, but the visual effect was absolutely unique.

The Code Red phone was located at the front desk, so the lower rank medic slept on a cot nearby. The senior medic and physician would pick the two most comfortable exam tables they could find. Some were better than others, but exam tables aren't built for sleeping. Emergencies were infrequent. Boredom and the limited sleeping options were the worst part of being on call, but we weren't in the jungle trying to ward off mosquitos and rain with a poncho, so there were few complaints.

The physician-on-call usually spent the early evening in his office reading. The two medics hung out near the front desk to read or talk, since someone needed to be in that vicinity. After a few hours, most of the doctors would wander up to the front and join our conversation. Apparently, several of the physicians noticed that I asked a lot of questions when the topic was medically related. Some of the doctors began saying hello to me when we passed in the hallways during the day. The usual relationship between doctors and medics was cordial, but not personal. In fact, the Army had regulations to discourage "fraternization" between officers and enlisted men (and women).

One day, several of the M.D.'s and I converged on those *Wild West* front doors at the same time, as we exited the Dispensary for lunch. They asked if I would like to join them. This was decidedly unusual. I accepted, and off we went to the cafeteria. The docs made a point of including me in the conversation and asked a number of questions about my background. I was pleasantly surprised by their interest, but ill at ease with conversation, afraid that I would appear immature and uneducated.

A few weeks later, I was returning from the cafeteria with a tray, anticipating lunch at my desk. Several of the physicians, also with lunch trays in hand, arrived back at the Dispensary entrance at the same time. One of the group asked if I would like to join them. I cheerfully agreed, without contemplating their intended destination.

Most of the doctors ate lunch in a large room which served as the medical library and conference room. Unless enlisted men were attending a class, or needed to use one of the reference books, this space was reserved for officers. We were instructed to ask any officer already in the room for permission before entering. My lunchmates headed for the library. As we entered, I could see several other doctors already at the long conference table, eating. I stopped at the door, explained to my hosts that I wasn't supposed to eat in this room, thanked them for their invitation, and started to back out.

One of them said, "Oh, don't worry about it. No one here objects, and besides, we invited you." He then turned to the officers at the table, "None of you mind if Turner eats lunch with us, do you? Anyone discussing any top-secret medical projects?"

Two of the physicians, usually more reserved in their interactions with the medics, looked surprised but nodded their assent. Another of my hosts nudged me into the room. Once again, the physicians seemed to go out of their way to include me in the conversation. As I was to learn, small talk amongst physicians differs very little from other men, with the exception of recent unusual cases. I was fascinated by it all. From that day on, I ate lunch with some of the physicians more and more frequently.

During a midday meal some weeks later, one of the docs said, "So, you are going to do pre-med when you get out of the Army." His comment was made with the tone of a declarative rather than a question. "Where do you plan to go to school?"

"Oh, no, Sir." I replied quickly. "I find all this stuff really interesting, but I'm not smart enough to be a doctor. I'm not sure what I will do after the Army." (I didn't want to admit that Plan A was to return to work in the foundry.)

Another of the physicians piped up immediately, "That isn't true, Jim! I have listened to the questions you ask. You are plenty smart to go to medical school. Don't run yourself down!"

Referring to me by my first name was also something new. Officers almost never referred to enlisted men by their first names, or even knew their given names.

I protested, "You guys don't understand. I barely got through enough science classes to graduate from high school. I nearly flunked out of college. None of my mother's brothers even graduated from high school. My dad has an education, but I am nothing like him."

Now, another physician spoke up. "I don't know what happened to you in school, but we have been watching you. You display an interest in medicine. You ask very insightful questions and follow our answers with other questions which indicate you understand what we say. There is no doubt that you have the intellectual ability to become a physician if you so desire."

With a sense of resignation that felt like a weight on my chest, I replied, "I am very flattered by your comments. I think being a physician would be a dream job... but it is only a dream. You don't know me very well. I have done poorly at nearly everything I have tried in school. I'm just not very smart."

. . . .

In retrospect, I think I kept describing myself as not very smart because I was increasingly confused by my uneven performance in everything related to schooling, and I had no idea how to explain this contradiction to someone else. Privately, I was beginning to accept the idea that I was smart in *some* ways, but these unexpected bursts of intellectual prowess occurred with erratic and unpredictable timing.

In fifth grade, I was the most successful reader in my class. A surprising and rapid transition for a kid who couldn't identify individual words on a page, less than three years before. My eighth-grade language arts teacher had pronounced me a gifted writer (and she was a published author), although the school principal refused to transfer me from the remedial class I was in, to the accelerated class which she recommended. My performance on the SAT, ACT, and county scholarship tests as a high school senior, plus the grades I received in advanced placement classes in history, English, and biology that year should have been compelling evidence that I wasn't stupid. However, the teachers in those courses were almost the only people who noticed these marked excursions from my usual mediocrity (with the exception of the school administrator, whose explanation was that I must have cheated).

The first year of college had been a disaster, and besides an A in psychology, the second year hadn't been much better. Then came the Army. On a series of written tests taken shortly after induction, I did well enough to receive an invitation to Officer Candidate School. (I declined because the position required spending an additional eighteen months in the Service.) Then, there was the letter of commendation from Ft. Sam Houston. I was completely bewildered by these contradictions, but my dismal performance in most of civilian education remained incontrovertible. Choosing an occupation requiring a lengthy exposure to a scholastic environment didn't seem prudent or realistic, and the idea of me becoming a physician was preposterous!

. . . .

Unbeknownst to me, a process was set in motion during the discussion of my abilities that would profoundly alter my future. Several of the physicians participating took my comments as a challenge. They began to teach me everything about medicine they thought I could absorb, considering my limited background... and some things that were way over my head. More importantly, they started to systematically work on my self-confidence. At least once or twice a week, one or more of them hunted me down at lunch time. On call nights, the physician would usually spend an hour or more talking with me. Sometimes we talked about his experiences in school and residency, sometimes about life in general, and sometimes we just talked. They treated me almost as an equal and insisted I do the same with them.

I think every one of the physicians in the Dispensary contributed to this process, in one way or another, with the exception of COL

DiLorenzo. No one fraternized with the Colonel. During one of our library lunches, we were in the midst of an animated discussion when he suddenly stepped into the room. The CO had an announcement to make and knew most of the doctors would be here. As he scanned the room for attendees, his gaze reached mine. He stopped suddenly, looking a bit displeased. "Oh, Turner, I didn't realize you were here."

The tone of his voice reminded me of someone who had just discovered the dog indoors on the carpet. I stood immediately. As I gathered my lunch things onto a tray, one of the other physicians broke in, "It's alright, Colonel. Turner here is going to med school after he gets out of the Army. We've been giving him some pointers."

The Colonel's voice softened only slightly as he continued, "Well, that's good, Turner. Now, I need to discuss something with the physicians if you will excuse us."

I was already heading for the door as this interchange took place. "Yes, Sir. Sorry to be in the way."

. . . .

Over the next few months, my relationship with several of the physicians became even more personal. Some invited me out to dinner and into their homes. Dr. Rustad arranged for me to attend medical conferences in the area and took me with him to Dermatology Rounds at Walter Reed Army Hospital. Ross Fletcher, M.D., our cardiologist, was the designated director of the Emergency Medical Response Team. He was a natural teacher and spent hours teaching me and quizzing me about cardiovascular physiology and resuscitation. He deferred leadership of the team largely to me, not because he wanted to get out of work, but to provide me with this important experience. He also went out of his way to ensure I was the beneficiary of every educational opportunity that came his way. When assigned to make an instructional film on resuscitation techniques for use throughout the military, Ross insisted I participate.

One day at lunch, on one of the many occasions where I thanked my new associates for their teaching and encouragement, the response was, "Most of us were drafted out of residencies. We were immersed in teaching students and interns. We miss those interactions. Now you are our medical student."

I had no doubt what he said was true. However, their interest in my welfare and success was often far more than just teaching. They treated me like a younger brother, who was their responsibility.

Douglas Goodin, M.D. was the staff psychiatrist. His office was next door to mine. Aside from our roots in the Lower Mississippi River Valley, or maybe because of it, we shared a common sense of humor and a close friendship. When neither of us had patients waiting, I was often in his office, just shooting the breeze. We joked about the differences between East Coast social customs and those at home. We had contests to see who could find the most ridiculous Army regulation, and who had seen the most neurotic patient that week. It was great fun, and in the process, I learned some practical aspects of psychiatry that were quite useful in my never-ending quest to understand the confusing world around me. Doug had a slow Southern drawl and a droll sense of humor. He also had a masterful way of telling stories that illustrated many of my unspoken fears and uncertainties. Any connection between the story and me was never mentioned, but I came to suspect that behind his calm, emotionless pause at the end of one of these tales, he was thinking, "OK, boy, chew on this for awhile. See if it helps answer your question."

I have met very few physicians who equaled Doug in the art of medicine.

. . . .

Toward the end of my time at The Pentagon, I was enjoying one of our frequent lunches in the library. On that particular day, those present seemed to be trying to sum up their advice for my future. One of them sat quietly, with a very reflective countenance. Finally, he said, "Listen, if for some reason, you don't end up going to medical school, don't try any of the other health professions, such as nursing. You're too smart. You will spend your life taking orders from doctors who aren't as intelligent as you are, and it will drive you crazy."

This observation, which was made with unmistakable sincerity, was the greatest compliment, and validation of my abilities, I had ever received. I tucked it away, like one stores life-preservers on a ship, for future use during heavy seas, of which there were many to come.

During a ten-month period, these men introduced me to the fraternity of physicians. In the process of making me feel as though I was a member of their group, albeit a junior member, they convinced me I might actually have the capacity to become a physician. Their kindness and effort in helping to build my self-confidence and conquer my existing perception of negative self-worth provided me with courage to challenge the educational hurdles that had previously appeared insurmountable. In spite of their encouragement, I remained quite doubtful this quest would succeed, but by the time I left the Army, I was determined to try.

— Memphis —

The spring of 1968 began full of promise. I had a very interesting set of responsibilities in the Dispensary, and I was reveling in the teaching and encouragement provided by the physicians. My enthusiasm was interrupted unexpectedly on Thursday, April 4, by the assassination of Dr. Martin Luther King, Jr. in Memphis, TN.

Shortly after news of the murder was announced, predominantly black areas in the Northeast and Northwest sectors of D.C. erupted in frustration and fury. By the following day, the number of protesters had grown to an estimated 20,000, some of whom began looting and burning buildings. Rocks and bottles were thrown at firemen responding to calls. The D.C. Police force of 3,100 officers was completely overwhelmed. Fire departments and police began declining calls for assistance from the neighborhoods where they had encountered physical hostility. By Friday afternoon, almost one quarter of our national Capitol was essentially ungoverned, and no one could predict how much larger, or more violent, the riots might grow. Units of the National Guard were activated in an attempt to control the violence. Although the closest points of destruction remained several miles from us, a team of medics was hastily assembled to reinforce our on-call team. I suspect our primary purpose was potential medical support of the troops on the street, if the violence worsened. I don't recall the Sergeant Major articulating that possibility, but it made sense. We had recent experience with a civilian demonstration, which included some violence, and our mission and staffing were better aligned with this type of assignment than either of the two military hospitals in the area.

As usual, SGM Gilbert's instructions echoed standard Army policy, "Be ready for anything."

Those of us assigned to the team headed for the barracks long enough to secure extra uniforms and toiletries and cancel our off-duty plans for the weekend. The newer medics were excited and had a lot of questions. For the few of us remaining from the team assembled for the October demonstration, this was a familiar exercise. Unless a particular need arose, our unit had no specific responsibilities, and therefore, little to do. Since radio and television reception within most of the building was blocked, our only sources of information during the weekend were reading the morning newspaper and occasional trips to the Mall Entrance of the building, which afforded a view to the northwest. Late Saturday evening, from this vantage point, I stared, mesmerized, at the skyline of the city. The Washington Monument appeared backlit by fires burning out of control in the distance. Even now, I am unable to find appropriate words to describe the confusion and sadness I felt while gazing upon that scene.

In spite of the ongoing chaos across the river, by Sunday afternoon, everyone on the team was thoroughly bored. We hadn't been called into the city or received any injured soldiers at the Dispensary. By early evening, most of us were gathered in the open area near the front desk, chatting idly to kill time. Unexpectedly, the entrance doors swung open. Several soldiers in combat gear and carrying rifles clattered through them, led by a member of building security. Our conversation turned to surprised silence. The squad leader, a buck sergeant, spoke. Word had been received of a reporter trapped in the rioting and thought to be injured. The information available was sketchy, but a reconnaissance mission had been organized to see if the individual could be found. Was there a medic willing to join the patrol?

I quickly volunteered. Two days stretched my capacity for staying inside, even with twenty-nine acres to roam. Besides, I was dying to get a closer look at the events in the city. I grabbed an aid bag, and we headed down the steps to the tunnel. Sitting by the curb was an Army jeep, with a .50 caliber machine gun mounted on the back. These vehicles didn't offer much protection from incoming projectiles, but this one sure was prepared to return fire.

As I climbed in a rear seat, the driver handed me a flak jacket. "Better put this on, Doc. Rumor has it they are shooting at people in uniform where we are going."

He didn't have to ask twice.

. . . .

We headed across the 14th Street Bridge and into the city. In the vicinity of the Mall, the streets were empty, except for police cars. A curfew had been imposed, and no pedestrians were in sight. To see the downtown area without people was vaguely unsettling, as in a sci-fi movie about an abandoned city. Aside from the sounds of frequent sirens, it was also eerily silent. We cut across a series of side streets, aiming for one of the thoroughfares, designed like spokes in a wagon wheel, by Pierre L'Enfant almost 200 years before. Thick layers of smoke lay just above the ground, partially blocking illumination from street lamps and bathing everything in an unnatural golden haze. During the past eight months, I had spent many weekends walking these lovely, tree-lined streets, marveling at the beautiful old homes and buildings, many with historical markers. Now, the appearance was sickening. Interior and exterior lights in the homes had been turned off to avoid attracting attention. No signs of life were visible. Front walks, which I knew should lead to immaculately maintained old homes, now disappeared midway across lawns, with only faint outlines of the residences in the smoke-filled distance beyond.

At Connecticut Avenue, we headed northwest, toward the area where the missing journalist had last been seen. After traveling for some minutes, we turned right into the target area, and soon encountered a military roadblock. A quick inquiry regarding new information about the missing reporter was negative. Now our advance became more cautious. Soon, a few residents appeared, mostly in furtive groups of three or four. They paid little attention to us. A few blocks farther on, we began to see broken windows and smoldering buildings, but no large groups of people, no active fires, and no injured journalists. We zigzagged across side streets, trying to visually inspect as large an area as possible. The neighborhoods here were almost as still as downtown. The only addition to the chorus of police sirens in the distance, were occasional building fire alarms, ringing plaintively in the dark. After searching for fifteen or twenty minutes, the sounds of scattered gunfire were added to the acoustic mix. The shooting didn't seem to be directed at us, but its origin wasn't far off.

The driver piped up, "What do ya' say we get out of here? We're never going to find this guy, even if he is around here somewhere."

The Sergeant hesitated only briefly before agreeing.

At the next corner, the driver made an abrupt turn southward, and we began working our way back downtown. Eventually, we intersected Connecticut Ave. once again. Approaching this thoroughfare, the Sergeant said, "Drive by the Capitol. I've never seen it up close."

Before long, we rounded Union Station, looking equally abandoned, and turned right on 1st Street. I was reasonably familiar with this part of the city but could only maintain my orientation by closely following the driver's maneuvers. Nothing looked the same as before. Fog was now rolling in from the nearby rivers, and combined with the smoke, visibility was cut to a few dozen feet. The Capitol dome, normally aglow through the treetops ahead, was nowhere to be seen.

We advanced slowly. A pair of vehicle headlamps, at intersecting angles, became visible in the darkness ahead. Continuing forward cautiously, we found their source to be two nondescript sedans, which blocked the street. Several soldiers leaned against fenders, talking. One of them signaled for us to stop and walked over to the jeep.

"What are you guys doing?" he asked, rather suspiciously.

The Sergeant explained where we had been, why, and added that he had never seen the Capitol up close and just wanted to drive by.

The guard replied, "What does it look like up in Northwest?"

"AFU, man. AFU," was the terse reply.

"We aren't supposed to let anyone down this street... but I guess you guys are all right."

With that said, he turned, walked back to the cars, and spoke a few words through an open window. One of the sedans backed up just enough to allow us to squeeze through, then quickly closed the gap behind us. The jeep's headlights, reflecting off the murky air, was now producing partial night blindness, which contributed to the surreal and disorienting scene. We inched forward. This was no weather for sightseeing.

The Supreme Court building suddenly appeared on the left. As we crept past, an imposing, ghostlike image became faintly visible on the right. Our attention and gaze shifted, straining to identify the shadowy mass. The Capitol materialized out of the fog like a shark in turbid water. My companions craned their necks, gazing upward at the massive building looming above us. I was the first to notice the steps leading to the main entrance. On each side was a machine gun nest, protected by sand bags and manned by four Marines.

I flinched in surprise; my mind struggling to absorb this picture. As the reality soaked in, I mumbled, more to myself than to my companions, "This is supposed to be the symbol of our country. Right now, it looks like a newspaper photo of a revolution in some fucking banana republic!"

"Yeah, man," came a dejected reply.

— Taps —

A Ft. Myer regulation required someone to man the desk in the lobby of our barracks and monitor who came and went. Everyone living in Train Barracks was on the roster for this guard duty, so the inconvenience only occurred about once per year. Adjacent to the lobby was a recreation room, or Day Room in Army vernacular. The Day Room was equipped with a television, chairs, and a ping pong table. The barracks joke was that the purpose of guard duty wasn't to sound the alarm if we were overrun by the Viet Cong, but rather to ensure no one stole the TV set. Considering the variety of entertainment available in nearby Virginia and Washington, D.C., the Day Room got little use.

As luck would have it, my turn for guard duty fell on 5Jun68. Only one thing was remarkable about this minor disruption to my otherwise cushy life. It happened to fall on my twenty-first birthday. Several friends devised a work-around. They took me out for pizza and beer the evening before. Eating and drinking establishments stayed open late in the D.C. area, and our muted celebration lasted well into my official birth date. We returned to the barracks about 4:00 a.m. To our surprise, the normally uninhabited Day Room was half full of people, and the TV tuned to a news program. Bobbie Kennedy had just been gunned down in a hotel in Los Angeles.

. . . .

Once again, world attention was focused on Washington. Over the next week, sporadic rock throwing and looting took place in a few areas, but nothing compared to that following the death of Dr. King. Until the spring of 1968, my most indelible memory of a public event was watching President Kennedy's funeral procession to Arlington National Cemetery on television. Now, the body of his younger brother would follow the same path, crossing Memorial Bridge to a burial site nearby. I have only vague recollections of the next few days. Initially, we wondered if a medical team would be assigned to provide coverage for the expected crush of spectators. This did not occur. Some of the guys debated watching the procession in person. Most just wanted to avoid the glut of visitors this occasion would undoubtedly attract.

My enthusiasm for witnessing historic events had waned. Any sense of excitement was replaced by a vague numbness. In less than five years, three of our national leaders had been murdered, two within the past two months. This was not how our society was supposed to solve problems, no matter what political opinions one held. JFK's death had shocked me. I felt it personally, as many people did. The deaths of MLK and Bobbie affected me differently. They were abstract rather than personal.

During my entire time on active duty, I deliberately maintained the attitude that a line company in 'Nam was never more than twenty-four hours away. No matter how many or few days until discharge I might have, shit happened, as we all well knew. In spite of the great job, and the comfortable barracks, when I looked out the mental window of my immediate existence, the war was right there: in the back yard, the front yard, and on the street. The weather outside had the atmosphere of sudden, violent death, at any moment. I resided in the climate of war. The fact that an American male got wasted by gunfire in 1968 no longer shocked me. One more didn't add much to the daily body count, even if death came on a hotel balcony or a kitchen in L.A., rather than a jungle ambush in Tay Ninh Province.

However, these two assassinations, so close together, produced a feeling of disorientation in me. At first, this was confusing. I had assumed life would be very different in the military. In fact, a common distinction was made by almost all young soldiers between life in the Army and *the real world*. Now, slowly, I began to realize there had been some constants of civilian society during my generation's childhood, which served as *real world* reference points, at least for me. I had assumed the immutability of a set of social and historical traditions which I now recognized as foundational to my orientation to self. Many of them were currently being upended. I felt as though magnets had been placed too near my inner compass. True north was increasingly difficult to identify. This confusion, no doubt, also related to the maturation process common for my age, as well as my roots in small town, rural America. Whatever the reasons, the sensation produced was unsettling.

Life seemed a lot more complicated at the age of twenty-one than it had been at nineteen.

. . . .

On the day of RFK's burial, I reconsidered my earlier inclination to avoid the spectacle. I left the barracks, taking the same path along the small road winding down the hill and through the woods I had followed on my first evening at Ft. Meyer. For reasons I can't fully explain, I now felt a need to watch *this* Kennedy funeral procession cross Memorial Bridge. As I approached the Marine Memorial, I turned back. The crowd already visible was enormous. Finding a worthwhile observation point would be impossible. While retracing my steps, I briefly considered hopping over the low stone wall by the barracks and walking through the cemetery to a vantage point near the Custis-Lee Mansion. I imagined that portion of the cemetery would be closed to visitors and the view unimpeded. I chose not to.

I remembered my feelings the first time I gazed upon this cemetery. The sea of crosses had been a stark symbol for me of the personal cost of wars past. Over the ten months I had now been a next-door neighbor to the place, the carnage of *this* war had continued unabated. Daily reports of boys who weren't coming home appeared regularly in local newpapers. The true combat statistics... carefully hidden from the public, but common knowledge at work, were even worse. Stories told by new arrivals to the Dispensary, just back from Vietnam, simply reinforced a growing frustration we all felt. We were expected to win a war with a deck our own political and military leaders had stacked against us. And every morning, from the barracks window, I could see the incessant work of the backhoes digging new graves... and occasionally hear the twenty-four measured, mournful notes of *Taps*, floating across the rolling hills.

. . . .

When my efforts to ignore the activities beyond that stone wall failed, which they usually did, the words of Abraham Lincoln at Gettysburg echoed in my thoughts.

"The world will little note, nor long remember what we say here, but it can never forget what they did here."

I now had a much clearer understanding of the symbolic purpose of this place to *never forget* both the soldiers of 1863, and those who had fallen since. For me, Arlington National Cemetery had truly become sacred ground. I was not going to use it as a shortcut to aid in viewing one more spectacle.

RFK gravesite, 10Jun68

— A Spring Stroll... with Snipers! —

I am reluctant to tell this story because it describes one of my occasional lapses into the depths of stupidity. However, it also offers another example of the very strange life I was leading, and why I sometimes felt as though I had fallen down Lewis Carroll's rabbit hole.

This day began with another trip to the White House. A long since forgotten foreign dignitary was visiting. The planned festivities included an appearance on the South Portico with President Johnson. As usual, a cadre of government workers, pressed into service for the event, would be observing the outdoor portion of the ceremony and eagerly waving their little flags. A communication glitch caused my partner and I to arrive considerably earlier than necessary. Start time was still almost two hours away. It was a beautiful June day, and our faithful evergreen awaited us patiently. Although the tree suited our camouflage needs well, even for the young and nimble, the contortions needed to maintain a standing position amongst the branches could become pretty uncomfortable after an hour or so. We saw no reason to increase that time by another ninety minutes. I believe this was my fourth trip to "the People's House," as Thomas Jefferson called the residence, and I was beginning to feel pretty comfortable with these assignments.

I decided to walk around the portion of the South Lawn where the guests would be standing, reasoning that if they were allowed in this area, it should be acceptable for me to also explore and admire the flowerbeds. The other medic wasn't interested in landscaping, so I started the inspection tour alone. The plantings were lush and beautiful but took me farther and farther from our assigned post. A small grove of trees lay ahead which I hadn't spotted on previous visits. This should have set off an internal alarm. It didn't. A picturesque winding brick path led into the woods. Like Snow White, I took the bait. Completely forgetting where I was, I started down the path; my attention drawn to the trees. I tried to identify the species and guess their ages. I had progressed thirty or forty yards when I first noticed the understory. The ground was almost completely covered by ivy.

The thought, *this must have been planted and receive frequent attention, to be so uniform,* drifted across the back row of my inner musings. Then, I noticed small cameras and sensors on short stalks, just high enough to clear the ivy. I looked around quickly. They were as thick as dandelions in a summer pasture.

Holy shit! What was I doing here!? I stopped in my tracks and glanced up to plot my withdrawal. Trotting toward me, quite purposefully, was a man in a suit, wearing Dirty Harry sunglasses. His right hand had disappeared under the left lapel of his jacket.

I quickly raised my hands. He was easily within hearing range.

"I'm sorry. I wasn't thinking." I said, and started walking backwards down the path, while still facing him.

His pace slowed. His voice was authoritative but not menacing, "That's all right. Just keep backing up until you reach the South Lawn."

As he spoke, he removed his hand from his jacket, then looked upward and to his right. With his right arm now extended in the same direction, a flick of his wrist and fingers gave a signal. I followed his gaze just in time to see two snipers pull back to port arms and duck behind the parapet surrounding the White House roof.

Clearly the Sergeant Major had not been exaggerating when he told me a fella could get shot for making the wrong move around this place.

– The IG –

The appointment policy for most Dispensary clinics was "first come, first served," with the exception of generals and admirals. Flag officers went to the head of the line. One morning, I received a call from the front desk that a major general had registered and was on his way to my office. The secretary added, "This isn't just any ol' major general. This is the Inspector General of the Army."

The Inspector General's office (collectively referred to as the IG), included hundreds of staff, who fulfilled a function roughly similar to the external auditor of a large corporation. However, the responsibilities of the IG included much more than financial accounting. Each military facility underwent an inspection tour annually by a team from the IG's office. In addition to financial records, the visits assessed compliance with Army policies and procedures for almost everything. The IG touched nearly every member of the Armed Services, from lowly Private to Commanding General, and the inspections were anticipated with more dread than civilians reserve for the IRS. A Post Commander's career could be derailed by an unfavorable review. Consequently, considerable pressure was exerted on the various lower level officers to ensure their areas of responsibility were buffed, polished and the records squared away. As in most organizations, the misery rolls downhill. Before an IG inspection, the rank and file enlisted personnel worked overtime for weeks to ensure the buffing and polishing was high gloss. In terms of the ability to inflict harm, the Inspector General was one of the most powerful men in the Army. There was a widespread joke that the two biggest liars in the U.S. Army were the ranking officer on the IG inspection team, who said on his arrival, "It is nice to be here," and the Post Commander, who replied, "We are delighted to have you."

· · · ·

The General soon arrived at my office. I ushered him into the cramped space, and discovered he was suffering from a common skin rash.

However, this was not a patient I was going to manage unaided. Excusing myself, I stepped next door to Elliott's office, informing him that the Inspector General of the Army was in my office with a rash, and it would be best if he saw the patient. After his confirmatory, "I'll be right there," I returned to my office, so the General would not feel he was being kept waiting.

Dr. Rustad entered the exam room shortly thereafter. He wore a mischievous countenance that I had learned was associated with his playful moods. A flicker of anxiety crossed my mind. My experience with Dr. Brown a few months before had made a powerful impression. In this place, decorum was like a flak jacket in the jungle, sometimes uncomfortable, but essential to personal safety. Dr. Rustad's pranks were usually hilarious but, like most humor, designed to push someone's boundaries.

Not today, Elliott. Not with this audience! I thought to myself.

His examination of the rash was reassuringly business-like and followed by an explanation regarding the nature of the ailment and treatment needed.

I began to relax.

As the General retrieved his uniform jacket from the coat rack, Elliott took a step back (the most this room permitted), and said, "So... General, I understand you are the Inspector General."

Our patient confirmed his current position.

"The big cheese, the main man himself!" Dr. Rustad continued.

I didn't like where this conversation was going at all, but Elliott was on a roll. There was no stopping him now.

"I have a question for you, General."

"Certainly," came the reply.

Elliott grabbed my arm, pulled me forward and yanked up the white smock I was wearing, thereby exposing my waist. "What am I to do with a soldier like this? Look at this belt buckle!"

The brass buckle on my military belt was literally green from neglect, rather than the shiny yellow demanded by regulations. Our medical smocks extended well below the waist, and one of our several small rebellions against Army regulations was to postpone shining our brass, until forced by an occasion requiring our regular uniform, in which case, the buckle would be visible.

As I gasped, Elliott went on, "And look at those shoes!"

This was another bit of Army decorum we stretched as far as possible. Our shoes were supposed to be shined every day. Most of us could extend that rotation to over a week if we were careful. On this particular day, mine were well into the grace period we allowed ourselves and bore numerous scuffs.

I was in a panic! I knew Elliott only meant this as a joke, however as an officer and a physician, he really didn't understand how capricious other officers could be, nor how disastrous the potential consequences for a lowly enlisted man. Neither of us had any idea whether this particular General had a sense of humor, but the organization he commanded had a reputation for displaying no more mirth than its civilian comparator. I was now having visions of the unlucky physician caught sleeping on the O.R. table a few months before. What irony it would be, if I was banished to Vietnam and ended up getting killed because my shoes and brass weren't shined.

The General paused and remained still for what seemed an eternity. Finally, he turned to Elliott, "Dr. Rustad, I have been in the Army for twenty-seven years. During that length of time, I have learned there are three people you don't fuck with: the cook, the supply sergeant, and the medic."

With that said, he put on his jacket, adorned with the two very shiny stars on each shoulder, then looked at me and smiled as he exited the office.

— Go Get Those Boys —

It is now difficult to imagine what life was like before cell phones. When the White House requested our presence for an outdoor ceremony, a staff car and driver were requisitioned from the Motor Pool. The two medics were picked up in the transportation tunnel under the Concourse and dropped off at the White House service gate sufficiently early to be in position before the ceremony began. Staff cars are a military version of taxis. Ours did not wait for us. The driver had assigned trips throughout the day. At some later time, estimated to be well beyond the conclusion of the ceremony, the car would circle back to pick us up. In case of a change in plans, we had no way to inform either the Dispensary, the Motor Pool, or the driver. Walking up to a White House door and asking to use their telephone didn't seem like a reasonable option.

That day was typical for mid-summer Washington. The temperature had been stuck in the 90's, accompanied by the usual insufferable humidity. This type of weather pattern often broke with the sudden appearance of thunderstorms, sometimes developing in no more than an hour or two. On this occasion, by the time we were in place for the celebration, a brisk breeze was blowing, and towering thunderheads soon replaced the morning sun. Before long, the crack of lightning could be seen and heard, demarcating the leading edge of the approaching storm. Anyone who has ever spent a summer in the South could predict what was coming next.

The location of the festivities was quickly moved indoors. Public appearances by the President are carefully choreographed by White House staff and stage-managed by the Secret Service. For each location, down to the specific room or outdoor area, the head of the Secret Service team has a list of approved people. If you aren't on the list, you are not supposed to be present at *that* location. If you *are* present, you won't be for long. We were not part of the approved staff for indoor ceremonies, and so were left in the yard along with the abandoned decorations.

Soon after the move was announced, the rain began. Fortunately, our tree provided excellent cover. Nor were either of us much concerned about taking refuge under *this* tree during a thunderstorm. We assumed the array of antennae on the White House roof would provide a more tempting target for any lightning strikes.

. . . .

For lower ranking soldiers (E-1 through E-4), there is a cadence to military life quite different than life on the farm. In the Army, daily tasks were usually assigned in the morning. Throughout the day, when commissioned or non-commissioned officers were present, it was best to at least appear industrious. However, in the absence of these superiors, work slowed dramatically. If the assigned task was completed, one *never* went looking for additional work. Such industry risked a more onerous project being assigned that might otherwise have befallen some other unfortunate grunt. There were three basic rules of existence for the lowly draftee:

1. Never volunteer for anything.
2. Always appear busy.
3. In 730 days, if I live that long, this will all be over.

So, on this rainy summer afternoon, my compatriot and I were quite content to stand under a tree, invisible to the outside world, hopefully surviving one more of those 730 days in relative comfort. The storm continued to increase in severity, with sheets of rain and gusty wind, but we remained dry and relaxed.

My partner was gazing absentmindedly at the White House, approximately thirty yards away, when one of the non-descript doors at ground level opened slightly. An arm darted from the narrow aperture, waved briefly, like a flag fluttering in an erratic wind, then withdrew. The black metal door slammed shut.

"Did you see that?" the other medic asked quizzically.

"No." (I had been looking in the other direction.)

"Watch that door closest to us."

Soon, it popped open again, just enough to allow the arm to reappear and repeat the frantic waving, before closing once more.

"What the hell do you suppose that's all about?"

"Beats me."

The door opened a third time. A face now appeared where only an arm had been previously visible. The disembodied countenance grimaced in the drenching rain, then yelled, "Hey, you GI's!"

We stepped partially out of our cover and hollered back, "Us?" (Since we were the only people remaining on the South Lawn, there weren't many other choices.)

"Yeah, you!"

"What do you want?"

"Get over here!"

Once more, the portal closed abruptly after the command.

We looked at each other, shrugged, and made a break for the building. Upon reaching the door in question, it opened just enough to allow a person to squeeze through. We hesitated. The light coming from within was dim, and our vision was blurred by the rain.

"Get in here!" commanded the disembodied voice.

An arm reappeared and pulled each of us into the room. The door closed behind us with a bang.

We were in a space just below the South Portico; its purpose apparently to store lawn mowers and landscaping equipment. The man now attached to the mysterious arm and face looked to be a groundskeeper.

"What do you want?" my associate asked.

"*The President saw you guys standing out there in the rain and told me to get you inside. You can stay in here until your ride shows up.*"

. . . .

I have been a people watcher for as long as I can remember. This habit probably began as an attempt to interpret the social cues I so often got wrong as a child. With experience, I learned that it was easier to interpret conversations and actions not involving me, so I began watching other people nearby. Washington, D.C. offered almost daily opportunities to observe well known and influential individuals. They were fascinating subjects for study. As the staff car ferried us back to The Pentagon that afternoon, I reflected on the day's events. It was an eerie feeling to realize that, *today*, the most powerful man on earth had been watching *me*.

— Knox! —

One evening in late August, I had the overnight duty for the Emergency Response Team. After dinner, I sat at the front desk, relaxing, thinking about nothing in particular. My postprandial reverie was cut short as those large green doors swung open. A soldier, in dress green uniform with a duffel bag slung over his shoulder and an uncertain look on his face, walked in.

"Knox!" I exclaimed.

SP5 Knox flinched perceptibly, then stared in my direction. He was no more expecting to see me than I was to see him. After a brief period of confusion, he recognized me. We had attended 91Bravo school together the year before. He had gone to Vietnam immediately thereafter.

I assured him that the paperwork needed to report in could be easily squared away. An extra chair was retrieved, and the duffel stowed behind us. I was anxious to hear about his experiences in 'Nam, and what he knew of other members of our company. He told me that most of the guys, himself included, had been sent to Tay Ninh Province near the border with Cambodia. This area was known as the Parrot's Beak. Throughout their year of deployment, most of the medics had remained in contact, either directly or by word of mouth. Every one of them had been wounded, but he hadn't heard of any deaths.

This portion of the border between Cambodia and Vietnam, with a shape suggesting its namesake, was relatively close to the capitol city of Saigon. The Ho Chi Minh Trail and several routes through the interior of Cambodia terminated in this geographic protuberance. Supplies and reinforcements for the NVA and VC were funneled into South Vietnam from the terminus of these crude thoroughfares. If the continuous infiltration of North Vietnamese troops and war material supplied by the Russians and Chinese was to be stopped, disruption of these routes was imperative. Consequently, the frequency of contact with the enemy, the intensity of the firefights, and the resultant American casualties were high.

"By the way," Knox added, laconically, "You know that bullshit we heard in training that if you were wounded, you wouldn't be sent back into combat? I was hit five times."

I glanced at the Purple Heart ribbon on his uniform jacket. It was carpeted with oak leaf clusters, each signifying an additional award.

"They would patch me up and send me right back. I didn't get out of the field until I contracted the resistant form of malaria and was too weak to stand up."

Falciparum malaria is endemic to Vietnam. It produces more severe illness and is more resistant to treatment than the other forms of malaria.

We talked into the evening. He related some of his experiences, and those of others we knew.

Finally, I had to ask, "What about Kilroy? Do you know what happened to him?"

A wry smile appeared on Knox' face.

"Yeah, I know what happened to Kilroy."

He paused, "Shortly after joining his unit, they went into the field. His company was ambushed and shot up real bad; a lot of casualties. When they came back into Base Camp, Kilroy looked like a ghost. He went to one of the battalion surgeons, and said, 'Man, I fucked up! I didn't pay attention in school, and I don't know what I'm doing out there. You gotta teach me!'

The docs and senior medics started working with him. His unit continued to see frequent action, with large numbers of casualties. When at Base Camp, he was bugging someone to show him how to do stuff. In the field, he was a wild man; all over the place during firefights, going after guys who were in exposed positions, and shit like that. His CO put him up for a Silver Star. A general came out from Saigon for the ceremony. When the General tried to pin the medal on his uniform, Kilroy ripped it out of his hands, threw it on the ground, and said, 'I don't want your fucking booby prize!'

Boy, that caused an uproar!"

One thing about Kilroy had certainly remained unchanged. Whatever he was told to do, he never went along quietly.

There was a good deal of cynicism amongst enlisted men about the awarding of medals for heroism. First, the awards were capricious. Many soldiers performed heroic acts, most of which either weren't recorded by their NCO's or weren't forwarded through the necessary chain of command by their superiors to result in medals being awarded. An even greater irritant was that officers were much more likely than enlisted men to receive medals, and often for doing much less. Most soldiers simply did what needed to be done under the circumstances. Quite often, that required incredible bravery and sacrifice.

In listening to Knox' stories, I noticed an interesting similarity to the tales of WWII that I heard during childhood. The stories told were limited to everyday events, often humorous ones. My uncles almost never talked about the traumatic experiences of war. If the story involved combat, the horrific aspects were omitted or minimized. Listening to Knox, I recognized the same pattern. His most graphic descriptions were, "Man, we saw some shit on that patrol!" or "They just cut us up!"

For many soldiers, the most disturbing experiences must be processed alone, before being shared, if they ever are. Only two of my uncles ever shared details of emotionally upsetting combat experiences with me, and I didn't hear any of those stories until more than twenty-five years after their war was over.

— "I Forgot" —

As the summer of '68 drifted toward fall, I reached another milestone in my brief military career. The Army had a policy of not deploying soldiers to Vietnam with less than six months remaining in their enlistment. This policy was driven by the expense/benefit ratio of relocating the soldier, not by empathy. On August 9th, I hit the magic date. I had been at The Pentagon for one year and on active duty for eighteen months. I was now relatively safe. Although my future included a good deal of uncertainty, the threat of death or disability from combat was rapidly fading.

As my new status became progressively more secure with the passing days, I wasn't the only person in the Dispensary curious about the source of my good fortune. Most people who offered an opinion favored the theory that my long anticipated tropical relocation had been overruled because of the work I had done, and was doing, for the Colonel. It was common knowledge within our unit that Colonel Di was a close friend of the officer commanding the administrative section responsible for unit assignments for almost every military member throughout the world. The de jour hypothesis was that a phone call from our Colonel, or dinner and drinks, had secured my pardon from the draftee's version of Devil's Island.

During the year I awaited the orders which never arrived, I had suppressed any desire to make an inquiry. It seemed preferable not to call attention to an oversight which might then be corrected. I had entered the Army determined to do what was asked of me to the best of my ability. A steady litany of information over the past year from people actually doing the fighting suggested that, whether right or wrong, the war could not be won by current methods, and most of the American lives being lost there were being wasted. Any thought of volunteering for duty in Vietnam entertained in the early days of my enlistment had been extinguished long ago. Like almost every other soldier I knew in the latter half of 1968, my definition of winning the war was to escape the Army before being sacrificed on the funeral pyre of futility that Vietnam represented to most of us.

The only significant remaining risks of being sent to combat would be a horrendous breach of protocol on my part (earlier scrapes, such as with Dr. Brown, had made me very aware of my potential for these lapses), or if there was a national emergency. Draftees during the Vietnam era were required to spend no more than two years on active duty, however we were officially obligated to the military for a period of six years, the last four to be served as members of the Army Reserves. In the event of a national emergency, our active duty service could be extended, or we could be returned to active duty at any time during that six-year period, *at the pleasure of the Department of Defense.*

. . . .

Several months after I entered the six-month protective umbrella, I had a routine meeting with Colonel Di, for reasons I can no longer remember. As the business of the meeting wound down, I decided to gamble on this opportunity to satisfy my curiosity.

"Colonel DiLorenzo, I have a question, if I may be permitted to know. Did you influence the orders to Vietnam which I never received?"

The Colonel leaned back in his chair, gazed reflectively into the distance for a moment, then smiled. "No, I did not. However, I was supposed to report that your orders had failed to arrive. I just sort of forgot."

He then smiled more broadly. The mystery was solved.

— The Office of Inscrutable Events —

This is probably the strangest of my Pentagon adventures, and I remain uncertain as to the identity of the person of interest who prompted the mission. However, the hint later provided regarding the actual purpose of this strange assignment came from someone with unimpeachable credentials. Years later, I stumbled across a description in a newspaper story which seemed to corroborate his explanation.

. . . . .

I was called into LTC Kilmer's office one day, probably sometime in late September. He was the Executive Officer of the Dispensary and second in command, administratively. The first thing he said to me was, "What are you doing on November __ (a date six weeks in the future)?"

"I have no idea, Sir. I assume I will be here at work."

"You aren't going on leave then?"

"No, sir."

"You aren't planning any long weekend trips just before that date?"

"No, sir."

LTC Kilmer had a reputation for approaching subjects in a rather circumscribed manner, but this was unusual, even for him. Enlisted men didn't normally have the luxury of taking long weekend trips. Although some of the medics occasionally took advantage of the Sergeant Major's liberal sick call policy, I never had.

The XO continued, "Is there any reason why you wouldn't pass a security check?"

"No, sir. I can't think of anything that would be questionable."

I then added, "Sir, I already have an enhanced security clearance, or so I have been told."

"Never mind that. This is a different matter."

The Colonel's questioning continued but made less and less sense to me. His demeanor was oddly mysterious. "You're sure you can pass a security check?"

"Yes, sir."

"And, you're sure you won't be out of town during the month before Nov. __?"

"I have no such plans, and I won't make any, Sir."

"Good."

. . . .

In covert military operations, the personnel involved frequently aren't told mission details beforehand, and sometimes, they receive fabricated stories in place of the truth. The fewer people who know the details and goals of the plan, the lower the risk of information leaking out. When considering the risk of foreign espionage, the wisdom of this method is obvious. Although we sometimes were exposed to highly sensitive information in the jobs we performed, we weren't in the business of covert operations... as far as I knew.

I could not fathom the purpose of the Lieutenant Colonel's questioning, but my curiosity was growing. "Any chance you can tell me more about this assignment, Sir?"

"No."

"Very well, sir."

"Dismissed!"

. . . .

A few days later, I passed MAJ Raimundo, our Chief Nurse, in the hallway. "Did you talk to Kilmer?" she asked, rather conspiratorially.

"I did." (SOP for confidential information: answer the question in general, but do not provide additional details.)

"What do you think is going on?"

"I have no idea. I assume you also talked to him?" (Get the questioner to confirm his/her need to know. I had no reason to think the Chief Nurse was a spy, but I grew up in a family with a very straightforward and candid approach to conversation. Learning the military style of guarding information was not easy for me. I had to think about it constantly when talking to others. Besides, whether or not this project was important, it sure was secret.)

The Major confirmed that she had indeed spoken with the XO and found his questioning oddly mysterious, too. "I'm dying to know what this is all about." She grinned.

"I asked him but got no information." I added.

Some weeks later, MAJ Raimundo and I were called to a joint meeting with LTC Kilmer. Rather brusquely, he informed us that the purpose of the mysterious assignment was to teach CPR to a group of Service members and civilians. This still didn't make any sense.

MAJ Raimundo countered, "But, CPR classes are available. Why don't they just take one of those?"

The XO simply looked at her in silence.

"OK," the Chief Nurse persisted. "What are we expected to cover: basic CPR, bag-valve-mask ventilation? Should we take Resusci-Annie and have them practice?" (Resusci-Annie is a mannequin used to teach CPR.)

I was glad the Major was in attendance. Those possibilities hadn't occurred to me, and I certainly wasn't as comfortable grilling a senior officer for information as she was.

"Take everything," was his reply. "Take the gurney and the medical bag we use for Emergency Response calls. If the team gets a call, we will deal with that. Take Resusci-Annie, too — *take everything!*"

MAJ Raimundo remained unsatisfied. "But, the aid bag has the medications and everything. You don't want us to try to teach them about cardiac medications, do you?"

"Take everything."

The Chief Nurse wasn't going to give up easily. "How long is this class supposed to last? If we talk about all that stuff, we could be there all afternoon!"

"Yes."

This meeting was clearly at an end.

The Major and I walked out of LTC Kilmer's office together. "I don't get it," she muttered. "This makes no sense whatsoever. I still don't understand exactly what we are supposed to do, or why we are doing it."

"I think that is the point," I replied.

. . . .

Over the next several weeks, whenever I encountered our XO in the hallway, he would repeat the same refrain, "You remember the mission on Nov __, right? You aren't going anywhere, are you? Do you have all the equipment? Is there anything else you can think of you might need?"

During the first of these interactions, I responded to his question about additional equipment with, "Since I don't know where we are going or what we are doing, that is a hard question to answer."

I received the same blank stare he had delivered to the Major. "Be ready for anything," was his only recommendation.

On further encounters, I limited my reply to, "Yes, Sir," for each of his questions. It was easier.

On the Friday afternoon before our seemingly all-important CPR class, there was a knock on my office door. It was LTC Kilmer.

"Are you ready?"

"Yes, Sir."

"You aren't going anywhere this weekend, are you?"

"No, sir."

"I want you to stay in town this weekend. Do you understand?"

"Yes, Sir."

"In fact, I would prefer that you remain on Post." (Meaning within the confines of Fort Myer, the location of our barracks.)

I hesitated, then answered, "Yes, Sir." knowing he had no way of tracking my movements without going to a lot of trouble. If he wasn't telling me where I was going on Monday, then I wasn't telling him where I was going on Saturday and Sunday. I had already decided not to stray more than a few miles from Ft. Myer in case I suffered some unanticipated catastrophe.

"Oh..., you don't drink, do you?" he added.

"Not much." I replied.

"Well, whatever you do this weekend, don't get drunk!"

"No, Sir."

"You promise me?"

By this point, I thought I might need to knock on Dr. Goodin's wall, in the office next to mine. The XO was acting as though he might succumb to a panic attack.

"I won't get drunk this weekend, Sir. You can count on me."

"Good! Good! I'll see you Monday morning, bright and early!" He hurried down the hall, as my office door closed behind him.

I sat and reflected on the most bizarre conversation with a lieutenant colonel I ever experienced. First, he had come to my office. Lieutenant colonels do not come to visit enlisted men; they have someone fetch them. If any walking is involved, the enlisted man does it, not the colonel. Second, he was repeating information and orders he had previously provided four or five times. Third, the tone of his voice sounded almost like begging. By comparison, we never experienced this type of preparation or anxiety with our trips to the White House. On those occasions, I would be notified of the event about one week in advance, and that was the extent of the planning. Whatever this assignment turned out to be, it was going to be a doozy!

I decided to report the Lieutenant Colonel's anxiety level to Dr. Goodin, as my entry for the most neurotic patient I had seen that week. Although, when I checked my neighbor's door, the office was dark, indicating he had taken advantage of a slow afternoon and started his weekend early. Lucky him!

. . . .

I arrived at work at 08:00 the following Monday, as usual. Our mysterious appointment was scheduled for early afternoon. The Major and I started packing about 10:30, since we still didn't know the location. While we were assembling gear, Colonel Kilmer appeared. He had a small slip of paper in his hand, which he passed to MAJ Raimundo conspiratorially. The note contained a Pentagon room number.

"This is where you are to go," he muttered tersely. "Is there anything else you need?"

We reassured him that we were taking everything available. He seemed calmer than on Friday, subdued even. I wondered if he had a hangover? He then turned and walked down the hallway without further instructions or well-wishes.

When he was out of earshot, I said, "I'm surprised he didn't tell you to memorize that room number, then either burn the paper or swallow it!"

"No kidding!" was her incredulous reply.

We embarked on our secret mission earlier than should have been necessary, considering the location indicated by the room number. If this assignment was as sensitive as our XO's behavior had suggested, the location might require more time to find than expected. Fortunately, this was not the case. The room was exactly where the number predicted. The door, which was closed, was non-descript and had no other identifying information.

Our knock wasn't answered, but the door wasn't locked. We peeked inside to find a small conference room with blackboards covering two walls, a raised platform at one end, and a lectern for speakers. We were the first to arrive. As we unpacked and positioned our equipment, people began filing into the room, mostly from a door near the rear. They had lunch bags and coffee cups. I overheard one of them ask another, "What are we doing here?"

Hmmm. So, this was a sham audience, just like the flag-waving crowds at the outdoor White House ceremonies. Well, on with the charade! The room held thirty to forty people and was soon almost full.

The Major leaned toward me and whispered, "You do the talking. Speaking before crowds makes me nervous." Fortunately, my role orienting new medics and providing some of the continuing education classes for the rest had given me some experience talking before a group and covering this subject.

The door we had entered opened abruptly. A full Colonel entered and approached us hurriedly. We exchanged names, and he thanked us for coming.

Before he could start for the lectern, I said, "Colonel, we weren't given a lot of information about this presentation. What information would you like for us to cover, and how long should the presentation be?"

As he brushed past me on his way to the podium, his answer came over his shoulder, "Just keep talking."

"Ladies and gentlemen, these representatives from the U.S. Army Dispensary," (He had made no effort to learn our names.), "have graciously offered to give a presentation on emergency medical situations this afternoon. Please welcome them." He then stepped aside quickly and lead the brief, polite applause that followed.

I turned to MAJ Raimundo and whispered, "I don't think hands on CPR practice is going to be practical with this many people."

She nodded her head in agreement.

"OK. I'll start. If you think of anything, please jump in. I don't know where I am going here."

The Colonel who introduced us was already working his way to the back of the room. He quickly disappeared through the rear door.

. . . .

I took my place at the podium. "There are many types of medical emergencies. Our staff at the Dispensary responds to most of them frequently." I quoted the number of patients seen by Dispensary staff on a daily basis. "Obviously, the medical emergency that first comes to mind is cardiac arrest. So, let's start the discussion with this event."

I went on to describe the symptoms and signs of cardiac arrest and how to identify them. I talked about arrhythmias and ischemia, the difference in symptoms and possible differences in etiology. I reminded them of the telephone number to call, if someone developed the characteristic appearance or complained of worrisome symptoms. Then I discussed the mechanism of CPR and how to perform the maneuver correctly.

Following this description, the Major and I moved Resusci-Annie to the front of the platform and demonstrated chest compression and mouth to mouth breathing. We stretched this bit of performance art as far as we could, then took turns describing potential problems that might be encountered, such as oral foreign bodies obstructing the airway.

I described the various means of summoning help, and which was preferable, depending on the circumstances. I talked about the role of other bystanders, and methods for coaxing reluctant participants to assist with activities they found less intimidating. We had now lengthened what should have been a forty-five-minute presentation to a little over an hour, but I was running out of material. My reticent co-presenter wasn't providing much additional information, and the Colonel who had introduced us was nowhere in sight. Now what?

I have always enjoyed the study of history, so in desperation, I launched into what little I knew of the history of resuscitation. I related the Biblical stories that have been interpreted as possibly representing resuscitation, such as Jesus raising Lazarus from the dead. I mentioned pictures of ancient Egyptians with a hollow reed placed in the mouth of drowning victims. I talked about the spontaneous conversion of ventricular tachycardia or ventricular fibrillation by a blow to the chest wall. (One of the physicians had explained this phenomenon to me one night when we were both on call.) As I frantically searched my memory for any medical story even remotely appropriate for this audience, the Colonel briskly re-entered the front door. He immediately mounted the stage, interrupting me in mid-sentence. He thanked us for our presentation and dismissed the audience.

Our mysterious assignment was apparently completed. We packed up the gear and headed back to the Dispensary. I think I earned a lifetime membership in the creative storytelling club that afternoon, but I'm still waiting for the certificate. However, two weeks after our presentation, I received a letter from this same Colonel thanking me for the excellent CPR presentation. The letterhead was some obscure agency in charge of third world political affairs.

Shortly before leaving The Pentagon, in an unrelated conversation, an officer confirmed to me the background of our mysterious CPR class. During our presentation, a very high-level meeting was occurring immediately adjacent to the conference room we occupied. The purpose of the meeting was to deliver some frank and discouraging news about the progress of the war to a very senior civilian official. This official was suspected of being in ill-health. There was concern that the impact of the information to be delivered might prompt a medical emergency. Our vaguely-defined presentation to an uninformed audience provided a cover to ensure we were immediately available for any medical needs next door.

During the Autumn of 1968, the veiled description of "a very senior official, suspected of being in serious ill-health" applied to only one person in Washington, D.C., President Lyndon Johnson. Whoever the senior official requiring our immediate availability was, any further information fell within a "need to know" security firewall, and a determination had been made that we did not need to know.

The newspaper article many years later described just such a meeting, occurring at approximately the time of our mysterious mission. There are many reasons why our choice to provide medical coverage for the President would seem unlikely. However, in thinking about the circumstances, I can also imagine why the Chief Nurse and I were the most logical choice of first responders. We had training and experience in field emergency medical care, and I probably knew the logistics of transporting a patient through the building on a gurney better than anyone else in the Service at that time. The White House medical staff would have been at a considerable disadvantage in that setting.

As Forrest Gump would say, "Life is like a box of chocolates!"

— The Academy —

A few weeks before my scheduled departure from the Dispensary, I was called to COL DiLorenzo's office. The summons was unexpected. My initial assumption was that the Colonel had a question about one of the several projects currently assigned to me, or wanted to discuss who would assume those tasks when I left. I had been wondering about that, myself. By then, most of my daily activities were somewhat beyond the training in the 91Bravo course. Nevertheless, as I walked down the long hallway to his office, the old suspicion that I must have done something wrong came creeping back. Repeated experiences throughout life with the consequences of my social blind spots and wayward tongue had made me wary.

On my arrival, I found Colonel Di, LTC Kilmer, and SGM Gilbert all present and looking rather triumphant. By now, I was pretty comfortable around these men... not back-slapping comfortable, but comfortable. Yet, I had never before been called to a meeting with all of them at the same time. Was I guilty of some unrecognized violation of protocol about to be brought to my attention? I quickly scanned the faces in the room. I had rarely seen Colonel Di laugh, but this morning, he looked like someone guarding a pleasant secret.

"Turner, how are you!" he boomed, while motioning for me to take the remaining chair.

"Quite well, Sir." No longer anxious, I remained perplexed.

"I understand your tour of duty is coming to an end soon," he continued. "What are your plans for the future?"

"Well, Sir, some of the physicians have convinced me I should try to go to medical school. I'm not sure I have the ability, but I am going to give it a shot. I have enrolled in a pre-med program at college, beginning the first of the year."

His face fell perceptibly, as did those of the other two men in the room. Now, I was really confused.

After a moment, the Colonel went on, "Well, that is an admirable goal. Medicine is a fine profession. However, the reason I asked to see you this morning is to offer you an alternative opportunity."

He went on to explain that the Army maintained a private preparatory academy. Each year, a few soldiers who had shown unusual potential during their initial enlistment were invited to attend this school. For those individuals, additional academic testing was performed, and a personalized study program developed. Tutors were provided as needed. Upon completion of the prescribed studies, the student was admitted to the next class of the U.S. Military Academy at West Point. Admission to the program required the approval of the Joint Chiefs of Staff and was very selective. Colonel Di had submitted a recommendation on my behalf several months before and had just now received notification of my acceptance.

I was stunned beyond words. No matter what anyone thinks of a military career, admission to one of the Service Academies is an honor without parallel. The United States Military Academy at West Point has trained many of the leaders of our country, including two Presidents. In addition to academic performance, appointment to the Academy usually requires the recommendation of a member of Congress. The Colonel's compliments and proposal washed over me like a warm ocean wave. I don't know how long I sat there, motionless, but it seemed like a long time.

Once recovered sufficiently to speak, the problem of what to say remained. Frankly, I loved my job at The Pentagon, but my experience there couldn't have been more remote from the *real Army* my peers, such as SP5 Knox, had lived in *their* assignments. Even though I was becoming acclimated to the ways of the military, it wasn't the best fit for me, as a culture or career. I remembered something SGM Gilbert said on the first day we met. "This will be the best assignment you ever have in the Army, no matter how long you spend in the Service."

I was pretty sure he was correct. I was living in a cocoon in this assignment. I had thrived here, in part, because I was given an unusual degree of flexibility to experiment, by superiors who were very supportive of my efforts and remarkably tolerant of my failures. This was not the way the Army usually worked. Even if I managed to survive the math and engineering curriculum at West Point, what would I have at its conclusion? I would be a Second Lieutenant in the real Army; an organization not noted for its flexibility or fondness for innovation. Medical school might be an improbable goal, but I suspected my success in the officer corps was even less likely. Uncle Red had attained true fame and tremendous respect in the Submarine Service, but had retired with the rank of Lieutenant Commander, not Captain or Admiral. After observing the ways of the officer corps and the means of advancement inside this building, the citadel of military success, the explanation for Red's limited advancement in the officer ranks seemed clear, and it directly impacted me. My uncle and I shared a characteristic which wasn't valued in organizational politics; the inability to resist saying the wrong thing at the tempting moment.

I did not accept the appointment.

— The Black Dog —

Under certain circumstances, the Army allowed soldiers to be discharged from active duty up to ninety days prior to their official release date. In military slang, this shortcut to civilian life was called an *early out.* (To be entirely accurate, we weren't being *discharged* from the Service. We were being separated from active duty and transferred to the Army Reserves.)

The most common justification for an early out was return from an overseas assignment with less than ninety days of active duty obligation remaining. The expense of travel and orientation to a new duty station was not cost effective. Another acceptable reason for early separation was to begin or return to college or skilled trade school. To be eligible, the soldier must be formally admitted to an approved school for a term beginning within that ninety-day window. Consistent with its usual degree of pomposity, the reason listed for the amendment to the discharge order was *for the convenience of the Department of Defense to return to school.* My scheduled separation date was 9 Feb 69. During the fall of 1968, I was accepted to Southern Illinois University Edwardsville (SIUE) for the winter term, beginning the first week of January 1969.

One of the reasons I chose this particular school related to its admissions policy. Illinois residents who were military veterans and possessed a high school diploma were given priority for admission. This addressed the awkwardness of a 1.9 cumulative GPA during my previous college experience. If the early out was granted to begin school, a few days travel time was customarily included. This meant I would probably have a release date sometime during the last week of December. I was hoping COL DiLorenzo and SGM Gilbert would display their usual flexibility regarding the exact timing of my departure. If so, I might make it home for Christmas.

When my orders arrived, the date of discharge was listed as 23Dec68, a Monday. I wasn't scheduled for call the weekend before, so had no assigned duties. SGM Gilbert arranged my appointment to complete the separation paperwork for Friday, Dec 20. Although I would still be on active duty, technically, until Dec. 23, I wasn't required to be in any particular place. As hoped, he also agreed that I might as well spend my last two nights in the Army sleeping in my own bed, at my parent's home in Illinois. His only admonition was, "If there is some kind of national emergency over the course of that weekend, you better hightail it back here!" (Since the DOD considered my release to be for their convenience, they certainly reserved the prerogative to cancel it at any moment if a perceived need arose.)

. . . .

December 19 was my last scheduled workday... but there was nothing for me to do. My duties had already been transferred to other people, or simply left in limbo. If I previously entertained any ideas of being indispensable to the organization, that illusion was abruptly dispelled. My name had simply disappeared from the duty rosters. I wandered the halls, visiting with friends and saying goodbye. Rather than the elation I had anticipated upon my escape from the Army, I found the mental process of disengagement unsettling.

In the administrative hierarchy, the USAD, The Pentagon, was under the command of Walter Reed Army Medical Center, and so, on the morning of Dec. 20, I drove to that facility for the processing of reams of paperwork necessary to change my military status from active duty to inactive reserve. The office was located in a nondescript ancillary building near the hospital. The entrance opened to a converted conference room, containing sixty to eighty standard brown folding chairs. To my left, a counter intersected most of the width of the room. A civilian employee stood behind the counter, awaiting my approach. Behind her, another door led to an office where conversation and the clatter of typewriters could be heard. After presenting my military ID and paperwork, she said, "Take a seat. We will call you when we need you."

She then disappeared into the room behind her with the manila envelope I had surrendered.

Don't lose that! I reflexively thought to myself. There was a reason military personnel always carried their records with them.

I turned from the counter and surveyed the gallery of chairs filling most of the room. Their appearance was unusual by military standards. Most noticeably, they weren't positioned in absolutely straight and uniform rows. Although some semblance of order remained, the chairs were not perfectly aligned, as would be expected. The center aisle was uncharacteristically wide, and the areas in front of the counter and at the rear of the room were also spacious. Classrooms and conference rooms used by enlisted personnel in the Army typically economized on space. A few soldiers were sitting near the rear of the room, some of them in uniform, others wearing uniform trousers coupled with one of several choices of hospital attire. Although this mix and match was a violation of military dress code, no one else seemed to notice. The chairs these men occupied had been moved into positions facing each other, as they chatted nonchalantly. After two years of military order, all of these small elements of disorder actually produced a sense of unease in me. I imagined an officer suddenly appearing and yelling to straighten up this room and get into uniform! How quickly new habits become ingrained.

The necessities of this environment slowly came into focus. Of course! These men had been patients at the hospital or associated rehab facilities. Several still sported casts, braces, and other paraphernalia related to their treatment. The position of their chairs had been adjusted so they could look at each other while talking, because some could not turn easily in their seats. The reason for the unusually wide aisle and spaces front and rear was probably to accommodate stretchers and wheelchairs. I had anticipated other personnel being discharged that day would be medics and technicians working at the hospital or clinics.

I hadn't considered the fact that patients being discharged from the hospital were often discharged from the military simultaneously.

I chose a seat several rows from the group and settled in for a long wait. Oh well, this would be the *last time* I had to wait for the Army. Occasionally, the front door opened, usually with some difficulty, and another soldier would join us. A few were on crutches, and some in wheel chairs. In between these interruptions, I sat lost in my own thoughts. My plan was to leave for Edwardsville that evening, a distance of nine hundred miles. I would be driving, and the trip would take all night, but I didn't want to waste even a minute of my first weekend at home. Packing wasn't much of a challenge. Military life discourages the accumulation of *stuff*. Another soldier from my hometown was catching a ride with me, to begin his Christmas leave. In one of those unexpected intersections in life, he and I had entered the Army on the same day and completed Basic Training in the same Company. However, he had enlisted rather than wait to be drafted, in exchange for guaranteed training in a particular specialty. Because of that guarantee, he owed the Army one extra year of active duty.

I mentally relived some of my experiences over the past twenty-two months. In a few hours, the most intense period of my life, up until now, would be over. I tried to imagine myself in the role awaiting me. I could not. I was no longer one thing (soldier, medic, Dispensary team member), but I was not yet another (student, civilian, small Midwestern town resident). I really hated to leave D.C. I loved it here, and the area had begun to feel like home. Unfortunately, there was no way I could afford to attend school, or even live in Washington. By returning to Edwardsville, I could live with my parents, thus avoiding rental expenses, as well as enjoying frequent meals at home. I was eligible for the federal G.I. Bill, which would provide $140 per month for school expenses. The Illinois legislature had also been very generous to veterans. I could attend any state-sponsored college for $50 tuition per quarter. The foundry, where I worked summers before the Army, had agreed to rehire me. The pay was modest, but Charlie would allow considerable flexibility to accommodate my classes. With a full-time pre-med curriculum, this latitude was essential. I needed to focus on being a student if I was to have any hope of success in this highly improbable quest. By living with my parents, I should have just enough money to cover other expenses. After two years of independence, I didn't relish living at home, however working enough hours to attain complete economic independence while tackling a difficult college schedule seemed unrealistic. I would swallow my pride.

My mind wandered to other things. I reviewed the paperwork needed to enroll for the Winter Quarter at SIUE, and mentally checked the list of things still to do. I imagined Mom dusting my bedroom in preparation for my arrival. Dad would be acting like nothing unusual was happening, but I knew he would be glad to have me back home in one piece. Several of my friends had already returned from Vietnam and were out of the Army. There would undoubtedly be some celebrating tomorrow evening. The most pleasant thoughts were of my grandmother. She was nearing her eighty-sixth birthday. Miraculously, my record of having spent every Christmas of my life with Grandma would remain unbroken.

Eventually, I ran out of daydream material. I glanced at the clock. It was almost noon. Within a few minutes, an employee came to the counter to announce the office would close from noon until 1:00 p.m. for lunch. She added that we were allowed to remain in the building but recommended getting something to eat and warned that once they resumed work in the afternoon, if a name was called and the person wasn't present, their file would be moved to the back of the queue. I had visited the hospital campus only once before and had no idea where to find food. Some of the other guys left purposefully, but several remained. I joined their conversation. Those still present confided that they hadn't been off their hospital wards long enough to learn the location of anything but the X-ray and rehab departments. A couple of us who were the most mobile went on recon. Vending machines were located, and a supply of peanuts, candy bars, and soda secured. We returned to the waiting room and passed out the rations. Soon, the other guys began drifting back. Apparently, no one wanted to risk going to the back of the line.

. . . .

I began to examine my companions more closely. The first thing that struck me was the paucity of rank. Most of them were PFC's, sporting one stripe on their uniform sleeve. Only a few were Corporals or SP4's. One of them was even a slick sleeve (no insignia, indicating the rank of Private). Surely, he was at least an E-2, although maybe he had gotten in enough trouble to get busted back to E-1. (A standard punishment for all but the most severe infractions committed by enlisted men was to be demoted to a lower rank.) The Private was a big guy with a ready grin. His hair was as short as a Basic Trainee, and I was quite sure that his most recent haircut had been administered by a neurosurgeon's assistant. The scar resulting from a curvilinear incision arced over his right ear from the front to the back of his scalp. It was the telltale streamer of an exploratory craniotomy and appeared to be six to twelve months of age. Multiple other divots and smaller scars adorned his cranium. A tubular elevation of his scalp, with the appearance of a mole tunnel in a lawn, began at a large protrusion near the top of his skull and snaked downward to his neck, where it disappeared beneath his collar. The large bump at its north end was the reservoir and valve of a ventriculo-peritoneal shunt, and the mole tunnel was a drainage catheter which ended in his abdominal cavity. Another, unseen, catheter connected to the underside of the reservoir, passed through a keyhole in his skull, then wove between the mass of neurons below to reach one of the fluid-filled cavities in the center of his brain. The purpose of this device was to bypass an obstruction to the flow of cerebrospinal fluid; a common complication of severe head injuries.

As I watched him, I also noticed the characteristic abnormal speech pattern and enunciation often seen in patients with these wounds. Some of his thought content wasn't too good, either. In medical terminology, this dude was jacked up. Maybe he had been involved in a fight in a Saigon bar and got the worst of it, both physically and administratively, but the number of other scars visible was more suggestive of shrapnel.

I remained puzzled by the lowly rank of his companions, as well. I was the highest-ranking person in the room. Maybe they had all been injured shortly after their arrival in 'Nam. Even so, months had now passed in the hospital and/or rehab; for some of them, more than a year. Military promotions were based on the amount of time a soldier had been in the Service, the time spent at his/her current rank, and the individual's performance. I had been promoted to Specialist 5th Class (E-5) in twenty months. This was pretty fast but not unusual. Several of the other medics at the Dispensary had made E-5 in less than two years, too. And, during 1967-68, anyone in the Army who showed up every morning, and didn't screw up too badly, could expect to make E-4 (SP4 or Corporal) well before completing a two-year tour of duty. These guys seemed like regular Joe's. What had derailed their promotions? Surely, some of them had the requisite time in service to make SP4?

A possible explanation occurred to me. Did the period of treatment and recovery from wounds not count toward time in Service and time in grade? If true, it seemed grotesquely unfair. I hoped my suspicion was incorrect, but I was too self-conscious to ask any of them. There were twenty-eight of us awaiting discharge that day. I was the only one who still had all of my parts, and all in working order.

I didn't contribute much to the conversation that afternoon. I was too embarrassed. I just hoped no one would ask what I had been doing in the Army for the past two years.

· · · ·

In listening to the men talk, I realized almost none of their conversation was related to going back to school, or a job waiting for them. They didn't talk about going home to marry their girl. She had deserted long before now. They didn't even talk about looking forward to hanging out with their friends. Most of these guys weren't going to be playing any pick-up basketball. Many of them wouldn't even be able to drive until fitted for artificial limbs and approved for adaptive devices on a vehicle. That sequence of procedures and paperwork would drag on for months.

Most of their conversation related to the percentage disability they had been awarded, how far they would have to travel to their rehab appointments, and, in some cases, how long before their wound closure would allow a permanent prosthesis, or their next reconstructive surgery could be scheduled. In addition to those with mangled arms and legs, there were burns and facial deformities from bullets and shrapnel. One guy had a tracheostomy below his deformed jaw. That would be a real show-stopper at the dances on Saturday nights. A thick-chested SP4, who looked like he had played football in high school, kept himself carefully positioned in his chair. His right arm was flexed at the elbow with the lower portion supported by a sling. His wrist was visible, but its terminus was sewn to the skin of his abdomen. I knew his shattered hand was still present, but now resided beneath the fatty layer of his belly for protection, while damaged bone and tissue healed sufficiently to perform the next stage of reconstructive surgery. The series of operations and healing required would take years.

· · · ·

The military maintains an extensive network of hospitals and clinics, staffed by active duty medical practitioners. The priority for this system is to return as many injured personnel to the battlefield as possible. For soldiers who have been injured more severely, treatment in military hospitals is routinely continued through the acute phase, primarily because of the unique nature of wounds of war. Once this phase has progressed to either a prolonged period of recovery or permanent disability, the soldier is discharged from active duty, and further medical care is deferred to a quasi-civilian medical system operated by the U.S. Department of Veterans Affairs, more commonly known as the VA. Service members are promised life-time medical care for any *service-connected disabilities* i.e. the persistent effects of injuries suffered while on active duty.

In addition to medical benefits, the disabled soldier receives a financial stipend based on the severity of disability remaining after treatment. His/her functional capacity is estimated and expressed as a percentage of normal. This determination is made by a military board of physicians, surgeons, therapists, and administrators. The amount paid is calculated by multiplying the soldier's pay grade by the estimated percentage of disability awarded by the medical board. Obviously, this is a very arbitrary number, and the association with rank defies logic. Once discharged, the injured soldier receives this monthly stipend to *assist* with living expenses.

The guys in the room with me had recently been through their disability hearings. Those decisions had enormous implications for their future. It was the hot topic of the afternoon. The comments typically ran, "I got 50%," or "I got 70%."

One guy, with his leg off below the knee, complained, "I got 30%. What the fuck am I supposed to do with that? How am I going to find a job? Do they think I'm going to make a living working for Good Will?"

The big guy with the head injury piped up, "Man, I got 90%!" and beamed triumphantly.

The room fell briefly silent after his pronouncement.

As the afternoon progressed, I gained an increasing awareness of the degree of his impairment. His speech was distorted but understandable. He could walk, although with a wide-based, reeling gait which resulted in occasional falls. However, his worst impairment, as with many head injuries of this severity, was his lack of judgement and insight. His level of maturity was that of a six to eight-year-old child. He clearly did not have the ability to care for himself unaided. At best, he would need to live in a half-way house for the rest of his life. At worst, he would be confined to a locked residential care facility… but none of this would happen immediately. The Army was going to release him that day. He would get his discharge pay, a bus or plane ticket to the major city closest to his site of enlistment, and a phone number to call for an appointment at a VA Medical Clinic. If he made it to the destination specified on his ticket, and no one was there to meet him, *he was on his own*. In that case, if he was lucky, the police might detain him for some minor infraction. Hopefully, a sympathetic policeman or judge would contact a social services agency to request an expedited competency evaluation. A proper evaluation should have been done before he was discharged from Walter Reed. Apparently, either the Psychiatry Department had dropped the ball, or the evaluation was deliberately being deferred to the VA System, which in his case was medically inappropriate. Now, under the best of circumstances, the process would require months of hearings and deliberations, with responsibility for his medical needs being lobbed back and forth, like a live grenade, between the VA and whatever services for the indigent were available in the county of his residence.

If he was unlucky on the trip home, or while waiting for the VA to act, someone would cheat him out of his paycheck in a bar, or he would get rolled in the alley out back. Maybe he would survive another head injury, maybe he wouldn't. His war wasn't over yet. He was just transferring to a different Theatre of Operations.

At one point, our cheerful friend stood up and announced that he "had to pee." All eyes were upon him, as he stumbled into a few chairs on his way to the latrine.

Once out of the room, one of the other guys said, "That dumb son-of-a-bitch thinks he has it made with 90%. He's a fucking E-2! He got hurt almost as soon as he stepped off the plane in 'Nam. He makes $104 per month!"

Based on other parts of the conversation, this guy had apparently been in the hospital and rehab for almost a year, which seemed to confirm my suspicion.

Someone else added, "Yeah, $104 times 90%. I wonder where he thinks he's going to spend all that money?"

The room fell silent again. A cold, nauseating sensation, like a bucket of ice water, seemed to pour in through my neck, down the interior of my chest and into my belly. At a fundamental level, my identity was linked with these men. We were all soldiers, and they were my brothers. But the war had divided us into two groups. There were twenty-seven in the most obvious group, and I, the only person physically still intact, was in the other group... alone. Even if I fell flat on my face in pre-med and had to relinquish that dream, I was still going home with a job waiting for me. I was on my way back to college, to chasing co-eds, and running with my buddies. For the other group, life was going to be very different. No matter how hard they tried, their wounds and the experience of war were going to impact and limit everything they did for the rest of their lives.

. . . .

About 15:00, the woman at the counter called my name. I spent the next twenty minutes answering questions, signing papers, and receiving instructions on how to apply for veteran's benefits. At 15:25, I walked out of the building. Although I wasn't yet officially released from active duty, for all intents and purposes, I was out of the Army... or was I?

Nearly two years and one lifetime ago, I had been immersed in the preparation for war, followed by training to assist in the care of its most horrendous results, with the unspoken knowledge that I might meet those same ends. Then fate had intervened, and I traversed only the first portion of that valley before two roads diverged, as in Robert Frost's poem. My companions of today, and most of my brothers from those days of training in early 1967, had taken the road that bent into the undergrowth of the jungles of Vietnam, while I had been diverted to the path consisting of concrete walls and marble floors at the Department of Defense. We had all obeyed the orders we received, but the outcomes had been starkly different.

As I stood in the pale afternoon sun, in the uniform I would never wear again, I was more conflicted than I have ever been in my life. The thought of the multiple tragedies I had just observed, and the knowledge that those must be multiplied a thousand times over, was suffocating. Part of the healthy processing of a near-death experience includes a celebration of having escaped the grim reaper, at least for the moment. However, allowing myself any elation right then felt like dancing at a funeral; irreverent at the least. The magnitude of my good fortune during the past seventeen months had just been rubbed in my face. Briefly, I teetered on the edge of a bottomless pit of despair.

I shook it off. I was simply an unspent cartridge the Army had chosen not to fire, and I was too contrary to allow them to make me into a psychological casualty of this war now. As I stepped off the curb and started determinedly toward my car, my immediate goal was to be done with wounds and done with war stories; to get away from here and back to the *real world*.

After carefully placing the envelope containing my all-important DD-214, the Army discharge document, behind my seat, I headed out of the parking lot, made a right turn onto the street, and accelerated into the next chapter of my life.

· · · ·

Unknowingly, I picked up a companion that day at Walter Reed. He has stayed with me ever since. Most of the time, he remains out of sight, but never farther away than just around the corner. The shrinks call him survivor's guilt. Winston Churchill described his bouts of depression as "boxing the Black Dog." When I first read that description, the Black Dog seemed a perfect metaphor for my companion from Walter Reed.

My Black Dog appears unexpectedly, summoned by a melody or a phrase that I associate with the Army or with Vietnam, and that chapter in my life. Sometimes, thoughts of a friend from those days will call the cur. At others, the mongrel just appears. He scatters any of my existing thoughts like a bunch of cats. They are always replaced by the same questions. "Why the fuck am I here? Why didn't I die in some rice paddy, or MedEvac helicopter crash, or mortar attack on a forward Aid Station, back in '67 or '68?"

I visualize one or more of those alternate universes. The sensations are vivid. I can smell the stench of the mud, the cordite tang in the air, the JP-4 running down a helicopter fuselage. I have learned that, if possible, it is best to postpone what I am doing and just let the feelings wash over me. Sometimes, they recede in minutes, sometimes, hours may go by. Occasionally, I can't get my mind off the war for several days. Then, I put the Black Dog back on his leash and tie him to a tree, around the corner and out of sight. But I know, sooner or later, he will get loose again. I suspect that damned dog won't die until I do.

C.I. Starnes Foundry, author in foreground

Chapter V.   SIUE
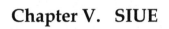

— Back Home —

January 4, 1969 was a cold, but brightly sunlit, winter day. I drove to my new college campus for the first time, parked in a massive lot that had been a cornfield just a few years before, and headed for the cluster of buildings in the distance. I was back home and once again a college student.

Edwardsville is the third oldest incorporated city in Illinois (1812). Beginning life as a frontier trading post, it served as a land grant office for the Illinois Territory until statehood supervened. Farming the rich prairie soil was an early attraction for settlers. Coal mines opened in the late 1800's, and these two occupations dominated the local economy until 1940. My childhood home was built, literally, on top of a mine. The view from our living room window was dominated by a man-made mountain of slag, hard by the nearest vertical shaft, located two blocks from our house. WWII forced the closure of most of the mines, and by the late 1940's, the influence of agriculture was also diminishing steadily, as farms retreated in the face of the post-war housing boom. By the time of my earliest memories, manufacturing and petroleum re-fining, located along the nearby Mississippi River, exerted significant economic influence and many local residents were either blue or white-collar workers in these industries. However, the heritage of farming and coal-mining, and the cultures of the immigrants who came for those opportunities, remained strongly imprinted. The architectural style and names: of streets, buildings, and homes, was like examining rings on a tree describing the evolution of the city and its inhabitants. Up until my departure in 1967, the population had slowly increased from 2,000 to 10,000 souls over the previous one hundred years, but in spite of its modest size, one would be hard pressed to find a more cul-turally diverse, All-American town than the Edwardsville of my youth.

During the two years I was away, the area experienced the begin-nings of another demographic and cultural evolution. The new state university campus at the edge of town opened in the fall of 1965. Edwardsville had long held a reputation as a well-educated community, but this accomplishment was certainly relative. Many of the new, highly educated university faculty members chose to live in the community. Some were widely traveled and had a taste for more cosmopolitan choices in *everything* than had previously been available locally. Now in its fourth year, the campus was already attracting students from other parts of the country, and a few from overseas. The student population was approaching thirty percent of the previous city census. *Hippy* dress and political opinions had become fashionable on many Midwestern college campuses, including this one; a dramatic departure from the more conservative "Old World culture" prevailing until recently.

Veterans of our generation were regarded with suspicion by some of the university students. Although we had not yet acquired the epithet *baby killers*, that label would be added soon enough. Returning from military service, my friends and I received a few handshakes from older adults, but we sure didn't get any parades. My home town had evolved into something quite different than the place I left. For the high school class of '65, some of us had gone to Woodstock, and some of us to Vietnam, and some of us were ricocheting between those two poles, trying to determine what planet we were currently on.

.   .   .   .

I wanted to resume the life of a student as quickly as possible, although it wasn't the classic image of college, with dormitories, football games, and pep rallies. To save money on administrative costs, the new university was designated an auxiliary campus of the pre-existing Southern Illinois University at Carbondale, ninety miles to the south. Additional cost-saving measures included an absence of dormitories and football program. Stadiums were expensive. Soccer was cheaper. Besides, this was designed to be a *commuter college*. Its purpose was to expand undergraduate capacity for the growing population, and to address the needs of working adults for access to higher education. Even though manufacturing had become an economic powerhouse of the region only twenty-five years before, by the mid-1960's, the number of jobs in this sector was already shrinking. The uncertainty of continuing opportunities for these occupations wasn't lost on community leaders. Memories of the Great Depression, only three decades in the past, still lurked.

In retrospect, I imagine this unusual sensitivity to signs of what lay ahead, decades ahead of many national policy-makers, was also prompted by the pioneer and immigrant cultural beliefs still present in the area. The opportunity to learn a marketable skill and the availability of work, were of penultimate importance to people in the generations before mine. Maintaining that perspective on life, most of my classmates and I displayed a very utilitarian attitude toward our education. I knew what I needed from this phase of my life, and I knew where I wanted to go next. For me, SIUE was a toll road that provided a financially viable means to travel the path I had chosen.

Along with beginning classes, I resumed work in the foundry immediately. My days were consumed with school, work, and study. Before leaving the Army, I had longed to stay in D.C. to attend Georgetown University. But my previous academic record precluded admission to a college of its stature, and my financial condition also prohibited that option, even if G.U. had shown the academic generosity to permit my enrollment. Like several other branch points in my life, SIUE turned out to be a fortuitous decision.

Most students pursuing admission to medical school earn a bachelor's degree first. Colleges generally require the student to declare one major and one minor field of special emphasis. To qualify for admission to medical school, there are no restrictions on the choice of a major field of study, however, a core group of courses must be successfully completed. These comprise the pre-med curriculum. When I entered SIUE, the required pre-med courses included one year of biology, one year of physics and two years of chemistry. At the time, calculus was not a requirement but was recommended. If it had been a requirement, my medical career would have ended abruptly. With false bravado, I registered as a biology major, with a minor in chemistry. In retrospect, that may not have been the best tactical approach for winning acceptance to medical school. If I had chosen a major from one of my strengths, such as history or literature, my grade point average would almost certainly have been higher. However, I have never regretted the additional knowledge I gained as a science major. I can also say there has never been a time in all of my training or subsequent career when I needed to solve a calculus equation.

My new home at SIUE was the Science Building. Considering my previous difficulties with science and math, I was now attempting a one hundred-eighty-degree pirouette, academically. Predictably, I was rather unsteady on my feet. First quarter classes included three general studies courses, and the first of three quarters of inorganic chemistry. The doctors at The Pentagon had advised me to announce my goal of a medical school education without reservation from the time I arrived back home, while predicting correctly that I would want to keep my aspirations to myself.

"Don't do that," was their counsel. "Get your plans right out there in public. Let everyone know. It will provide impetus for you to keep going if you get discouraged. No one says this is going to be easy, but we are confident you can do it."

I took a middle path. I did not trumpet my intentions to the world, but if anyone asked, I admitted my plan of applying to medical school. This goal was greeted with everything from disbelief to laughter by people who knew me. And, no one was more astounded than my parents. I was expecting these reactions. I had to admit, my previous educational record made the idea of medical school seem pretty laughable.

When first quarter grades were posted, these same people were even more surprised. I had earned three A's in the general studies courses, and a B+ for inorganic chemistry.

— Vanzo's Tap Room —

A group of my close friends from high school had also interrupted college for a stint in the military. Like salmon to a spawning ground, most of us returned home when our tour of duty ended. Everyone in our group had survived, and none, at the time, appeared to have lasting physical injuries. However, for some, the pale rider had brushed their sleeve, while others had watched him take comrades. A few saw less trauma than I did. We bonded with other acquaintances returning from the war, prompted by shared experiences. Among this wider circle, some had been hurt badly and a few mortally. There really weren't any other people we could talk to about what we had seen, heard, and felt, no matter where we fell on the spectrum of risk or injury experienced. I had hoped to leave the Army behind when I returned to college. I soon learned that the war wasn't finished for any of us.

. . . .

It is a physiologic fact of nature that college students need a place to hang out. When not in class, studying or working, we gathered at an eclectic establishment called Vanzo's Tap Room, owned by brothers Frank and Jim Vanzo. The ambience and decor were unique... almost indescribable... and the place was populated by one of the most diverse and interesting groups of people I have ever known. Vanzo's had been a favored destination before we left for the Service, and it was second in priority only to the homes of our parents when we returned. We fondly referred to Vanzo's as our home away from home. In fact, it was our living room. Here, surrounded by our peers, we discovered how much we had changed in the past few years.

I would walk into Vanzo's and see someone I had known since grade school. Warm greetings would be offered, followed by some variation of, "So, what have you been doing?"

If the respondent had remained at home, the answers could be separated into two themes:

- "I'm at SIU; going to graduate next spring. Then, I don't know... it depends on the draft."

- Or, "I'm married, got two kids and I'm working at the mill." (As in steel, or the myriad of other heavy industry in the area.) This group was well along an uninterrupted path of early adulthood and would probably remain unscathed by the war.

Those were the choices available to most males in early 1969, unless, of course, the family was wealthy. Few in Edwardsville were. In any case, the conversation soon dwindled. If he was working at the mill, the fact that he bowled two ninety-seven in league play last Thursday night had virtually nothing in common with the recent experiences of us returning veterans, whether we had been jumping out of helicopters in the jungle or managing the Emergency Medical Response Team at The Pentagon. I could rarely think of anything to say in reply except, "Gee, that's great!"

Conversely, I struggled to find acceptable answers when asked about my recent activities. If I told the listener what I had really been doing, most people thought I was either bragging or lying. So, I usually condensed the narrative to, "I was stationed in Washington, D.C. at The Pentagon."

Typically, there weren't many follow-on questions. Both of us would shift from one foot to the other in awkward silence, finally broken by, "Well, sure was nice to see you again." These attempts at social reconnection seemed like dreams from another lifetime to me, and I probably elicited the same sensation in them. We had taken very different paths into the woods.

Even amongst friends, I was reluctant to talk about many specifics of my military experience. No one else had gone through 91Bravo school. Some of my escapades remained classified, while others might be interpreted as boasting. What concerned me the most was that some of these guys, with painful memories of Vietnam, would be resentful of

my good fortune. I certainly didn't tell anyone except my parents of being offered the possibility of admission to West Point, and I'm not sure
Mom and Dad ever realized the significance of that honor. After relat-
ing the story, neither of them ever mentioned it again. I had returned
from a different universe to a profoundly changed home planet.

The anticipated feelings of excitement and euphoria upon re-
entering civilian life intact were also absent. A sense of isolation was
more common than elation. I had looked forward to celebrating with
my friends, particularly those who had also served, but now, I didn't
feel much like celebrating... nor did they. When we were together, I
noticed sudden lapses in conversation, as the speaker was unexpectedly
pulled back into a memory from his recent past. Despite the superficial
laughter, a somber undercurrent was often present as we each processed these experiences, together but alone.

I do not mean to imply that we were morose. We had a blast! Social-
izing at Vanzo's, going to parties and music performances, playing
softball, football, and camping in the Ozarks near where I had under-
gone Basic Training. Some of the best times of my life happened during
those three years of college. But each of us was more introspective than
prior to the military. The pure joy we had experienced drinking beer in
a parked car on a country road back in high school could never be rec-
reated.

·   ·   ·   ·

During the transition back to civilian life, almost all of us took turns
trying to drown the Black Dog in alcohol. Fortunately, in my immediate
circle, everyone eventually realized the Dog was a strong swimmer and
could tolerate bigger doses of spirits than we could. Unfortunately,
some of our other friends amongst the vets did not survive the swim. I
watched two guys I had known since early childhood die prematurely
of alcohol-related injuries. One of them, a Marine, could not adjust to
the reality that he had survived while many in his unit had perished.
The other, just a crazy kid who stares back at me from a photo of my

fifth birthday party. Another, a friend since first grade succumbed to mental illness and death before the age of forty-five.

Survivor's guilt is a curious thing. It touches many of us who might be presumed to have escaped the war unscathed. Some might even say it is the price we pay for having gotten off easy. But I watched survivor's guilt kill or cripple soldiers who had been in the thick of battle, too. There is something intangible about facing the prospects of war. It induces or reveals a sense of responsibility in many of us; the impulse to step up when required, and sacrifice ourselves for others, if necessary. For some, those feelings become misplaced and exaggerated, with very destructive consequences.

That war killed a hell of a lot more of us than our government has ever acknowledged.

In war, there are no unwounded soldiers.
- Jose Narovsky

I have used the term survivor's guilt in my stories because I think it is more descriptive and understandable, and better suits my purposes, than post-traumatic stress disorder. I continue to find the phenomenon that has become PTSD very confusing.

— The Long March. —

As I settled into the laborious process of earning a degree in biology and chem-
istry, I made several unexpected discoveries. Amongst them, I found that I
liked the subtle irony with which many scientists view the world. The Biology
Department office had glass walls facing a hallway. A sign placed near the en-
trance was a favorite of mine. It proclaimed a simple truth that engineers and
many social scientists never seem to understand, "Mother Nature bats last."

After one more quarter of mostly general studies courses, I dived into
science, head first. My class schedule for fall semester included introductory biology, organic chemistry, and physics. Because enrollment in
the physics class required a beginning course in calculus, that rounded
out my schedule. I had last suffered through a math class, geome-
try/trigonometry, as a high school sophomore. After that experience, I
promised myself to *never* take another class in mathematics for as long
as I lived. So much for promises. Predictably, I was completely lost. As
the deadline for dropping approached, I waved the white flag and exited calculus. Surprisingly, I was keeping my head above water in physics, in spite of a chilling pronouncement by the instructor on the first
day of class. After introducing himself, he said that he needed to make
a confession.

"I am a particle physicist. I study high energy chemical reactions,
such as nuclear fission and fusion, and try to explain the behavior of the
various subatomic particles involved. I have been doing physics for so
long, I can no longer remember what it is like to not understand physics. I haven't taught an introductory course in general physics since I
was a graduate student, twenty years ago. I'm afraid I won't be very
good at this, but the administration insists I teach this class."

This misappropriation of resources wasn't really the fault of the
administration. The previous year, the Illinois legislature, in its infinite
wisdom, had passed a law that all faculty of state funded colleges must

teach at least one undergraduate course per year. Although the reasoning behind this legislation was uninformed, and wreaked havoc with faculty schedules at state universities, as the saying goes, it is an ill-wind that blows nobody good. Our overqualified theoretical physicist instructor was a very nice man, and a much better teacher than he claimed. There was an added bonus for me. Because the problems he studied involved complex mathematical solutions, the basic calculus of fundamental physics was boring to him. So, he minimized the math and emphasized the theory. That style of teaching and testing unquestionably saved me.

The introductory physics course was designed to provide the non-physicist science major with an acceptable basic understanding of the physical laws that impact the other branches of science. The full course extended over three quarters and covered everything from gravity to thermonuclear fusion. Approximately one hundred students registered for the class that fall. When we took the final exam for the third portion of the class the following spring, fifteen students remained. My performance throughout the year was consistently near the class median, which was rewarded with three course grades of C. Some of us who were still present after the final exam of the final quarter thought the professor should have applied a survivor's multiplier to our grades. It didn't happen. One portion of his *mea culpa* from the preceding fall did hold true. He really couldn't remember what it was like to not understand physics.

I attempted calculus one more time, with the same results, and gave up on mathematics, erroneously believing I had no other courses awaiting me with calculus requirements. As the year progressed, a stark reality became more and more apparent. Although my accomplishments in biology, chemistry and physics were much greater than anyone who knew me would have predicted, I was simply not an "A" student in science by the criteria used to determine letter grades. Whether or not teaching or testing methods affected my performance, or my study skills were still not sufficiently honed, the evidence of my limited abilities steadily accumulated. I was a B student in biology, and a C student in chemistry and physics. Although, for me, this level of performance was stellar compared to just a few years before, it was unlikely to be sufficient for medical school admission committees. Switching majors would extend the time required to complete my degree by at least one year, probably longer. And I suspected that admissions committees looked more favorably upon applicants with degrees in science than in humanities. (This assumption later proved to be false, at least at Northwestern.) What to do? Pre-med students, with grade point averages similar to mine, were dropping like flies.

Midway through the year, I engaged in an *agonizing reappraisal* of my options. The reality was that my chances of being accepted to medical school were slim to none, but when I tried to think of acceptable alternative careers, the list remained unpopulated. Grandma was fond of saying that when you don't know what to do next in life, you should just get up every morning, put your boots on, and keep going to work. The answer would eventually become clear to you. Finding myself in exactly that predicament, I followed Grandma's advice, and simply continued on, one day at a time.

. . . .

The great football coach, George Allen, once observed, "Many people with mediocre talents produce superlative results because they don't know when to quit. They never give up."

I sure was hoping he knew what he was talking about.

— I Wonder... —

As I began my senior year at SIUE, the future remained uncertain. I had survived the academic hell year just concluded, which winnowed our group of pre-professional students (intent on either medical, dental, or veterinary school) by approximately ninety percent. I had a solid B average in my major field of study and would soon earn a degree in science; a goal thought impossible by almost everyone who knew me, myself included, just a few years before. However, my classmates and most of our professors thought my persistence futile, some even laughable. The only person in the biology department who seemed to be solidly in my corner was my advisor, Nancy Parker, Ph.D. From the first time I had met her, two years before, her attitude had always been one of encouragement.

For students applying to medical school, the process began early. Acceptance was based on four sources of information: the student's grade point average (GPA), performance on the Medical College Admission Test (MCAT), the information provided in three letters of recommendation, and the written opinion of the student's faculty advisor. For the best chance of admission, all of this information needed to be completed and mailed in one packet to each of the applicant's choice of medical schools no later than the end of November in the year preceding one's hoped-for medical school start date. In addition to classwork, autumn of our senior year was consumed by these tasks.

My GPA of 2.7 was mediocre by medical school standards; 3.5 was regarded as average and 3.2 minimal. I was hoping my military experience and performance would partially offset this blemish. The MCAT was intended to measure a student's mastery of the fundamental information provided in a four-year college education and emphasized the basic sciences. The test was multiple choice format, included approximately one thousand questions, and was given over two, consecutive, eight-hour days. It is similar to the SAT exam in high school, cranked up several notches. Most schools used MCAT scores as a convenient means of filtering the enormous number of applications received each year. Usually, only students scoring in the top one third on this mental exercise in humility received further consideration for admission. One couldn't even hope for a slow year populated with blockheads and ambulatory psychotics. (There are a significant number of each in every college class.) Each MCAT score was compared to all others for the current and previous two years and ranked accordingly. With great trepidation, I took the MCAT at the first opportunity that fall. It seemed prudent to attempt this particular hurdle early. Unless my scores were within the upper third, chances of me being accepted to any medical school in the U.S. were nil.

I gave considerable thought to the choice of people to ask for letters of recommendation. Letters from three individuals were required. Most students chose two favorite faculty members and a physician who knew them personally. I took a different approach, hoping to leverage my greatest strength. I contacted two of my former mentors amongst the physicians at The Pentagon. As a long shot, I also requested a letter from Colonel DiLorenzo. I didn't know if he was still in command at the Dispensary, or if the letter would be forwarded to him if he was not. But he was the only person who could document some of the more unusual aspects of my experience and honors during that time. I was desperate for proof of any attributes that might convince an Admissions Committee to overlook the mediocre grades. I could only hope he would be supportive of my potential as a medical student.

I discussed the plan with Dr. Parker. She agreed that her letter could serve a dual purpose if Colonel Di did not reply. Letters of recommendation were to be sent directly to the student's advisor. They were not to be shared with the applicant, in an effort to solicit more candid appraisals. Once the required elements of the application packet were received, the advisor was expected to write a cover letter with an evaluation of the student's strengths and weaknesses.

Dr. Parker served as student advisor for all of the pre-med students in the biology department. She was an embryologist by training, ran one of the most productive research labs in the department, and amongst students, was regarded as the most intellectually gifted of our faculty. Although my interactions with her had been limited to an introductory embryology course the preceding spring, and occasional student-advisor chats, she had been consistently supportive of my efforts, in spite of their lackluster results. As a new university, I found most of our faculty quite good, and surprisingly interested in our welfare, but Dr. Parker was clearly my biggest advocate.

In November, results of the MCAT were sent to me, and separately to Dr. Parker. My score was in the sixty-seventh percentile (within the upper third of students). I was elated. When I dropped by Dr. Parker's office, knowing she would already be aware of the results, she smiled expansively and congratulated me. Now, only the letters remained unknown.

In another few weeks, all letters of recommendation had been received, and Dr. Parker asked to meet with me. I hoped the purpose was simply to confirm my list of schools, but I also worried that one or more of the letters might include a tepid appraisal. I arrived at her office accompanied by my typical level of anxiety in interactions such as this. She greeted me with that ever-present, welcoming smile, but also, a mischievous twinkle in her eye. She motioned to a chair.

"Well," she began, "I have your transcripts, a copy of your MCAT scores, and all of your letters of recommendation. As we have discussed, your GPA is a potential problem. However, your MCAT scores are perfectly acceptable. *And your letters!* In my entire career, I have never seen letters such as these! I wonder what the medical schools are going to do with you now?" With that said, she leaned back in her chair and almost cackled with laughter.

One of the things I had always liked about Dr. Parker was her candid opinions, including opinions of people. You always knew where you stood with her, and when Dr. Parker was in your corner, there was never any doubt about her support. I grinned back at her conspiratorially, and said, "I hope this works."

As I headed out of her office, basking in the glow of her approval, a thought occurred to me. Even if I didn't make it into medical school... to some degree, I would regard my college career as a success. I had won the respect and support of this faculty mentor, who I respected highly, and who knew me better than any of the others.

— The Door that Would Not Open —

Most acceptance letters from medical schools began arriving in December. If the student wished to attend that particular school, he/she needed to confirm their acceptance of the position. If no confirmation was received within a set time, or the student declined the appointment, the position was offered to the next person on the school's list of draft choices. This process was much like a nationwide game of musical chairs. Students were encouraged to apply to more than one school, since acceptance at any given school was uncertain, no matter how illustrious the application packet. On average, students applied to six schools. I applied to twelve. No stone unturned, was my motto. Students constituting the academic cream of the crop might be accepted to multiple schools. Typically, two or three rounds of invitations went out before each school filled its class. I did not receive any acceptances in the first round, but I wasn't expecting any. I was prepared to be delighted if I was the last damn student picked anywhere in the continental United States. (I hadn't applied to the University of Hawaii.)

A physical chemistry class occupied most of my waking moments during Winter Quarter. When I came up for air in late March, I had to face the fact that medical schools were now through round two of the acceptance process, and well into round three. I hadn't made anyone's dance card, but regrets from a few schools were beginning to trickle in. A successful conclusion to my quest was looking more and more unlikely.

. . . .

On a cold, grey day in late March, I picked up my mail and sat thumbing through it. There was a letter from the University of Chicago. I stared at it awhile, then opened the envelope. Inside was the usual form letter saying my application materials had been reviewed and did not meet their criteria for admission, then the author wished me luck in another career.

Looking back on the entirety of my efforts to gain a medical education, I think this was the absolute low point. Not only was the author informing me of the denial, he was implying that I was not qualified to be a medical student anywhere. Remaining motionless in the chair, I looked out at a rather desolate late winter landscape and absorbed the sting of his words. I reflected on the path my life had taken during the past seven years. What a roller coaster ride it had been! From the despair of high school and a failed attempt at college, to a brief, but remarkable string of successes in the Army. And now, back to another failed attempt at something I had come to want very badly. One of my friends, an avid golfer, is fond of saying you can play a really good hole or two in golf, but then the course puts you back where you belong. I felt like I was being put back where I belonged; a failure.

I reread the letter. Aside from the disappointment of the rejection, there was something about his words that angered me. This man didn't know me. He, and the committee he represented, had no more information about me than what was provided in the application packet, which included letters from some physicians who had an entirely different opinion of my abilities. The conclusions of those physicians were based on personal experience observing me in a medical environment. Not only was this jerk insulting me, he was insulting them.

I began to sense the familiar feeling of Uncle Red sitting across the table from me. He had that "Well, what are you going to do now?" grin on his face, and I *knew* what he was going to say next.

"The surest way to get a Darnell to do something, is to tell him that he can't!"

I threw the letter in the trash with the rest of the junk mail, took a deep breath, and turned to the other things needing to be done that day.

. . . .

In April, I received a letter from Howard University. Although their freshman class had filled, I was being placed on an alternate list. If one of their chosen students dropped out unexpectedly, I would be eligible for admission. This was at least validation that I was a qualified applicant, and certainly the most encouraging news so far. The letter listed additional requirements in order to remain eligible for admission. One necessity was to remain a full-time student.

Well, that settled the question of what I would do after graduation, unless I was accepted somewhere else. I needed to find a receptive grad school. At that time, the SIUE graduate program in biology usually did not fill all the positions available. I had a solid B average in biology, not stellar, but probably good enough to get one of those positions... although that assumption wasn't assured. The Department Chair had always seemed reserved during our chance encounters in hallways, and I had never taken one of his classes. He was an ambitious man and worked diligently to forge a competitive reputation for this new department in a new university. I suspected his disinterest in me was related to my grades and a presumption I was not destined to be an illustrious alumnus. I couldn't argue with his conclusion. No matter, I needed to take the GRE's for biology *fast*! I barely made the application deadline, and a seat in the last offering of the exam, just a few weeks away.

For the basic sciences, the Graduate Record Exams are the equivalent of the MCAT. They test the student's general knowledge of science, plus the fundamental body of information in the student's major: biology, chemistry or physics. For once, I actually purchased a study guide and read the entire document. If I was going to enroll in graduate school, I had no idea what I wanted to study, but the GRE was an absolutely necessary first step.

On the evening prior to the exam, I planned to stay home, review a few notes and go to bed early. About 10:00 p.m., I got a call informing me a friend from out of town had returned unexpectedly, and our crew was at Vanzo's. I protested the importance of the looming exam, but finally succumbed to the siren's song of, "Oh, you can have just one!"

I'm sure the reader can fill in the remainder of the story. I returned home at a wholesome 4:00 a.m., overslept the next morning, and had to beg admission to the exam because I was thirty minutes late. The tests consumed the next seven hours. During that time, I dozed off at least three times, that I can recall.

The results arrived surprisingly quickly. I ranked in the top 17% of candidates, nationally. This certainly wasn't genius level, but I was pleasantly surprised. The Chairman was also surprised, but not so pleasantly, since mine was the highest score in his department for the academic year. When I saw him a few days later, he actually looked disappointed.

His response to my unexpected success was a subdued, "Well, I suppose I will have to offer you a position for next year."

I have always wondered how I would have done on that exam if I had stuck to my original, austere plan for the evening before. I suspect my score would have been lower.

The visiting friend who had disrupted my study plans was a student at the University of Illinois, home for the weekend. The next week, he sent me an announcement, confiscated from a bulletin board in the physiology building. Attached to the poster was a note, saying he thought I might be interested. The announcement described a new multidisciplinary graduate program in the neurosciences, to be directed by C. Ladd Prosser, Ph.D.

When I was in college, Ladd Prosser was one of the editors of a textbook of comparative anatomy used in almost every college in the country. He also had an international reputation for research on the structure and function of the nervous system. The description of this new program was indeed fascinating. Several traditional departments, ranging from psychology and physiology to electrical engineering would be involved. For successful candidates, writing a master's thesis would not be required. Integrated course work and research would lead directly to the doctoral dissertation and degree. At the time, this was a new approach to graduate education. I was sure all positions had been filled with brilliant candidates within hours of the announcement.

My friend, the source of the announcement, was a marketing major. He was fond of saying, "It doesn't cost anything to ask."

I called the number listed. An administrative assistant answered the phone. When I told her why I was calling, she asked if I minded being put on hold. Within a minute or two, Dr. Prosser came on the line. This, I was not expecting. I was brutally frank in explaining my predicament with the medical school alternate list and last minute need to find a home for the coming year.

He asked about my GPA. When I answered, he replied, "Hmmm." Then, he asked about the GRE. I could report this result with a little pride, but I suspected all of his grad students had scored in the top ten percent.

With surprisingly little hesitation, he said, "I think we can make a place for you, but I've committed all the grant money I have for this year."

I hadn't even considered the possibility of getting financial support. I thanked him and was returned to the office assistant to exchange addresses for the necessary paperwork.

Now, it was decision time. I had two graduate school acceptances in hand; one paying a stipend (SIUE) and the other not. Although I had accepted Dr. Prosser's kind offer, it was of no consequence to him if I changed my mind. I certainly wasn't going to keep him waiting. The Department Chair at SIUE was a different matter. My consideration of the two options required less than five minutes. I was willing to pay for the opportunity to work for Ladd Prosser.

Following his grudging offer of a position, the Biology Chair had added the admonishment that I shouldn't take too long making a decision. His attitude irritated me. Rather than being pleased by the possibility he might have misjudged my potential, and I might actually be of some value to his program, he seemed to regard my success with a mixture of annoyance and suspicion. He reminded me of the high school administrator who had accused me of cheating on the SAT exam.

After speaking to Dr. Prosser, I avoided the SIUE biology department office, and its principle inhabitant, for as long as possible. When we met in the hall a week later, his usual gruff manner was in full display. "Well, Turner, are you going to take the position or not? I can't wait forever!"

"No, Sir," I replied. "Thank you, but I am going to decline the position here."

"What are you going to do?" he asked petulantly. (I would have been willing to bet my name was already penciled into a grid to supervise a lab for an undergraduate course.)

"I have accepted a spot in a new neuroscience doctoral program with Ladd Prosser at U. of I." I replied, nonchalantly.

The look on his face was priceless.

.   .   .   .

Our graduation ceremony, held a month later, was one of the most anticlimactic events of my life. Many of my classmates were justly proud of the degree they received that day. We had all performed a considerable amount of work in order to earn it. However, my goal was never to simply earn a Bachelor of Arts degree. My goal was to go to medical school. The possibility of that goal being achieved now looked dim. A few weeks before graduation, another medical school added me to their waiting list. By the time the letter arrived, I was so dispirited that I can no longer remember which school made the offer.

— Arriba, Arriba, Ándale! —

I moved to Urbana, IL in September 1972 to begin graduate school. For housing, I partnered with the friend, Mike Douglas, who had alerted me to Dr. Prosser's program. We bought a house together; sales price $9,500. With that information alone, one can easily imagine the appearance of this little gem. However, Mike had some experience with the basic construction trades. I had somewhat less but knew which end of the hammer to hold. We hoped to make the place habitable before school started, and eventually rehab it to sell for a profit. We both qualified for a G.I. Bill loan, so with only a ten percent down payment, our monthly mortgage payments were $92. This was half the cost of renting an apartment. Only partially in jest, Mike assessed the transaction succinctly, "What the hell! Even if we can't sell it when we finish school, we'll just burn it and walk away. You're never going to find rent cheaper than $46 per month!" He had a compelling argument.

. . . .

Enrolling at the University of Illinois was a humbling experience. I felt like a high school kid just starting college. SIUE enrollment was about 3,500 by the time of my graduation. Total enrollment at the U. of I. was more than tenfold that number. The campus was huge. The first few weeks, I kept a campus map stuffed in my pocket, just like the freshmen, and I used it often. Shortly after my arrival in Urbana, I met with Dr. Prosser to discuss choices for first semester classes. When I arrived for the appointment, his office assistant explained apologetically that he was tied up on an important phone call elsewhere. She ushered me into his office, pointed to a chair and left the room. Like most academic offices, the walls of his were lined with bookshelves. I have always believed one can learn a great deal about a person by knowing what they read. So, I began scanning the rows of books, noting the authors and content. The array of subjects was surprisingly broad. Eventually, my gaze worked its way back to the shelf adjacent to my seat. At eye level was a large, imposing tome; its cover sheathed in luxurious, deep red leather. Gold leaf lettering on the spine announced II Neuroscience World Congress.

Hmmm. I wonder which bigwigs attended this meeting? Gingerly, I slid the heavy book from its resting place and opened the cover. The frontispiece said it all. Second World Congress of Neuroscience. St. Petersburg, Russia. Chair: C. Ladd Prosser, Ph.D. 1972.

Oh, Lord! I knew Dr. Prosser was widely respected in the U.S. I had heard that he possessed an international reputation... but this? He was the Main Man! I carefully eased the sacred book back into its place of honor, trying to avoid even fingerprints on the shimmering red leather.

Soon, Dr. Prosser hurried into the office, sat down at his desk, and broke into an apology for keeping me waiting.

Keeping me waiting?!

"No worries," I replied.

Conversation soon turned to the choice of courses for the first semester. The subject of math came up. I cringed, then tried to explain my history of failure in mathematics. His response was both reasonable and terrifying. "Gee, it is hard to imagine taking full advantage of the variety of subjects available in this program without a mastery of integral and differential calculus, as a minimum. Most of my students go beyond that level. Why don't you sign up for introductory calc? I'm sure you can do it!"

Graduate level biochemistry, a course in human ethology (the study of human behavior from the perspective of animal models), and a graduate seminar rounded out my schedule. I left his office with a feeling of gloom. I should have heeded the advice of my other friend, the golfer, and stayed where I belonged.

I have had the good fortune to meet a few genuinely brilliant people in my career. People who have perceptibly moved the needle of scientific knowledge a bit. In my limited sample size, all of these exceptional individuals shared several characteristics. Every one of them was self-effacing and attempted to minimize the impact of their contributions in casual conversation. Each of them also displayed consistent kindness and consideration towards the people around them. Ladd Prosser was a member of that group in every respect. In that first meeting, he asked what my interests in neuroscience were, and if I had identified any particular goals I wanted to pursue. I replied that I was overwhelmed by the possibilities the program offered and felt it would take some time and investigation before I could narrow my interests to a single topic.

He burst out laughing. "Thank God! What a refreshing answer! I am so tired of new grad students coming in here and answering that question with, 'What I really want to do is cure cancer.'"

Although I felt hopelessly underpowered in terms of mental horsepower in this program, Ladd Prosser never intentionally contributed to that feeling. The sense I always came away with from interactions with him was that he was in my corner, just as Nancy Parker had been, and he was fully committed to helping me succeed.

The first meeting of our graduate seminar completed my humiliation. My classmates had all transferred from other departments into this promising new program and were several years ahead of me in their training. Each week, one of them presented the work they were doing in the lab. Dr. Prosser and other students would then ask questions and offer suggestions. I had virtually nothing to contribute. I have never felt so intellectually out of place as I did in those weekly meetings. In retrospect, first semester graduate students aren't expected to contribute much to these conferences. The purpose of our presence was to get a glimpse of what lay ahead. There are sound reasons why earning a Ph.D. in the sciences requires five to seven years of hard work.

I dug into grad school. I had never studied harder than for that calculus class. Three hours per day were set aside for that subject alone. I signed up for tutoring and found there were plenty of others struggling with higher math. It was hopeless. I was simply too far behind to be able to bridge the gap. Interestingly, as in physics and physical chemistry, I could grasp the fundamentals of how calculus contributes a framework for verifying scientific hypotheses and understand how an equation could determine the shape of a curve on a graph, but manipulating those equations was completely opaque to me. After the first month, I dropped the class. My usual pattern of grades was reemerging, a solid C in biochemistry, and an A in ethology. Mercifully, the graduate seminar was not graded. We were simply required to attend.

. . . .

Dr. Prosser had regular meetings with each of his graduate students. At least in my case, they were informal and devoid of pressure. During one of those appointments, late in the fall, he had just returned from a large neuroscience meeting.

My casual greeting, "How are you doing, Dr. Prosser?" received a surprising reply.

"Depressed."

This was a marked departure from his usual sunny demeanor.

He then added, "There were 2,200 neuroscientists at that meeting, and 2,000 of them were looking for a job. I'm afraid I am encouraging young scientists to follow in my footsteps, when their chances for employment will be almost hopeless." He looked forlorn. Then, he stared at me, and his face brightened. He sat forward in his chair and said, "You shouldn't be here! You should be in medical school, pursuing what you want to do. This is a waste of your time. We need to get you into medical school!"

He pressed the button on an intercom. "Would you get the Dean of the Medical School on the phone for me, please."

"Yes, Sir," was the crisp reply.

I had learned at The Pentagon that one measure of a person's power was how fast other powerful people answered their calls. Dr. Prosser leaned back in his chair and began chatting. In less than five minutes, the intercom squawked, and the secretary announced the Dean was on the line. Dr. Prosser picked up the phone and greeted him warmly. Obviously, they knew each other well. Then my boss explained that one of his grad students was in the office at the moment, and we were wondering what it would take to get him (me) into medical school.

There was a brief silence as the caller asked Dr. Prosser a few questions.

Ladd hesitated a moment, then said, "Why don't you just ask him yourself?" and handed the phone to me.

I literally jumped in my seat. What was I going to say? Fortunately, the Medical School Dean was just as cordial and informal as Dr. Prosser. I explained that I had applied to grad school because of the medical school waiting lists, and their requirements for continuation in school. Then he asked for my GPA and MCAT scores. I provided them and squeezed in the additional information of my experience as an Army medic and the encouragement by the doctors in my unit.

He replied without hesitation. "Well, your grades are the problem. There are so many students interested in medicine at present, the GPA bar has been set ridiculously high, in spite of the fact we don't know if grades have any correlation with skill as a physician. If you are one of Ladd Prosser's grad students, I have no doubt you have the ability to successfully complete medical school. In fact, compared to his program, you will find medical school a snooze!" (Those were his exact words. I nearly burst out laughing when he made that comment.)

He went on, "And, in my opinion, many schools are being unscrupulous in how they use alternate lists. Frankly, you could die of old age before you reached the top of many of those lists." After a pause, he continued, "I just returned from six weeks as a guest lecturer at a school in Guadalajara, Mexico. There are 5,000 American students attending that school. They fall into two categories. Some of them went down there to party. They won't last long. But, a lot of them are just like you.

They have worked hard and have the qualifications to become fine physicians. They simply couldn't get over the admissions hurdle. I don't know if this is the right path for you, but I would consider going to Guadalajara. Not all of the teaching down there is high quality, however by this point in your education, you have to do all the work yourself anyway. The school simply provides the opportunity. I can't teach our medical students unless they are willing to do the work of learning. There is a possibility of transferring to a U.S. school after completing two years in a foreign school. It isn't easy, but it is possible. The big roadblock to medical school is freshman admission. There is room to accommodate more students in the second two years. However, if you are unable to transfer, and you continue to work like I'm sure you are working in Ladd Prosser's program, in four years, you will have a medical degree. You won't still be sitting on some alternate list. You can then return to the U.S. for post-graduate training, and you will have accomplished your goal of becoming a physician."

In less than ten minutes, this man had yanked me from despair to hope. Serendipitously, I had seen an advertisement for the Guadalajara school in our building just the day before. I thanked him for his time. He wished me luck and hung up.

Dr. Prosser was still sitting there, now with a curious look. "Was he able to help you?"

"Very much so," I replied. "He laid out exactly what I need to do to go to medical school. It looks like I am going to Guadalajara."

Chapter VI.   The Guad

— **You Can't Do That** —

Deciding to attempt medical school in a foreign country on the basis of a ten-minute telephone conversation may seem impetuous. However, by the conclusion of that call, I possessed most of the information I needed to make a rational decision (at least on my scale of rationality). The U. of I. Medical School Dean had assessed my past performance and concluded I was capable. He had explained the various pathways potentially available for further training and medical practice in the U.S., once certain milestones were achieved in Guadalajara. And, he had described pretty clearly what I would need to do in order to successfully negotiate that path. Many people have marveled at my audacity in tackling medical school, a training program well known for its academic rigor, in a foreign language. I already knew the answer to that challenge. My high school courses included two years of Spanish, and I had acquired a mastery of the language that high school tutelage usually provides. I could say: hello, good night, and where is the bathroom? I had also taken three semesters of Spanish while at Blackburn College, which further enabled me. I could then say, 'Where is the *men's* bathroom?' Otherwise, I was a functional illiterate in Spanish. However, both of my Spanish teachers had been practical people. They had assured us that we could get by in a Spanish-speaking environment with a rudimentary knowledge of sentence structure, mastery of approximately twenty verbs and their conjugation, and a working vocabulary of the twenty most common adjectives and adverbs. I had no reason to doubt their opinion. Besides, the language of medicine is Latin. Medical terminology in English and Spanish is very similar.

My greatest obstacle to beginning school in Guadalajara was economic. Tuition for American students was $5,000 per year. I had managed to complete my degree at SIUE without acquiring any debt, other than a debt of gratitude to my parents. In Mexico, I would no longer be eligible for assistance through the G.I. Bill, and I would be unable to

work part time. The cost of tuition, books, room and board in Guadalajara was only slightly less than Dad's after-tax annual income. He had
saved a little money over the years, in addition to social security and
the teacher's retirement plan, but not much. And, he was now nearing
retirement. Growing up during The Depression produced a cautious
approach to life for both of my parents. This level of economic risk was
completely foreign to their nature. Besides, the idea I might actually
have the ability to complete medical school and someday repay them
required a level of faith that tested even my devout parents.

I avoided mentioning my new scheme until I completed finals and
returned home for what my parents assumed was semester break. Their
reactions to the bombshell I dropped after dinner one evening remain a
vivid memory. I explained the proposal as calmly as I could. Dad
looked shocked but, as was his style, said nothing. Mom wasn't so reticent. The first words out of her mouth were, "You can't do that!"

I had heard that assessment of my talents before. Fortunately, during my time in the military, especially the period at The Pentagon, I acquired at least a modicum of emotional armor. Mom's persistent lack of
confidence in me wasn't as devastating as it would have been five years
before. I tried to see it as the classic comparison of a glass half empty, or
half full. My grades in pre-med had been inadequate for admission to
an American school, however, it was inarguable that I had made remarkable progress over the past six years. I had pursued the opportunities presented by the Army and received recognition and encouragement for my performance. I had earned a degree in biology and chemistry in a program with a very high attrition rate. I had been placed on
the alternate list at two medical schools, which documented their belief
that I could perform at the medical school level. I reminded her that no
one who knew me throughout childhood and adolescence would have
predicted I could get this far. So why was it such a preposterous idea
that I might be able to climb a little farther? My mother was always a

stickler for logic, and she acknowledged the logic of my argument, but I could tell she remained unconvinced.

Then, it was time for the heavier shoe to drop. I reviewed the concerns Dad had yet to say aloud. Obviously, the only realistic source of funding for this venture would be their retirement savings. After describing the financial implications that I knew were on their minds, especially Dad's, I changed the subject. Rightfully, they would need time to digest this information. Over the next few weeks, I explained every aspect of the plan to them, as outlined by the Medical School Dean, and the possible outcomes he had described. Eventually, Mom and Dad agreed to fund one semester of tuition plus living expenses... but only one. I would need to find another benefactor for the second semester.

If you are going to succeed, sometimes you have no choice but to address challenges one at a time.

. . . .

The day after speaking with the medical school dean in Dr. Prosser's office, I mailed a request for an application to the school in Guadalajara. A thick packet of paperwork soon arrived, and I began the tortuous process of completing forms and requesting transcripts. The information requested was surprisingly detailed, including transcripts from junior high school. Finally, all paperwork was assembled with the exception of my seventh and eighth grade records. My parents had been scrupulous about saving report cards since I began first grade, in spite of the disappointing results they documented. But none of us could find anything from seventh or eighth grade. Surely, they didn't really need documentation from junior high school. I mailed the packet without the missing records and requested an appointment for the required interview.

In a few weeks, a very official-looking letter arrived with a return address listed as Universidad Autonoma de Guadalajara. The letter was in English, confirmed receipt of my application, and provided a date for an interview. It didn't specify a time or location. A list of things to bring to the interview was included. Nothing was mentioned of the missing junior high school data. The last item on the list stated that all fees must be paid in advance, in the form of a cashier's check in U.S. currency, which was non-refundable.

The do or die inflection point for this final attempt to scale the mountain was now in sight. The information at my disposal was maddeningly contradictory. On the one hand, was the assessment and advice provided by the medical school dean. He was obviously quite familiar with the various paths to a medical career in the U.S. He also had first-hand knowledge of the school in question. And finally, who could have better insight into the academic demands of medical school? He had pronounced me capable. On the other hand, what little I knew about business transactions in Mexico was not reassuring, and the amount of money at risk was considerable. If all this fell apart, it would take years for me to pay back the money I owed Mom and Dad, while working at the kinds of jobs available to me. Once more, I reviewed my options. Realistically, this was my last chance at a career in medicine. I wanted to be a doctor. It was now or never.

. . . .

I booked an airline reservation for the day before the interview. The letter from the school had been vague about the timing of tuition payments or other fees. It only stated they must be paid in advance. I tried to imagine what the interview would be like. The Dean at U. of I. had described UAG as a *proprietary medical school.* In other words, they accepted foreign students as a source of profit for the university, not out of any altruistic desire to train more physicians for the world. I wondered what surprises might await me at the interview. I decided on a strategy that, in the worst case, would hopefully contain my losses. I bought a cashier's check for $2,500, made out to the university, as stipulated. If more fees were revealed during the visit, I could protest that I had no additional funds with me. This would give me some time to reassess the risk, and if significant additional costs were revealed, to explore whether or not I could even raise the extra money. Ideally, I should have stayed for several days, to get the lay of the land and gather information about housing and other necessities. The university didn't provide student housing for foreigners, or much practical information. However, I was so short on money I limited the visit to just the two days needed for the interview. Further exploration would have to wait.

I arrived in Guadalajara late one afternoon in February. A local Holiday Inn provided the only familiar entity for this first trip. The hotel was on the outskirts of town, relatively close to the airport, but some distance from either the university campus or the central city. I had no idea what taxi fare would be for tourists, but suspected a special rate was reserved for Americans. The next morning, I set out for the school early, since no specific appointment time for my interview had been provided in the letter. Mercifully, the cabbie I drew was an honest one. The information from the university also failed to explain that the medical school was located on a separate site, five miles from the main campus. The cab driver had no knowledge of this either, which wasn't surprising. After many miles and multiple stops, we finally located the correct destination.

Upon entering the admissions office, the secretary motioned for me to take a seat, but said nothing else. The next two hours were spent waiting in silence. No other prospective students appeared, and I began to wonder if the secretary had misunderstood the purpose of my visit. Abruptly, and without further explanation, I was ushered into the inner sanctum. The office had an ornate, wooden desk and bookshelves lining the wall behind, just as one would expect at a U.S. medical school. An official soon entered the room. He was dressed in a tan cotton suit and sported an iconic pencil mustache. He was pleasant, but business-like. The interview was entirely in English, and his diction was impeccable, with just a hint of an accent. I presented the information requested in the letter. He thumbed through the material, without seeming to really look at the contents. After completing this exercise, he folded his hands on the desk, looked at me, and smiled. "Well, Mr. Turner, your paperwork appears to all be in order. Of course, we have many applicants for the medical school, from all over the world." He waved his arm expansively. "We will review your transcripts and inform you of our decision in a few weeks."

This was unexpected. I had assumed if I documented an appropriate educational background and paid the exorbitant tuition fee, then acceptance was immediate. The gentleman folded his hands on the desk once more. His smile and body position remained unchanged... expectant. I sensed the unspoken challenge, your move.

The silence seemed to reverberate throughout the room. I had no prior experience with situations such as this and no idea how to proceed. Strangely, since landing at the airport the day before, I had felt as though on a movie set. Late afternoon sun now slanted through the office window. An old-style fan hung overhead; its blades turning slowly. If either Gary Cooper or Leo Carillo had walked through the door right then, it would have been right on que. Probably, no more than a minute passed, but this movie was proceeding in slow motion. Suspended within this imaginary scene, an idea came to my mind. *This is where the wily official extracts money from the rube!* The film sped up and I could visualize the conclusion of the scene.

I spoke hesitantly, "Oh, I apparently misunderstood." I reached into my briefcase. "I brought this cashier's check for $2,500 as payment of tuition for the first semester. Now, I'm not sure what to do with it. It will expire in less than thirty days, if not cashed."

The man behind the desk followed the script, perfectly. One of his neatly folded hands now darted across the desk, like a snake striking, then hovered, just short of its prey. His thumb and forefinger gently closed on the outstretched corner of the check. "I will take care of that for you. I'm sure everything will be in order." He eased the check out of my hand and dropped it into a desk drawer.

A few days after my return home, another letter arrived from UAG, congratulating me on my admission to the medical school freshman class.

This description may sound contrived to some readers, and corny to others. It is as accurate as my memory allows. For a long time, I was unable to explain why I experienced the intense imagery and sensations that occurred during my first visit to Guadalajara. I finally arrived at a theory. I was a young child during the 1950's. During that decade, boys were immersed in TV shows and movies about the Old West. The setting for many of these productions included Mexico. I think the scenery and language I was experiencing for the first time, plus a high-stakes social interaction of the kind which typically makes me ill at ease, prompted the only mental reference I had available. Once I made this connection, I realized the same sensation was evoked the first time I drove through Monument Valley in Southern Utah, also a frequent backdrop in cowboy movies. What can I say? I am a visual thinker and rely on patterns of cues from previous observations to help interpret social interactions.

– Mañana –

During the months between my formal acceptance to the UAG and the beginning of classes, only one additional item involving time and expense had arisen. The admission packet included a previously unrevealed requirement; we needed to complete a summer semester of classes designed as an introduction to life in Mexico for a foreign national. The classes included Mexican history, geography, a course on society and economics, and a Spanish language class. I found all of these classes interesting and useful, but they required moving my departure date from September to late June, which added three months of unanticipated living expenses. Fortunately, the tuition charged was considerably more reasonable than the medical school.

Thanks to the oversight of the U.S. Army, and the generosity of Colonel Di, my previous experience in a foreign country was limited to the interview at UAG and a six-hour trip to the northern tip of the Gulf of California while in college. Now, I was *moving* to Mexico, possibly for years. As the time of my departure approached, a growing list of needs and unanswered questions about the practicalities of setting up housekeeping accumulated. I had no personal contacts in Guadalajara, or anywhere else in Mexico, for that matter. The school didn't have dormitories for American students and didn't offer much information, other than the warning that we *must* have a student visa. If we tried to enroll with a tourist visa, the university would report us to the immigration service, and we would be deported. (Although this turned out to be an *official position* for political appearances only, I didn't know that then.) Fortunately, while working at a nearby hospital in the months before classes started, I met a doctor whose son was also preparing to enter medical school at the Autonoma. We decided to room together; in my case to lessen expenses, in his case for moral support. Although we shared information regularly, both of us were coming up with more questions than answers. He was a much more experienced traveler than

I, but had spent little time in Mexico, and none in Guadalajara. Our only choice seemed to be; jump in and deal with necessities when our options were clearer.

I applied for a student visa several months before the anticipated departure date, as recommended. The instructions stated that I would need to physically appear at a Mexican Consulate, with confirmation of my identity, in order to receive the necessary document and passport stamp once the visa was approved. As the weeks and days counted down, I heard nothing. When only a few weeks remained, I resorted to plaintive calls to the Mexican Consulate in St. Louis. The response to each call was the same, "Mañana por la mañana" (tomorrow morning). I was rapidly running out of mornings.

To further complicate things, correspondence from the school had warned that only three absences from class during the summer semester were allowed. If we exceeded this number, we would fail the course automatically. Successful completion of the summer classes was required before beginning medical school. If we had not fulfilled this requirement by the September start date, enrollment would be deferred until the following semester. This sort of delay would almost certainly doom my already tenuous financial plan.

· · · ·

With only one week remaining before I was to leave for Mexico, I stopped by Vanzo's one afternoon for a beer. Jimmie was in his usual position behind the bar. I described the problem to him and admitted, "I just don't know what else to do."

It is probably difficult for some people to imagine the relationship many of my friends and I had with Jim and Frank Vanzo. In our lives, they were much more than bartenders. They were also mentors, and Jim knew my background better than most people did.

"You worked in Washington, and became familiar with some folks in Mel Price's office (our local Congressman), didn't you?"

I nodded affirmatively.

"Well, why don't you call him?"

"Mel is a very powerful member of Congress, but I don't know how much contact he has with foreign countries. I would guess, not much. He is on the Armed Services Committee, not the Foreign Relations Committee," I replied.

Jimmie persisted, his trademark lopsided grin in place, "It won't hurt much to ask, will it."

I went home and called the Congressman's office immediately. The person I knew best wasn't in the office, but the fellow who answered the phone remembered me. I explained my predicament, apologized for calling about a problem which might be outside their area of influence, and asked if he had any ideas.

"I don't know. I haven't personally dealt with the Mexican government. Let me make a call. I will get back to you as quickly as I can."

I thanked him for his efforts and hung up.

About ten minutes later, the phone rang. I certainly wasn't expecting such a quick response. It was probably someone wanting to talk to Mom. I picked up the receiver. The caller was a man with such a thick accent I couldn't understand what he was saying. On the third try, I finally deciphered, "Your visa is ready."

"When?" I asked quickly.

"Now." Then, he hung up.

I tried to ask when the Embassy closed for the day, but he was already gone.

In that era, most businesses in Mexico closed for afternoon siesta. I assumed the Consulate probably adhered to this custom. The kitchen clock showed 2:30 p.m. I jumped in my truck and headed for downtown St. Louis. The trip would take about thirty minutes if all went well. I located the Consulate office, housed in a surprisingly old and run-down building. All I can remember of the entrance was peeling white paint, a door that was closed, and no door bell. Great! Now what was I supposed to do?

A small sign, hanging above the otherwise plain door, identified this as the Mexican Consulate. I tried opening the door. It was locked. I knocked and waited. No response. I knocked again... siesta time. Hopefully, I would have better luck in the morning. As I turned to leave, the door opened a crack... then a little farther. A hand and portion of forearm glided through the narrow aperture and waved an envelope. The afternoon sun on what remained of the white paint obscured my view of the building interior. The hand waved the envelope again, this time pointed in my direction. I took the envelope and looked inside. There was my visa.

— Bienvenidos! —

For anyone reading this section with the intent of gaining information about life as a medical student in Mexico, keep in mind that these adventures occurred forty-five years ago. Both the country and the school have changed dramatically since then. Readers who have visited Guadalajara recently will have difficulty identifying the city I am about to describe. Although I have not returned there since my days as a student, I am told I would recognize almost nothing visually or of life in the city as we knew it.

My prospective roommate and I landed in Guadalajara one week before summer classes were scheduled to begin. We had remained unsuccessful at finding a contact in the city, so the local Holiday Inn once again became our base of operations. The summer classes were going to consume every extra dime I had managed to scrape together. If I lived throughout the summer as frugally as I thought possible, by my calculations, four nights in the hotel was all I could afford.

On our first morning in the city, we encountered an American medical student just finishing his first year. My roomie's litany of questions was interrupted with, "You need to see Pedro. He has a shop located on the Glorieta Minerva traffic circle that caters to the needs of ex-pat medical students. All the buses pass through that circle. You can't miss it. You will probably want to rent a mailbox there, too. Everyone else does."

. . . .

Our visit to this little shop a few hours later began a practical introduction to the myriad of daily luxuries available only in a First World Country (think infrastructure). Pedro's two most important services were: the letting of mailboxes, and an enormous bulletin board covered with messages from one student or group to another. In 1973, residential postal service in Guadalajara was limited to a few areas, and private telephone service was rare. The bulletin board at Pedro's served as an important method of communication amongst the U.S. students. Squeezed in between the personal notes were hand-written offers of goods and services from local individuals. Houses and apartments for rent, people looking for roommates, housecleaning, home furnishings, repairs for almost anything, translation services for documents, legal services, money exchanges; just about anything the uninitiated foreign student might need.

The remaining space in the small shop was crammed full of display cases and wall hangers. There were maps of city bus routes, small flashlights and lanterns (the city had outgrown its power generating capacity and frequent blackouts occurred), booklets listing stores and services providing needed commodities, and travel brochures describing local attractions. These things were available at nominal cost, or for free. Pedro was one hell of an entrepreneur and, for us, a lifesaver. The first item he pushed across the counter after our introduction was a bus schedule and maps. "You'll need this," was his knowing advice.

The American consulate had recommended not taking a car to Mexico *without having a thorough knowledge of local laws and customs*. My beat-up old truck had been sacrificed to help pay for the unexpected expenses of the summer semester, so driving wasn't an issue for me. My roommate didn't have a car, either. However, this was the second largest city in Mexico; a metropolis of two million people. The maps indicated ubiquitous bus routes. What wasn't explained was the need to adapt to a completely new conceptualization of time. In reality, the individual coaches arrived and departed each stop at the whim of the driver. Buses followed the designated route... sort of, unless the driver needed to do an errand... or happened to engage in a race with the driver of another bus to a common destination. During those contests, which were surprisingly frequent, the driver might take a shortcut, or simply ignore one or more stops along the route in order to win the race. Bus service generally commenced at 7:00 a.m. and ended at 10:00 p.m.... except when the driver was late getting to work (frequently)... or was either tired or sufficiently drunk by the end of the day to prompt shortening his shift by omitting his last scheduled stops (also frequently). I still maintain that you haven't really known excitement until you've careened through the narrow streets and blind curves of a barrio at seventy miles per hour on a Guadalajara bus. We were soon to know excitement.

The main campus was located several miles from the existing edge of the city. A small neighborhood of houses and apartment buildings, located near the front gate of the university, was adjacent to a large street connecting the school and urban area. The residents of this neighborhood were mostly foreign students. The medical school campus, as I had discovered in February, was within the developed boundaries of the city, about five miles from this Norteamericano enclave. (*Norteamericano* was the term used by most Mexicans for citizens of the U.S. and Canada.) Although bus service ran from the city to the campus, we were at the end of the line. Most of us were therefore subjected to the vagaries of public transportation on a daily basis.

. . . .

Since our first priority was finding housing, the bulletin board ads at Pedro's drew our immediate attention. While perusing this little mecca of information, several more experienced students dropped by the store to retrieve mail and exchange news. We mined each of them for as much information as they would divulge, in particular if they were familiar with any apartments advertised on the board. We soon hit pay dirt. One student knew of a listing that was in our price range. He said the building was owned by a surgeon and located in the neighborhood adjacent to the main University campus. He only rented to American medical students and had a reputation for being a nice guy. The ad included a phone number but no address other than the apartment building.

This prompted the next question. Where were public phones located?

"That is a problem. There are two public telephones in the entire city of Guadalajara."

"Two telephones, two million people! You have got to be kidding me!"

"No."

Of these two lifelines to the outside world, the one recommended was in the parking lot of a pharmacy almost halfway across the city. Soon we were on the first of a series of buses which ultimately passed reasonably close to this sentinel of communication. The telephone was a standard pay phone with coin slots, but rather than being enclosed in a booth, the only cover was a plastic shroud shaped like an ice cream scoop. Standing beside the phone was a line of people waiting to make calls.

Phone calls were *very* expensive in those days, requiring a cache of coins for even brief local conversations. So, our next stop was inside the pharmacy, and another line of people, waiting to exchange paper money for a mass of coins... with a transaction charge, of course.

Then, we joined the end of the line outside, to wait for that single, overworked telephone. That visit was misleading. Our total time spent in both lines was about an hour. On subsequent trips, the wait was usually two to three hours, sometimes more.

Our call was answered by a receptionist in the doctor's office. Yes, a two-bedroom apartment was still available, however it was being painted and wouldn't be ready for occupancy until sometime the following week. After explaining to the receptionist that we would be homeless by then (or at least I would be), the surgeon agreed to meet us at the building the following morning. During the interview with our prospective landlord, we learned that he had completed his surgical residency at a St. Louis University hospital. He spoke warmly of his experience there, and of the community. He owned several apartment buildings in Guadalajara, but said he reserved this one, his nicest, for American students, as a means of repaying the many kindnesses afforded him while he was in the U.S. He agreed to let us move in the next day.

Before leaving, he offered one of his business cards, with the comment, "Customs and laws in Mexico are very different than in the U.S. While you are here, if you find yourself in trouble with the police, or if you become seriously ill, call me. I will help you to the best of my ability."

This was one of the first of many examples of kindness and generosity the people of Mexico extended to me during the year I was a guest in their country. Habits and customs vary from place to place, but expressions of genuine good will create universal bonds.

— Think You Will Die —

A major part of our acclimatization to Mexico involved diet and disease. Almost everyone had heard the admonition, "Don't drink the water!" when traveling south of the border. However, the risks of communicable diseases were considerably more nuanced than simply avoiding a glass from the tap. In restaurants, even when purified water was used for drinking, the ice cubes frequently were not. Fresh fruits and vegetables were to be avoided, unless carefully disinfected at home (we used a dilute solution of iodine), as they had usually been washed in tap water or contaminated in the field. So many benign little habits had to be unlearned, and so many new precautions needed to become automatic.

As we were gathering to go to school one day, a neighbor, Brett, came running down the steps with a worried look on his face.

One of the guys asked, "What's wrong with you?"

"I've just been poisoned!"

This got everyone's attention.

Brett continued, "I was taking my shower, in a good mood, and singing loudly, when I realized I was standing under the showerhead with my mouth open!"

Fortunately, Brett escaped illness that time, but not for long. As the summer wore on, one by one, we were felled by the serious waterborne pathogens. These weren't cases of *tourista*, the effect of benign alterations in flora suffered even by the tourists who stayed in upscale hotels. What we feared was Shigella, Salmonella, Giardia, and the other pathogens that sickened, and sometimes killed, millions of people world-wide, annually. These more serious parasites usually required antibiotics, and/or IV fluids, and one or more weeks of convalescence. Occasionally, hospitalization was needed. We didn't know how the university handled absences due to illness, but we were learning their default position on most things was inflexibility.

. . . .

Two problems contributed to the ubiquitous disease threat. First, virtually all of the water in Mexico was contaminated with pathogenic organisms; bacteria and other microorganisms that will make most people very ill. Much of this contamination was the result of infrastructure inadequacies. In the cities, water lines were routinely constructed of open joint cement pipe, allowing contaminants to seep through the joints and into the water when pressure was low (a frequent occurrence). Worse yet, sewage lines, made of the same material, were commonly located next to, or above, the water lines. Additionally, natural water sources and foodstuffs were routinely contaminated because the bacterial theory of disease was still not being taught in schools. So, farmers, food handlers and cooks inadvertently contaminated their products because they didn't know any better. Some of these problems were understandable, given the educational level of workers. However, cities, such as Guadalajara, had paid hundreds of millions of dollars to foreign engineering and construction firms to design and build water and sewer systems. The people deserved better, for what they had spent. Bottled water, the most common local accessory in home and office decor, was of little help. Much of the water in these containers was also contaminated.

Eventually, I lost the daily game of roulette. Fortunately, my girlfriend, Donna, had arrived from the U.S. some weeks before. After supper one evening, I began to feel vaguely ill. In the middle of the night, I awakened abruptly, with a sense of something being terribly wrong. After a brief assessment, I discovered the twelve steps to the bathroom had lengthened dramatically. I barely made it. Over the next forty-eight hours, I lost approximately twenty pounds. By the third morning, just lying in bed had become painful, but I couldn't risk being any further away from the bathroom and was too weak to go back and forth to bed, except by crawling. Just to spend some time out of bed, I tried staying in the small confines of our toilet stall, which allowed me to brace myself against the walls in order to sit upright.

I wasn't as frightened as in Basic Training when I had pneumonia. I knew that IV fluids would probably improve my condition and allow me to weather the course of the illness. However, even with IV fluids, I had no idea how long this might last, or how much it would cost to go to a doctor in Mexico. On the other hand, no matter how modest the expense, we couldn't afford it. I was living on sixteen dollars per week. That wouldn't cover a doctor's visit. To make matters worse, I was burning through the acceptable number of absences from class.

By day three, I was hallucinating occasionally and drifting in and out of awareness of my surroundings. One of the few things remembered is of Donna being clearly frightened, and me refusing her request to go to a doctor... She took matters into her own hands. A meeting of our friends was convened, and a decision made. Someone called the landlord. The next thing I remember is the surgeon appearing in our bedroom doorway, with Donna and my friends peering over his shoulder. Fortunately, by the time he arrived, I had crawled back to bed but was still mortified for him to see me in such a state. At first, I didn't even understand why he was there.

The doctor entered and explained that my friends were worried about me. After asking a few questions, he said calmly, "I know you think you are going to die, but you won't. You probably have Shigella dysentery. I am going to prescribe some antibiotics. You should be feeling better within forty-eight hours. If not, your friends are to let me know."

His prediction was correct. Although my allowed absences were completely depleted, I was able to return to school in time to avoid having to repeat the semester. Our Spanish teacher was a wonderful young woman with an M.A. in literature from UCLA. She took one look at me on the day of my return and said to go home until I felt better. When I expressed concern about allowable absences, she promised to mark me as present. Her generosity did not solve the issue of my other classes, whose instructors were not so helpful, but it allowed me to shorten the school-day for that first week.

Over the next three weeks, most of my symptoms improved to a state of off and on vague abdominal distress, which persisted until I returned to live in the U.S. I regained some of the weight lost, but at semester break six months later, I still weighed fifteen pounds less than the summer before. Almost all of the Americans I knew in Guadalajara eventually had a similar event, with similar lasting sequelae. For most of us, this was just one more challenge to face in reaching our goal. However, those less committed began dropping out of school. Over the summer and first two months of medical school, I would estimate 10-15% of the Americans in the freshman class dropped out. Just as the Dean had described, there were two distinct groups of American students down there. Some of us were serious about getting an education, the other group, not so much.

The kindness and care displayed by my landlord and Spanish teacher in this incident were two more examples that shaped my opinion of Mexico, and its citizens. These two Samaritans were highly intelligent and successful in their fields of study. Both were eligible to stay in the U.S. and work when they completed their studies here but elected to return to their native country in order to contribute to its success, educationally and economically. They were also remarkably generous and kind to citizens of the country that had helped them. We couldn't hope for better people as international neighbors.

— Huesos —

In September, at long last, our first semester of medical school began. Although the methods of presenting information have changed significantly in the past forty years, the process of becoming a physician is based on an ancient set of rituals and rites of passage which have retained a distinctive pattern for almost three thousand years.

The first requirement is to develop a working knowledge of scientific information specific to the human species. This group of courses, collectively referred to in medical school as the basic sciences, uses the same methods we had learned as undergraduates, however, instead of poking, prodding, and measuring plants, trees, and polliwogs, we now applied those methods to the human organism. The curriculum in Guadalajara was almost identical to U.S. schools, and used the same textbooks. The quality of teaching was variable. Some professors were quite good, others pathetic. The dean at U. of I. had provided sound advice. Just keep studying as though you are in a U.S. school, and you will be all right. The goal is not the grade you get in these courses. The goal is how well you do on the National Board exam, and how well prepared you are to return to the U.S. medical education system.

The National Board of Medical Examiners offers a three-part series of tests for prospective physicians. The first part is taken after completion of two years of study in medical school, the second part just before medical school graduation, and the third part near the end of internship (first year of residency). These tests are offered at multiple sites, but the content is the same at each location and for each applicant, no matter which medical school was attended.

Classes were arranged into traditional lectures and laboratory sessions. The lectures were in auditoriums accommodating hundreds of students. Laboratory equipment was rudimentary, but satisfactory for the study of the basic sciences. My favorite class was anatomy lab, where most of the time was devoted to dissecting cadavers. The usual sources of study material were prisons and unclaimed bodies referred to the police for disposition. There was never any shortage of specimens for study, although heavily weighted toward males. Their origins allowed us to dabble in forensic science. These unfortunates had lived difficult lives, most dying no later than early middle age. We competed with the other lab groups to find the most unusual wounds and injuries on the cadaver assigned to us each week. After lab sessions, we speculated on how the injuries might have occurred. Gunshots and stabbings were common. The most memorable was a fellow with fresh bullet holes through both knee caps. Of course, he also had a bullet wound to the back of his head, which we presumed came after the shots to his knees. Sometimes, it's just not your day.

Human Anatomy had a reputation for being the most difficult course of the freshman year. Our first week in class confirmed that rumor. The lectures were by a Ph.D. anatomist. My laboratory group was taught by a surgeon who had trained in the U.S. He was proud of his education, and equally proud of his native country. He assured the Norteamericanos that *his* course would be just as rigorous as any we might find in a U.S. school. He proved to be well versed in anatomy, and a very good teacher. Students in the upper classes also warned us of a heavy emphasis placed on the anatomy of the bones, and the location of attachment of the various muscles to those bones. They described the first lab test. We would be handed a bone and asked to identify all of the muscles which connected to that bone, and where. Our mentors strongly encouraged us to acquire a skeleton for study at home.

Initially, this didn't seem insurmountable. A skeleton perpetually adorned the physiology lab at SIUE. It was made of plastic but was anatomically accurate. After arrival in *The Guad* (our nickname for Guadalajara), we had learned that a large and amazingly well stocked medical bookstore was located downtown. I figured several of us could pool our money and order a plastic skeleton from the medical bookstore, or a medical supply house, if necessary. Then someone said these plastic skeletons cost several thousand dollars in Mexico. Hmmm, on to Plan B.

"Where did the students in the upper classes find theirs?"

"They bought them from gravediggers," was the reply.

"What!" I exclaimed.

"You go out to one of the local cemeteries, find one of the grave-diggers, and buy a skeleton from him."

I could imagine a whole bunch of problems with this plan. A ready supply of skeletons was not in question. When people are buried in the U.S., the fees charged by the cemetery include something called perpetual care. Although the family of the deceased does not own the ground the grave occupies, the fee for perpetual care includes the right to remain buried in the same grave, and maintenance of the cemetery grounds around the grave site. In Mexico, where disposable income was considerably less, many families could not afford perpetual care, so contracts for shorter periods were also available. The standard contract was for five years. At the conclusion of this period, either the family paid an additional fee, or the corpse no longer had the legal right to remain on the property. Many families were unable to afford the ongoing charges. The deceased resident therefore became a squatter.

Usually, these unfortunates were not evicted immediately after the rent became past due. The first response was neglect. The ground around the grave was no longer mowed and trimmed. However, after the passage of another few years, the delinquent body was exhumed and transferred to a land fill. Herein lay a legal and spiritual contradiction in Mexican society. Mexico had a devoutly religious culture. The two major religions were Catholicism, claimed predominantly by the middle class and the wealthy, and a less structured, richly variable set of traditions, evolved from the Aztecs, Incas, and other great societies of Mexican antiquity. These later spiritual beliefs and practices belonged to the impoverished, many of whom had not integrated with the Spanish invaders, four hundred years before. One commonality of the two religious systems was a profound respect for the dead. Consequently, Mexican law forbade desecration of corpses, graves, or personal possession of dead bodies or parts thereof. The punishment for infractions of these laws was draconian. Therein lay the contradiction. If you couldn't afford the rent on your family member's grave, he/she went to the garbage dump. But, if you were trying to learn a profession that could address the abbreviated life span and exorbitantly high infant mortality rate present in Mexico, you risked going to prison for your studies.

I desperately wanted a medical education, but not badly enough to spend ten years in a Mexican jail. A group of friends congregated in our living room for an intense and lengthy discussion a few nights later. Of the people in this group, all were serious students. We had sacrificed considerably to attend this school and were determined to become physicians. This problem presented the biggest conundrum yet faced in our adopted country. One by one, the prospective felons provided their opinions on the importance of gaining this study aid vs. the risk involved. A third potential alternative, which initially seemed obvious, was also off the table. Skeletons secured by the classes ahead of us were not available to buy or borrow. A few had been saved for siblings or friends in classes below them, but the majority were disposed of as soon as anatomy class ended, to obviate the risk of being caught in possession of body parts.

Although serious, our group was not without humor. The evening was rife with Shakespearian quotes. (Alas, poor Yorick! I knew him...) Eventually, we all agreed that the deed must be done; the crime committed. Now came the choice of lackeys. Our investigation revealed an additional contradiction of life in Guadalajara. Just as with recreational drugs, sufficient demand will result in the creation of a supply. There were two medical schools in the City; the Autonoma and the government sponsored university. At the time, the Autonoma was reputedly the largest medical school in the world, with over 8,000 students. The state university contributed a much smaller number, however the total student population resulted in significant demand for this contraband. The profession of gravedigger is not particularly exalted in Mexico, nor well paid. Some of these professionals were willing to compromise their religious beliefs in order to supply the demand and supplement their wages.

Further consultation with students in the upper classes revealed the following; concrete vaults were not routinely used in Mexican burials because of the expense. Most of the corpses exhumed had decomposed to the point that only the skeleton remained. Any soft tissue still present once the body had been exhumed was quickly and efficiently debrided by rats, beetles and maggots. The quality of the skeletons was quite variable, depending upon the type of casket used and soil compression. Some of the gravediggers involved in this clandestine market were quite industrious and had studied the anatomy of the human skeleton sufficiently to ensure a complete specimen was being offered. It was important to buy from one of these more knowledgeable sources. Otherwise, significant parts of the product might be missing.

But, how did you find one of these guys? They couldn't exactly advertise in the newspaper. The method advised by those experienced in the caper was to drive to a cemetery during the afternoon (most funerals were scheduled for mornings) and hang out near the office in front. One of the suppliers would approach you. Then, you had to rely on gut instinct; either hire the guy or go back another time. There were two additional warnings. Stay away from visiting families, or worse yet, funerals in progress. Everyone in Guadalajara knew what young Norteamericanos were doing in local cemeteries, and emotions could run high. Also, one must avoid the cemetery administrative staff. They would call the cops. The presence of medical students in cemeteries was bad for business. One particular cemetery was strongly favored. We jokingly predicted that its name would be *Our Lady of Perpetual Commerce.*

Once a cooperative gravedigger had been found, arrangements were made to return at dusk in order to complete the transaction. Another commonality of Mexican spiritual belief was superstition. We were assured that any visitors would exit the cemetery before dark. However, waiting until after dark would make headlights and flashlights more easily visible to the guards. (Guards were posted at the more reputable cemeteries to ward off real grave robbers attempting to strip the recently buried of valuables.) Therefore, we must arrive just after sunset, once visitors exited, and complete the deed before complete darkness. The window of opportunity would be narrow.

. . . .

As we divvied up responsibilities for the caper, I quickly volunteered for the group assigned to retrieve the skeleton. This seemed far safer than the afternoon trip to locate a gravedigger. Two members of our not-so-merry band of grave robbers had automobiles. We decided to use one for the afternoon trip and the other for the evening visit, as an additional effort to deflect attention. The heist was carried out on a beautiful autumn evening. As we drove slowly through the cemetery gates, a brilliant orange sun sank below the mountain peaks. The grounds around the office and nearby graves were immaculately maintained. We located a service road that avoided the main route of entrance and exit on its path into the graveyard. Soon, someone darted from behind a maintenance shed and approached the car. He signaled for us to follow and took off at a slow run. Moving further into forbidden territory, our guide angled away from us, running between the graves, as we traversed the closest road while trying to keep him in view. Rounding a curve, we came upon exactly what we had hoped not to encounter. Cars were parked along the side of the narrow road, and a large family stood beside a fresh grave. As we squeezed past the parked cars on this one lane gravel path, the entire family turned to stare at us. Their expressions were not welcoming... but no one chased us with a pitchfork.

By now, our collective anxiety level was rising sharply, in part because, while keeping an eye on the mourners, we had lost sight of our gravedigger. Some of us were getting an edgy feeling that we might have been set up, and my fascination with new experiences was well past its limit. The road entered another section of the cemetery no longer maintained. Uncut grass quickly transitioned to dense weeds nearly as high as the car. We rolled slowly forward into the neglected wilderness of this section of the cemetery. Our only choices: to continue down this river of darkness, or reverse course and face the hostile family behind us. Occasionally, the outline of headstones peered through the vegetation in the rapidly approaching darkness.

Suddenly, the gravedigger jumped out of the weeds in front of us at a run and headed farther down the gravel path, motioning for us to follow. He soon skidded to a stop, turned to his right and pointed us in that direction. Once again, he disappeared. We couldn't see an intersecting road until we were right on top of it, as the weeds were now taller than our line of sight. There he stood, in the middle of this faint road, with a triumphant grin on his face. He beckoned us to follow. Once the car was well out of sight from the other road, he signaled for us to stop and exit the car.

The ambushes and kidnappings described to us since our arrival in Mexico sometimes had a similar pattern. Several of my comrades expressed reservations about leaving the car. Another retorted, "Hell, we've gotten this far!"

Everyone piled out of the car. The guide, wind-milling his arm for us to follow, strode quickly ahead through the brush. Twenty or thirty yards farther on, he stopped once again and held up his hand, indicating for us to wait. Our supplier once again dived into the brush and out of sight. It was now completely dark.

Within a minute, we heard rustling and crackling in the vegetation, and the gravedigger reappeared, dragging a black plastic trash bag behind him. A sliver of moon had appeared overhead but produced only enough light to create shadows. One of us turned on a flashlight, as the gravedigger reached into the bag and began quickly pulling out bones to document the loot. First, a skull, then humerus, femur, and a handful of ribs issued from his sack. By this time, we were sufficiently spooked that all we wanted to do was get out of there, complete skeleton or not. But our host refused to be deterred from his show and tell. He kept scooping out remnants at a furious pace. Finally, he held up a dirt-covered hand, holding what appeared to be a small clump of debris. Using his fingers to quickly brush away leaves and sediment, he announced triumphantly, "Hyoid!"

The hyoid is a small, delicate web of bone located anteriorly in the neck, near the top of the trachea. We were to learn that this is the bone least likely to be preserved and most difficult to locate when exhuming an unprotected skeleton.

The price of our ill-gotten study aid? Forty dollars, American.

The bones were quickly returned to the bag and deposited in the trunk of our car. The gravedigger led us back to another gravel road in the maintained section of the cemetery and pointed us in the direction of the exit. Within thirty minutes, we had safely returned to our apartment building. In order to spread the guilt, if we had been followed (paranoia was generously shared by all), the sack of bones was hidden on the roof of our apartment building, to await inspection another day.

. . . .

When someone asks how different medical school in Mexico was from my experience in the U.S., the answer is, *indescribable.*

Studying by lantern light. Summer 1973

— You Don't Understand —

The relationship between the Norteamericano students and the Autonoma administrators was less than cordial. They welcomed us with open hands but not open arms. The Autonoma, i.e. autonomous or independent, university had been established by a very conservative group of wealthy families in 1935. The purpose of the university was to provide an alternative to the National University, which the Autonoma founders felt had become unacceptably influenced by socialists and communists. These families had wielded enormous political and economic power for generations, and traditionally, the group was allied with the military and police forces, thereby amplifying their power.

Once our medical studies began, we had more exposure to American students in the upper classes. They quickly oriented us to the political realities of the university, and to a more accurate description of the legal system than had been described in class that summer. School officials were extremely paranoid about *American hippies* polluting the minds of their precious sons and daughters, or disrupting their school with demonstrations, as had happened in Mexico City in 1968. American popular music: rock and roll, folk, or worse yet, rhythm and blues, was not allowed on campus. Conversations about liberal causes or politics, recent political demonstrations in the U.S., or world events contrary to the official views of the university, were similarly banned. Students violating these prohibitions were summarily expelled.

In order to identify possible subversives, the university employed a group of spies, known as *tecos* (the Spanish word for owl). The *tecos* were primarily Mexican students, rewarded with financial or academic support for their services. The administration should have saved their money. We weren't there for political debate. Our purpose was to jump through whatever hoops were necessary to allow matriculation into the U.S. medical education system. During lectures, it was not unusual for a professor to go off on a rant about liberals or communists or that the

Estados Unidos (United States) was descending into socialism. We just kept our heads down, surreptitiously reading our English language textbooks, while the instructor shouted in the background. The only students I ever saw get into trouble because of teco espionage were Mexican nationals, usually because they weren't as conservative as their parents.

The necessity for self-censored speech at school and having to listen to frequent diatribes by some of the faculty, proved a source of irritation for almost all of us. We took turns breaking into our own rants about school, and the frustrations of adapting to life in a new culture, when our own tolerance reached its limits. However, our rants were carefully restricted to times and locations protected from teco observation.

Early in the year, some of us befriended a Cuban student. He was highly intelligent, well-travelled, and offered a more nuanced education about the history of Latin America in general, and the cultural differences amongst individual countries, than was otherwise available to us. One afternoon, our group was walking from one lecture hall to another. The class just finished had been completely uninformative and punctuated with a typical digression by the instructor on the sins of liberalism. His comments hadn't been any more offensive than others we frequently endured, and none of us even mentioned them, as we trudged along.

Unexpectedly, our Cuban pal began cursing loudly and launched into a tirade about this particular instructor, and the school in general. This was extremely dangerous!

Several of us immediately issued a cautionary "Shush!"

He continued, undeterred.

Not wanting to lose our new friend, we surrounded him and began laughing loudly to drown out his voice, while walking him off the campus, and out of harm's way.

After reaching the relative safety of the parking lot, someone said, "Oh, calm down. Just ignore the jerk."

To which he replied, still yelling, "That's easy for you! None of you guys understand what he is saying. I have to listen to it! I actually speak Spanish!"

His critique of our Spanish language skills was dead-on... and hilarious. Miraculously, this diatribe escaped detection by the tecos, and life went on.

. . . .

In some ways, the nation's legal system represented an even greater threat than the school's draconian conservativism. Although the Mexican Constitution and laws have many similarities to those of the U.S., there are important differences. The most worrisome was the lack of habeas corpus protection. In the U.S., a citizen detained by the police must be charged with a specific crime and appear before a judge or grand jury within a specified period of time. No such protection existed in Mexico. The police could arrest you, put you in jail, and theoretically leave you until you died of old age without ever charging you with a crime or conducting a formal trial. Not surprisingly, this led to frequent abuses of police power and rampant corruption. I have no idea what portion of the various police and military personnel were corrupt, but it was significant. Mexican citizens, with the exception of the wealthy, were terrified of these authorities.

A favored method of supplementing income for dishonest soldiers and police was to arrest a foreigner (usually from the U.S., but other visitors were not immune), inform the victim that he had committed a very serious crime (with or without fake evidence), and incarcerate the individual. Hit and run motor vehicle incidents were a popular alleged offense. This explained the U.S. Embassy recommendation not to drive in Mexico until thoroughly familiar with the *laws and customs*. The unlucky detainee was not allowed access to a telephone nor provided with an attorney until *bail* was deposited. The *bail* was set by the arresting officer, based on his estimate of how much money could be extorted from the victim's family. Of course, the *bail* never went any further than the officer's pocket, minus a cut for the jailer. As a convenience to the accused, if he or she had enough cash in their possession, the *bail* money could be given to the arresting officer, and the offender was then free to go. This was infinitely safer for the accused, because the black hole of incarceration was avoided. Mysteriously, no further communication from the court, regarding this matter, would ever be received.

The most expedient protection against this method of extortion was to always carry cash, in U.S. dollars, secreted somewhere on your body (money belts were popular). For the standard contrived stop and shake down, $20-50 was usually sufficient to persuade the cop to make a quick buck, rather than engage in the more complicated process of jail and attempted communication with the family. For those of us too poor to carry even $20, there were two alternatives. If someone suddenly went missing, the first step was for friends to make the rounds of the jails. For an additional bribe, the jailers would run down the list of inmates, or allow a walk through to look for a familiar face. These little bribes, in exchange for everyday government services, were called *la mordida* (the bite). If the missing friend was located, you could then take up a collection for *bail*, or notify the family back home in the case of more serious issues. The other alternative, unfortunately, relied completely on luck. A variety of police and military agencies had overlapping responsibilities for law enforcement. Although some individuals were corrupt, others were honest, hard-working people attempting to make their country a better place. If one remained in jail long enough, an honest cop might notice your predicament and arrange for a hearing before an honest judge, where the charges would either be dismissed, if appropriate, or a reasonable fine imposed for your transgression. This good fortune saved at least one of my friends.

. . . .

Another threat lurked on a daily basis. Although individual freedom of expression was theoretically protected by law, freedom of the press was not. Government censors monitored major newspapers and periodicals regularly and forced the deletion of any articles felt damaging to the image of Mexico or its government. When receiving advice from upper-classmen about the behavior modifications needed to successfully navigate the school, one story was always shared, and with emphasis. In 1968, a large group of students in Mexico City had staged a demonstration in support of worker and student rights. Independent observers described the gathering, which was held in a city plaza, as peaceful. Police and military personnel opened fire on the demonstrators with automatic weapons. We were told that two hundred students were killed. The government suppressed all reporting of this incident. When I was in Guadalajara, five years after its occurrence, accurate details of the massacre remained unavailable to the international press, although virtually all of the local citizenry seemed to know about it from word of mouth.

We were told the story as recounted above. Several additional sources of information have now been published, including a report on NPR "All Things Considered" which aired on Dec 1, 2008. As of this writing, the text is still available on the NPR web site.

One day during spring semester, I was in an area of trees and lawn on campus, similar to the quadrangle of many U.S. college campuses. This space was encircled by a six-foot high, wrought iron fence. Gates were present, but I had never seen them closed. It was a sunny spring day, a large number of students happened to be present on the lawn, and everyone was in high spirits. I wasn't aware of any focus of disruption. As far as I knew, this was just a bunch of college kids talking animatedly in multiple small groups.

Suddenly, the gates swung shut, and guards with rifles lined the outside of the fence. The rifles were pointed at us. Those students who could see what was happening called for the students nearer the center of the group, who could not, to quiet down. Within a couple of minutes, there was almost dead silence. Some of the guards appeared confused and ill at ease, while others remained hostile and aggressive. I was afraid that any outburst from the students might prompt gunfire, and there weren't any avenues of escape.

After several more minutes of silence, someone announced on a loudspeaker that the school was closed for the rest of the day. Anyone remaining on campus longer than fifteen minutes would be arrested. The main gate opened just enough for several guards to move inside its perimeter. They ordered us to form into two columns. We were then marched out of the quadrangle to the parking lot nearest the campus exit, accompanied by armed guards, and told to go home. The following day, everything was back to usual (not normal, just usual).

— Páguelos! —

Supermarkets, very similar to those at home, were present in Guadalajara, however they were too expensive for most student budgets. Unfortunately, meat in the small, local shops was of questionable quality and source. After one such experiment, which ended badly, I was informed that the word *res* is not the Spanish translation of *beef*. The proper meaning of *res* is *beast*.

On the edge of the city was a massive open-air market, which supplied nearly all fruits and vegetables to local groceries and restaurants, as well as individual shoppers. Every Saturday morning, we piled into Brett's aging Mustang, or another available vehicle, and headed for El Mercado. This trip was a weekly highlight. The vegetables were from local fields. The choice of fruits here in the sub-tropics was dazzling to a Midwestern boy. The market was designed so the produce trucks backed into a stall and simply drop their tailgates. Customers bought the wares straight from the truck bed. I commented to one of the vendors one day on how ripe and tasteful the fruit was. He replied, in Spanish, "Yeah, we send all the green shit to the United States and keep the good stuff for ourselves!" Then, he winked and smiled broadly, enjoying his little joke on us Norteamericanos.

The pinnacle of Saturday shopping was always a visit to *La Machina*. This was a machine that made tortillas and was located at the far end of El Mercado. A twenty-pound mass of dough lifted by hand into a huge funnel at one end of the contraption began the process. The operator then coaxed the gooey material downward with two huge wooden sticks. As a portion of dough exited the small end of the receptacle, a blade sliced off the hanging masa, which then dropped between two rollers. The rollers compressed the dough into a flat circle of perfect thickness. The maize frisbee now fell onto a conveyor belt driven by a chain and sprocket. The belt, carrying a never-ending row of these delicacies, clattered slowly and noisily into a rectangular sheet metal tunnel that looked like an old furnace duct. The sides were perforated by gas jets at intervals along its twenty-foot length. Warm, slightly browned, intensely aromatic tortillas reappeared on the conveyor belt at the far end where a line of expectant customers stood waiting. Upon reaching the head of the line, you handed the worker a tortilla container, usually a woven basket with lid, and indicated how many kilos you wanted. He or she held your container under the conveyor belt until the appropriate number of tortillas dropped off the end. We soon learned to bring an additional receptacle to accommodate an extra kilo of tortillas for the road. Otherwise, we never made it home with the tortillas needed for later meals. Of the gastronomic delicacies I have sampled in life, fresh, warm tortillas from *La Machina* are, unequivocally, the best.

. . . .

One Saturday, the return trip from El Mercado included a surprise. The day was warm and sunny, and the ration of road tortillas long gone. Everyone was in a good mood; the only lament being that we should buy two kilos of road tortillas next time. Our route, a rutted, barely two-lane, oil and gravel road, passed a few isolated neighborhoods separated by tracts of scrub brush and timber, then snaked around the periphery of the medical school campus. We were laughing and talking as we rounded a bend and encountered a carload of adolescent Mexican males stopped at the side of the road. Parked behind them was a nondescript tan sedan. Surrounding the carload of kids were six men, wearing incomplete military uniforms and holding semi-automatic rifles. The guns were aimed at the boys.

One of us commented, "Oh, man! I wonder what they did?"

Someone else added, "Whatever it was, they are in a heap of trouble!"

A third offering was more practical, "Don't look at them. I'll bet those goons don't want any witnesses."

. . . .

We continued on, our mood a bit subdued. Within a few minutes, a furious honking erupted behind us.

Our driver checked his rear-view mirror and exclaimed, "Oh, crap! It's the goons!"

He pulled to the right as far as possible, hoping they would pass us in pursuit of some other evildoers. No such luck. The sedan stayed right on our tail, and two of the occupants began waving their arms out the windows, indicating for us to stop.

This situation presented several potential problems. The uniforms were of immediate concern. Some of the men were wearing military jackets with civilian trousers, others vice versa. The state of Jalisco was swarming with gangs of robbers at that time. (This was long before the term narco was invented... or needed.) Some of the gangs were revolutionary groups hoping to overthrow the government, others were simply thieves. Roving bands of rogue police officers or soldiers rounded out the potential choice of assailants. Roadblocks and traffic-stops by legitimate Army soldiers, checking identification and looking for revolutionaries, were common, which further added to the confusion.

When confronted with a situation such as this, the first task was to try to determine the allegiance of the men holding the guns. This was critically important information because tactics and outcomes varied between groups. Unfortunately, identifying legitimate agencies was often difficult. Local police departments were so poorly funded that many officers did not receive a sufficient number of full uniforms. Consequently, even officers on duty might be wearing an incomplete uniform, if a needed spare was unavailable. Many jurisdictions could not afford a police car equipped with the traditional flashing lights and siren, either. Some cars didn't even have an identifying name or insignia. In those cases, if an officer wanted you to pull to the side of the road and stop, he would honk the horn incessantly and wave his arm out the window. However, there were almost *never* six policemen in the same car if the stop was for a traffic infraction.

Military pay was low and erratic, but legitimate soldiers usually had a complete uniform. Unfortunately, some of the gangs had sufficient strength to attack military or police supply depots in less populous areas, which they did regularly. Besides weapons, uniforms were a common target of the raids. The bandits would then set up road blocks, posing as military personnel. If accosted by armed men wearing only portions of military uniforms, this usually meant they were either bandits or revolutionaries. Outcomes of these encounters could be quite variable. If the stop was made by a group of corrupt soldiers, the target was cash and valuables, as extortion was inconvenient. If the stop was a shake-down by the police, and you were unable to produce a sufficient bribe at the scene, you might be taken *downtown*. That meant jail and attempted extortion from your family.

The bandits and revolutionaries had a different modus operandi. If you were a high value target, you were kidnapped for ransom. We weren't. If the stop was made on a road with occasional traffic, such as this one, you might be instructed to accompany them *downtown*. This trip, you never wanted to make. The actual destination was usually a more deserted location, where everyone in the car would be killed, and the vehicle ransacked. We heard stories of these incidents regularly.

From the available evidence, our current situation didn't look good. The driver reluctantly pulled over farther and stopped. We were immediately surrounded by the men from the unmarked car. Now, the rifles were pointed at us.

One of the assailants addressed our driver and demanded, "Sus papeles!" (Your papers).

No one knew what to do, so we simply sat there.

The demand was repeated in a more declarative tone.

The driver replied, "Qué papeles?"

(This was deliberately incorrect Spanish grammar, in an effort to convince the questioner that we did not understand.)

The officer now shouted, "Papeles, papeles!" and some other things we really *didn't* understand.

In desperation, the driver reached into the glove compartment and began fumbling around, as if looking for documents.

Someone in the back seat started to speak, which prompted the command "Silencio!" as another man jabbed the muzzle of his rifle in the open car window.

Finally, the glove box yielded a small piece of paper which was handed to the interrogator. It was a game token from McDonald's. The soldier apparently knew at least *something* about the U.S. because he threw the token to the ground, then barked, "Downtown!"

This was the only word of English spoken by our captors during the entire encounter, and it was the word we least wanted to hear. We were running out of time and options, and all of us were terrified.

Just then, a car came racing around the curve behind us at high speed. It was the teenagers who had been in this predicament a few minutes before. They started jeering at the soldiers.

One of the boys leaned out of the car window and yelled, "Paguelos!" (Pay them off), as their car sped out of sight around the next curve.

The soldiers jumped and stared in the direction of the teens.

Then, the leader yelled, "Vámonos!"

The men immediately jumped into the sedan, the engine wheezed to life, and the car spun out of the dirt and onto the road in pursuit of the insolent youngsters. As soon as our assailants were out of sight, we executed a U-turn, and took off equally hastily in the opposite direction. From overhead, I imagine this looked like a scene from a slapstick comedy. From the ground, it wasn't nearly as funny.

— Miss Settie —

Since leaving the Army, I had tried to follow Grandma's advice about facing problems one day at a time, and its corollary that if there was no apparent solution to a problem at the moment, just put your boots on and work on the problems facing you today. You might have to wait awhile, but an answer to the seemingly insoluble puzzle usually appeared. As the first semester of medical school progressed, one of those insoluble problems grew ever nearer. I did not have a committed source of money to pay for second semester tuition and expenses. My parents had agreed to fund the first semester, but no more. Since then, there had been no mention of that support being extended. In early December, I received a letter from Dad. It began, "I have some good news for you. Miss Settie has offered to pay your tuition for the second semester."

. . . .

During the majority of my childhood, Dad served as the pastor of the only church in Atwater, IL. It was a classic rural church in both appearance and function. The business district of Atwater consisted of the church and one general store. The city population hovered between thirty-five and fifty souls, depending on whether or not one family with thirteen children was currently renting a house in town or somewhere else. Some of the surrounding farms had been owned by the same families for over 100 years; a few by descendants of the original settlers. Both the store and the church were vital assets to the community. There was a sense of permanence to Atwater I have found in few other places.

Miss Lusetia Blevins was born in Atwater around 1880. As a child, she demonstrated an unusual aptitude for school and an independent nature, neither of which was encouraged in girls of her day. At the completion of eighth grade, she insisted on continuing to high school. Fortunately, her parents acquiesced. After high school graduation, she was admitted to the University of Illinois. During my childhood, she never told me of the struggles she faced in that endeavor, other than to say her interest in natural science, as biology was called in her day, had been discouraged by the faculty. In spite of this lack of support, she was ultimately awarded a Bachelor of Science degree in natural science and a Master of Science in botany; one of the first women in University of Illinois history to achieve those milestones. After a career with the U.S. Department of Agriculture in Washington, D.C., she retired and moved back to Atwater, assuming the honorary position of resident intellect, and the title, Miss Settie. During the years I knew her, spanning her eighth and ninth decades, she remained intellectually sharp and inquisitive.

In his letter, Dad recounted a recent visit with her. She had asked about me in detail. He told her of my degree from SIUE and brief stint at the University of Illinois, knowing the mention of her alma mater would be of interest. He then described my desire to become a physician, some of the difficulties I had encountered, and my current efforts in Guadalajara. Apparently, at some point in the conversation, he divulged the cost of tuition, and uncertainty whether I would be able to find sufficient financial resources to continue.

Her response was immediate and incisive; her usual style. She wanted to help with my efforts and would pay for my second semester tuition. Dad said he had protested because of the amount of money involved.

Ms. Settie replied, "You know, Charles, when I was in graduate school at U. of I., my desire was to go to medical school. The advisor recommended against it. He said to me, 'You are clearly smart enough to study medicine, and I will write a letter of recommendation to the school if you insist. But, I want to warn you. You will be the only woman in the class. You will not be treated equally by the professors or your classmates. And, once you graduate, you will struggle for your entire career to be allowed to do the things that you know very well how to do.'

"I decided to take his advice, and that is why I got my degree in botany. I understand what it is like to struggle to accomplish something that you know you can do. I have the money, and I want to help Jim."

Dad concluded his letter by saying he and Mom would continue to pay my monthly living expenses.

.   .   .   .

Solutions to problems sometimes come from unexpected places and in unexpected ways.

— Mi Abuelita —

Donna found a job as a tutor for adults learning English. The school was located in the central part of the city, and classes were held at a variety of times in the morning, afternoon, and evening, to accommodate the student's work schedules. Her assigned classes sometimes resulted in a ten-hour day, for which she was paid $1.25. Daily bus fare was twenty-five cents and took almost one hour each way. These were the only types of jobs available for a foreigner without a work permit, even a college-educated one. Her employment didn't last long. The evening class often meant she must take the last bus of the day back to our apartment. This was always dicey. The second to last stop was at the merger of several streets. All of the remaining riders usually disembarked there, leaving Donna as the only passenger. The distance to the last stop, near our little barrio, was approximately two miles, along a street bordered by forest, arroyos, and brush on one side. We had been warned never to drive on this street at night because of bandits. Walking was regarded as too dangerous even in daylight. On several occasions, the driver continued to our stop only after she argued with him. Finally, one night, he absolutely refused to go further, and threatened to physically throw her off the bus if she didn't leave voluntarily.

The forbidden road lay ahead, but there weren't many choices. After exiting the bus, she noticed a taxi parked a short distance. Upon inquiry, he was available and for a price within the expected range. But, it was more money than she had. When telling the story later, she described being so discouraged and frustrated that she just stepped away from the cab and started walking down the street towards home.

Before traveling fifty yards, the taxi pulled alongside, and the cabbie asked where she was going. When she told him of her intention to walk home, he became very animated, insisting she absolutely could not walk down that street! He then stopped the cab and opened the rear door, indicating for her to get in. When she confided having too little money for the fare, he replied that was no matter, but she absolutely could *not* walk down *that* street.

I was in the living room, studying, when Donna walked through the door. She asked if there were a few dollars in the emergency stash, explaining that she had taken a cab home without enough money for the fare. I retrieved the needed cash and headed out the door to pay the driver. The cabbie was standing just outside, waiting for me. Very firmly, he said I should never allow *mi amiga* to walk down the street in question, because she would probably be killed.

I assured him I was aware of the danger and thanked him profusely for keeping her safe. I offered him the five dollars we had (approximately twice the fare originally quoted) in gratitude. He refused to take *any* money. After several more attempts to pay him, he shook my hand, wished me a good evening, and drove off. Afterwards, we exchanged details of our separate interactions with the cabbie. She said the drive had been consumed by a lecture from the cabbie, such as a big brother might give, about the risks of travel at night in this neighborhood.

The next day, we decided the teaching job was too dangerous, no matter how poor we were. This ended Donna's surreptitious teaching career in Mexico. Just contemplating the possible alternative endings to that evening still terrifies me.

. . . .

Soon, the holidays were upon us. My surprising good luck of spending every Christmas with Grandma had finally run out. January 21st would be her ninety-first birthday. Although remaining in remarkably good health, and still living in the house at the end of Main Street, we all knew she couldn't last forever. However, UAG operated on a semester schedule, and fall semester wouldn't end until the third week of January. Christmas break was short. Airfare was out of the question, and driving, even if I could find someone headed in that general direction, was a grueling 1,300 miles each way through the mountains. Besides, I had already arranged a ride home for the semester vacation and needed to save every peso possible, in order to pay for my share of the gas during that trip. We would spend Christmas in Guadalajara.

This really wasn't so bad. Donna would be there with me, and I was curious to see how Christmas was celebrated in Mexico. A friend of Donna's was planning to visit for a few days, so there would be some extra activity to anticipate, and then Donna would be returning home to start nursing school at SIUE. Christmas shopping wouldn't take long. We had very little money. My parents were practical people. They would not be offended if no presents arrived from Guadalajara this year. My plan was to buy small items for them and save postage by delivering the presents at semester break. The most important shopping would be things for Grandma and Donna.

One weekend, I headed to the main market downtown, Mercado Libertad. It was housed in a converted parking structure with multiple levels. On each floor, vendors set up hundreds of small booths, selling everything one could imagine. We usually avoided this market because it was a favorite destination for visitors. The goods offered were largely directed toward the tourist trade and priced accordingly. The place was filled with people, unfamiliar aromas, food stands offering strange treats, and every imaginable item the American tourist might want to haul back home as a souvenir. A steady stream of these Norteamericano sheep were delivered by tour bus each day, for shearing by the local merchants, all the while convinced they were experiencing the real Mexico. Knowledgeable residents rarely shopped there. However, for this occasion, and without a car, traveling to individual stores was impractical. The tourist business was usually slow at Christmastime. I hoped that would result in more reasonable prices.

The choice of a present for Grandma was easy. Weaving and selling shawls were common means of employment for poor women in the city. The wraps were warm and brightly colored; a good choice for Grandma. Her central vision was almost gone, but she could detect color peripherally. I examined the items at several booths. As expected, the quality of shawls varied widely. One vendor was a middle-aged woman who had apparently spotted me as soon as I came into view. She approached and motioned for me to follow. Her stall had a modest selection of shawls and other items. She immediately began her sales pitch, assuming another tourist had been hooked. One of the shawls seemed satisfactory, if not great. The price quoted of $20, was of course high. I replied in Spanish that I lived in Guadalajara and would not pay the tourist rate.

My adversary then surmised correctly that I was a medical student at the Autonoma. After confessing to this, she deployed her next gambit. I must be rich, if able to afford the UAG, and therefore, should help an old woman struggling to make a living. (She was no more than fifty, but I wasn't about to contest her struggle to make a living.) Most people in the city knew exactly what the tuition for Americans was at the medical school. It was a fortune by local standards, so this was a tough argument to refute. There was a playful lilt to her banter; simply a game to act out with customers. I have always had a deep admiration for people who can maintain a sense of humor in the face of adversity. I liked her.

I also knew the working poor harbored a deep resentment towards the wealthy families who controlled the Autonoma. So, I protested her assumption of my wealth, telling her my parents were school teachers and didn't make large salaries. Furthermore, the *officials* at the University (using a term for thieves in place of *officials*) had taken all of my money. She laughed, and her eyes twinkled. I went on to explain the shawl was for *mi abuelita* (a term of endearment meaning my little grandmother). Now, she insisted on helping me. She took my hand and led me away from her booth. I protested that the shawl she was selling was satisfactory.

"There are shawls of much better quality available from other vendors," she confided. For the next thirty or forty minutes, we searched throughout the market, examining goods at a variety of booths, while leaving hers unattended, except by nearby vendors. Eventually, a very nice item was found, and the price negotiated down to $8. by my new friend.

As we walked back to her location, I thanked her for the help provided, and expressed concern that she had missed sales while we were away. I offered to pay her the difference between the advertised price of the shawl purchased, and the amount settled upon. She absolutely refused to take *any* money. When we arrived back at her stand, she shook my hand and said, "Feliz Navidad a ti y a tu abuela también." (Merry Christmas to you, and to your grandmother as well.)

— We All Look Alike —

Semester break finally arrived. Donna had returned safely to the U.S. a few weeks earlier. One of my classmates with a car was from Indianapolis. Five of us squeezed into his Camaro and tried to enjoy the twenty-five-hour drive to Edwardsville (and they still had another five hours to go). If Mom and Dad noticed my fifteen-pound weight loss, it was never mentioned. However, they did spring for air fare back to Guadalajara, so I could stay home a little longer. My grades for first semester were nearly straight A's. The more hair-raising adventures of the preceding six months remained untold. I did divulge the story of our trip to the cemetery for the skeleton, but decided to omit other escapades involving bandits, kidnappers and drunken bus drivers from my travelogue.

. . . .

Second semester in Guadalajara was considerably less adventurous than the first. By now, we were becoming acclimated to the culture, and more skilled at avoiding experiences best left untried. Life at school had become one of minor adjustments, rather than weekly crises. An intermediate goal in our quest to become physicians had been reached, and the day to day routine was now more enjoyable than stressful. However, as the completion of one year at UAG approached, I again faced a familiar dilemma. There was no identified source of money to return to school in the fall. Ms. Settie's generous assistance had been limited to one semester. A persistent search for loans available to students in foreign medical schools remained unsuccessful. My parents provided no indication they intended to alter their financial decision further. Their reluctance was understandable; their life savings were meager. They were members of the Depression Era. Dad had worked at two or more jobs throughout his career in order to accumulate modest pensions from the school system and Social Security. Both of my parents had seen bank deposits and job security disappear overnight. In their experience, no asset could be completely relied upon. Unless another bene-factor appeared out of thin air, my only opportunity to continue medi-cal school would require transfer to a U.S. school.

A few students from UAG successfully transferred each year, but only after taking Part I of the National Board Exam. In addition to its primary purpose, this exam provided a means for American schools to compare students in foreign schools to their own students. Part I cov-ered the basic medical sciences taught during the first two years of medical school. Students taking the exam after just one year were at a decided disadvantage. On the plus side, the American student presence in Guadalajara was so large that a test site had been established there. On the negative, another logistic problem arose. UAG was a proprietary medical school. American students were cash cows who financed much of the university budget. Consequently, the school was not eager for any of the herd to be culled. The board exam consumed eight hours per day for two consecutive days. So, the Autonoma scheduled examina-tions in every class during those two days and announced that anyone who missed the exams would fail the semester and need to repeat it. As an additional threat, the student would be dropped from school en-rollment and required to re-apply for admission. And finally, no excus-es would be accepted for missing the tests scheduled on those dates.

I had received A's in all but one class (B in that one) the first semester and was on track to receive similar grades for the second. If I failed to show up for the UAG exams, all of that work and expense would go out the window. Besides, even if I took the board exams, my chances of successfully transferring to a U.S. school were not encouraging. No one had ever heard of a student transferring after one year, and that type of information was closely tracked by the American students. This was agonizingly frustrating. After spending years working to improve my study skills, finding a career that really interested me, and proving my-self capable of doing the work, I was about to get washed out because of a lack of student loans. One evening, the problem came up in a discussion with some friends. They had no intention of taking the boards until after sophomore year but weren't under the same economic pressure I faced. Their families were able to pay for their education.

One of them, a shy conversationalist, was typically doing more listening than talking. Up until now, he had said nothing. Finally, after the alternative risks had been thoroughly examined, and the conundrum of unacceptable choices generally acknowledged, he said quietly, "I have a solution."

We all stared in his direction quizzically.

He continued, "I could take the exams at UAG for you, so you could take the board exam."

I countered, "But, you have to take the UAG exams, too. Are you planning on dropping out of school?"

"No. I can go to the classes, show my ID badge (which was always required for important events such as major exams) and take the tests. The tests never take us very long to complete (which was true). Once finished with my test, I can leave, put on your name badge, return to the front door, get another exam, and fill it out in your name."

The lecture halls were enormous, with doors front and back. For exams, we were required to enter the front doors and present our I.D. badge to a student monitor. Upon finishing, we would hand the completed exam to another monitor and exit the rear door.

He continued, "Even if there isn't time to finish them, you will have turned in exams, proving you were present. If you fail these exams, your grades are already high enough you won't flunk the courses."

"That's all true, but if you get caught, you will get kicked out of school along with me. You shouldn't take that chance."

"I won't get caught," he said calmly. "You know the Mexicans think we all look alike," at which point he broke into a conspiratorial grin.

On this point, we knew he was right. We were both slim and had sandy blond hair. I was a few inches taller and a bit heavier, but many of the Mexican students, and some of the Americans, thought we were brothers. We spent the next 15-20 minutes discussing the likelihood of the plan succeeding. There was general agreement that he could probably get away with it.

I was still very reluctant to allow my friend to take this kind of risk on my behalf. All of us had worked very hard to get to this point in our education and had invested $10-15,000 in the effort. He was adamant that he wanted to do it.

Finally, he said, "Look, here is the worst-case scenario. If I get caught and kicked out of school, they will let me back in next semester. The school isn't going to want to miss another $15,000. for six more semesters. They don't have anyone else applying to the sophomore year to replace me. My Dad can afford the $5,000 penalty, if I get caught, and I think he would agree with me doing this.

Now, it was our friend's turn to rant, something he rarely did. "I have been putting up with these bigoted, racist assholes for the past year, and it is driving me crazy! I may not be as vocal as you guys are, but I resent them just as much as you do. I want to do something to mess with them. It will make me feel just a little bit better about all the crap we have to endure."

The quality of teaching amongst the professors was variable, but their personal and political beliefs were pretty uniform. We all shared our friend's contempt for their attitudes.

I was stunned. None of us would have suspected this fellow was gifted with eloquence in those days, but he had just made a rational and well-articulated argument for taking on a very risky secret mission. For the next few weeks, he practiced my signature in an attempt at vague similarity. When the exam days arrived, I sneaked across town to the board exams, being held in another part of the city, while my friend doubled up on his exam load. At the end of the first day, I was anxious to hear how things had gone.

"Just as we predicted," he smiled. There was only one uneasy moment. In one of the testing rooms, there was only one door and only one monitor checking ID's on the way in and out."

"What did you do?"

"I turned in my exam, went out in the hall and waited about 10 minutes. Then, I went back in with your ID and made up a story about being late. The guy handed me an exam and never blinked!" My co-conspirator broke into a broad grin.

And so, I must add this eloquent imposter to the long list of people who helped me gain a medical education. My friend has requested anonymity in relation to this story, but my gratitude remains unchanged.

Some of the stories related in this section may be interpreted as unflattering to the country of Mexico and its people. This is not my intent. I disagreed with the political and cultural attitudes of the UAG administration, and many of their professors. This was the only group of people I had ever encountered who proudly identified themselves as fascists. The threats, not only to our freedom of expression, but also our lives, were real and deeply resented. Over the past forty years, Mexico has made enormous progress, socially and culturally, in spite of complex challenges. I hope the leaders of the Autonoma have changed as well. I suspect they have. I must also acknowledge that the Autonoma provided me with an opportunity in 1973 no U.S. medical school was willing to offer. Therefore, UAG also belongs on my sine qua non list of benefactors. I would never have achieved a medical education without them.

The authorities then in control of UAG had no effect on my memories of, and feelings toward, the country. My sentiments regarding Mexico were formed by my interactions with the common people, La Gente, in that beautiful land. Every society has its share of rude, inhospitable individuals; the drunken, threatening bus drivers of the human race. However, almost all the people I met in Guadalajara were exactly the opposite. They were like the cab driver, the woman who helped me at the Mercado, our landlord, and our Spanish teacher. They were kind, considerate, and amazingly generous toward strangers in need. I deeply love and respect the real people of Mexico.

Chapter VII.   Summer of '74

— Reality —

The summer after my year in Guadalajara, there were several things to feel really good about. I had successfully completed one year of medical school, even though in a foreign country. Almost all of my grades had been A's and nothing less than a B. I had achieved respectable scores on the first part of the National Board exam, including a passing score in two subjects we hadn't covered during the first year. I was enrolled in a summer program for medical students at a local hospital which was both fun and interesting. However, no solution to my financial problems had appeared. How was I to pay for the remainder of my medical education? Acceptance to an American school seemed to be the only path forward. If admitted to a school in the U.S., I was eligible for loan programs that would at least pay the cost of tuition. I had written letters to 35 schools over the spring months, inquiring about the possibility of transfer. Very few schools even bothered to reply, and those that did, declined to consider me until I completed the sophomore year. A growing number of American schools were beginning to accept a few students in transfer from foreign schools, but the uniform policy was fixated on entry at the third year of training. The new medical school affiliated with Southern Illinois University seemed my best possibility, but acceptance of their first class of students had been postponed for another year.

That summer, I called every school in Illinois that hadn't replied to my letter, except one. Although no response had come from Northwestern University, it was no surprise. Almost everyone I knew regarded Northwestern as the finest university in Illinois and one of the best schools in the entire country. The medical school was legendary. Any thought of me being accepted to Northwestern University Medical School was laughable... but laughable could no longer be accepted as a barrier. During that very discouraging senior year at SIU, the realization had come that if I gave up on my quest without exhausting every possible avenue, the omission would plague me for the rest of my life.

With the feeling of someone dropping his last dollar into a slot machine, I picked up the phone and called the main number for the medical school. The operator transferred me to the Admissions Office. The woman who answered the phone listened to my story. To my surprise, she said they were quite familiar with the Universidad Autonoma de Guadalajara and went on to explain that the Dean of the medical school had been a visiting professor at UAG during this past school year. He had lectured only in sophomore classes, so I was unaware of his visit. Then she mentioned the medical school had recently established a transfer program, and eight Autonoma students were being admitted in transfer to the junior class for the coming semester. However, she didn't see how she could help me at this time. Only students who had completed their sophomore year were eligible, and besides, the candidates had already been selected.

Suddenly, I was so close to an opportunity I had sought for so long, but still lay just beyond my grasp. Once again, I could not get through the door.

Now she was saying something else I didn't completely absorb, but the tone of her voice made it clear this was her prelude to ending the call.

I was frantic! My head was pounding. This lifeline could not be allowed to slip away. Think! Think! Think!

An idea pinged into my consciousness from some distant, overstimulated neuron, "I have read that, on average, one student drops out of the freshman class of each medical school each year. Did you lose any freshman this year?"

There was a pause.

"Why, as a matter of fact, one of our students contacted the office a few days ago to say she would not be returning this fall."

I could *feel* that imaginary door pause in its inexorable path toward closure.

"If you anticipated a class of sophomores that included her, then apparently you have the facilities to educate that number of students. Why let the spot go to waste, when new doctors are needed so badly in this country?"

"Hmmm. I hadn't thought about that, and I don't know the answer to your question. The Chairman of the Admissions Committee is in his office this afternoon. If you don't mind waiting for a few minutes, and he is free, I will ask him."

I was tempted to say, "Lady, I will hold this telephone until September if you want me to," but decided on something sounding less pathetically needy.

In less than five minutes, she returned to the phone. She sounded cheerful. "Dr. Berry says he has never considered this circumstance either. If you wish to come to Chicago within the next few weeks, he will arrange some interviews. However, he said not to get your hopes up. He really hasn't had time to think about this sufficiently."

The details were quickly worked out, and we ended the conversation.

Holy Cow! I had just wedged my toe in the door of Northwestern University Admissions. Even better, they were already entertaining the possibility that those of us from The Guad were not some kind of lepers. Maybe, there was a chance. *Holy Cow!*

The visit to Northwestern had been scheduled for one week from my first phone call. Now came the sobering prospects of having to explain to these exalted intellectuals, all of whom I suspected were eligible for knighthood, why anyone in their right mind would risk tarnishing the reputation of this renowned institution with a loser whose academic credentials fell so far below their standards. My euphoria faded. What would I say? I couldn't talk about my grades. Every student with mediocre grades has an excuse.

What if the interviewer said, "Well, you seem like a nice young fellow, but I am concerned whether or not you will be able to keep up with the work in this challenging environment. This is medical school, you know."

Ladd Prosser seemed to be my best defense for that type of question. Dr. Prosser's reputation in academia was beyond gold-plated. As the Dean from the U. of I. Medical School had said, "If you are good enough to be one of Ladd Prosser's grad students, you will find medical school a snooze!" Yes, hopefully that quote would do.

In defense of Dr. Prosser's reputation for recognizing talent, I don't think he seriously considered my abilities sufficient for his program. He did seem to recognize that my score on the GRE's was probably due to more than just luck. But primarily, he was a remarkably kind and generous man. He appreciated my dilemma and decided to help me. For that, and his many other acts of kindness, I will always be grateful.

My MCAT scores were acceptable for medical schools in general, but below those earned by typical Northwestern students. Dr. Parker had confided that my letters of recommendation were excellent, but almost all successful medical school applicants have glowing recommendations. That covered the three components used by medical school admission committees to select the chosen few. Northwestern students were exceptional. What was exceptional about me? Hmmm.

Trying to visualize the typical Northwestern Medical School student, produced a few presumed traits which might be leveraged as positives, rather than negatives. I would be a few years older than most of their students, especially those in the accelerated undergraduate program. I had diverse work experience, which translates as increased maturity and a broad knowledge base in most interviews. The offspring of the patrician families whose children were educated by Northwestern and the Ivy League schools for generations had probably never soiled their hands with common labor. I had also worked in medically related jobs, side by side with doctors for much of that time. Those physicians had judged me a good candidate. And, finally, with this degree of exposure to life in a healthcare profession, I was unlikely to lose interest in another year or two, as had befallen the former student whose departure created this window of opportunity.

Discussion of my military service needed to be carefully scripted in advance. By 1974, many people had very strong opinions about the recent war, and the conduct of some of its veterans. I had no idea where my interviewers would fall on the political spectrum. I decided to follow a standard rule used in Pentagon meetings. The less you say, the smaller the target created for hostile incoming artillery. I also needed to anticipate questions that might be asked of me, choose flame-retardant answers, and practice those responses. Considering my propensity for saying the wrong thing at the wrong time, or to the wrong audience, this would not be a good time to just wing it. I decided on the following,

I trained for the role of combat medic, however my orders to Southeast Asia were somehow lost, and I was diverted to The Pentagon. For seventeen months, I worked closely with physicians in a variety of specialties at that location, and occasionally, at the White House.

If asked for an opinion about the war, or any of the collateral damage now being discovered, the answer would be,

This has been a very complicated affair, Sir.

My military service and achievements should have been a source of pride. They were, and still are. However, 1974 was a very different time and possessed a very different atmosphere. Most of the vets I knew spoke very little of their experiences, except to other Vietnam-Era veterans, for the same reasons.

. . . .

I took the train to Chicago the evening before the interviews and stayed with friends. The meetings were scheduled for early afternoon. I do not have a reputation for punctuality, but I left for the medical school campus three hours in advance. If every means of public transportation in the city seized up at the same moment, I wanted to be able to walk to the Medical Center, if necessary, and arrive on time... I arrived way early.

I walked around, looking at the various hospitals and administrative buildings which covered most of a four-block area in downtown Chicago. I didn't allow myself to think about the possibility of actually belonging on this campus. In order to stay calm, I tried to induce the mental state practiced in combat medic training; a zone of awareness occupied solely by the task before me. The reality of the stakes riding on my performance in the next few hours *must* be banished from my mind. I imagined a comparison between the impending interviews and being captured by the Viet Cong. I would be questioned by an NVA interrogator. Survival hinged on my answer to every question. I must not fall victim to my typical weaknesses in social interactions, particularly those involving perceived *authority figures*. I *could not* allow my mind to wander. Answers to questions *must be* measured, deliberate, and appear well-thought out. No off-the-cuff remarks today! Probably, the biggest difference between the impending interrogations and the

Viet Cong was, in this case, I was trying to get *into* the prison. Self-doubts about my ability to successfully complete this gauntlet, just like mentally preparing to do a tracheostomy in the field, had to be excluded. Anything my brain identified as negative was banned. I needed that same focus, even if the bullets and shrapnel of mediocre grades and inadequate abilities were whizzing all around me. It was imperative that I successfully present myself as an attractive extension of the experiment the Dean had already initiated.

. . . .

With half an hour to go, I went up to the Admissions Office. I recognized the voice of the woman at the desk as the person I had spoken with on the phone. She expressed regrets the interviewers had not yet arrived and hoped there hadn't been a misunderstanding about the appointment time. I confessed to having walked around outside for an hour and a half, fearful of being late for the appointment, and offered to come back later. She laughed, brought me a soda, and pointed to a chair. While I waited, she mentioned that my first interview would be with Dr. Berry, the Chairman of the Admissions Committee. Soon after, I was ushered into a wood paneled office with a brass plate on the door announcing the name and title of my interrogator. Dr. Berry rose and shook my hand. I don't remember much about the interview, other than being quite dissatisfied with the rehearsed lines which I managed to squeeze into the conversation. He was polite and cordial, but I sensed he just wasn't very interested. He had probably already formed his opinion about setting another precedent. We talked for 15-20 minutes. He never questioned my abilities, which was certainly a relief. In fact, he mentioned the committee's frustration with trying to make decisions based on traditional measures of academic success when there was little evidence these indicators had relevance to the potential for a candidate to become a skilled physician.

Without much of a summation, he thanked me for coming and stood up, "I know this process can be quite stressful. We won't keep you waiting. I would anticipate you will hear from us sometime next week."

The young lady from the front office met me in the hall. She commented that I would now get an informal building tour, as the next interviewer's office was at some distance. We wandered through the Ward Building, the icon of the medical school campus, before descending to a classroom in the basement.

The second interviewer was very pleasant. He began his comments by explaining, apologetically, that although he possessed an M.D. degree, he was really a biochemist and had spent his entire career in the lab, doing research. A copy of my application packet was in front of him. He said he had been reading it with interest, then suggested I just tell him my life story.

I stumbled a bit, not knowing what he would think important. He asked why I had chosen to leave college and join the Army. His interest seemed so sincere, I let down my guard and launched into *the making of Jim Turner to age twenty-five*, complete with Grandpa and his Kentucky roots, Mom and Dad, the Depression, my acquisition of the *brain damaged* label and struggles in school. I told him about becoming interested in the subjects in combat medic training, and the doctors at The Pentagon encouraging me to pursue medical school. I described the conversation in Dr. Prosser's office with the medical school dean from the University of Illinois, and my subsequent diversion to Guadalajara. I finished with the story of surreptitiously taking the National Board exam. Before the interviews, I had no intention of revealing this much information. There were far too many elements that could be interpreted negatively. But this man acted so genuinely interested and nonjudgmental about what I had done with my life, and he kept asking more questions. He would have been a good trial lawyer.

Then, he asked a question I hadn't much considered. What interested me the most in medicine, and did I have a particular specialty in mind?

Again, I hesitated. "I am interested in proximate causes of death, and if these processes can be interrupted."

"Pathology?" he guessed.

I laughed. "No, I want to try to keep them alive. I suppose Emergency Medicine is the closest specialty to my interests."

"Well, emergencies are high stakes, stressful situations."

Damn! I just knew what was coming next!

"Let's see how you do under pressure. How about a little chemistry quiz?"

Rats! Things had been going so well up until now. I reluctantly agreed, not really having any choice in the matter.

"The primary purpose of red blood cells is to transport oxygen. The red cells contain the metallo-protein hemoglobin, which is the active transport molecule for oxygen. Oxygen binds and releases from hemoglobin differently, depending on the pH of the cell cytoplasm. Please draw a graph of the oxyhemoglobin dissociation curve on that blackboard, and then explain to me how it works." He leaned back in his chair expectantly.

This was almost certainly the first time in my life I felt lucky during a chemistry quiz. Of all the chemical reactions I had waded through in the past five years, this was the one most applicable to what I wanted to do with science. I had studied the phenomenon repeatedly, and thought I possessed a pretty good grasp of its fundamentals.

I drew the horizontal and vertical lines of a graph on the blackboard but couldn't remember which characteristic was the ordinate and which the abscissa. No matter. I could have reproduced the shape of the curve, and its position on that graph, in my sleep. But somehow, when I began to describe the chemical mechanism, the curve didn't conform to my explanation, and I couldn't figure out how to make it right. Finally, I admitted never having been very good at math and proceeded with an explanation of the reaction. Ignoring my botched artwork, I launched into a description of the four sub-units of the molecule, the variations in shape and affinity of the binding sites for oxygen, and the effect of pH on those shapes and affinities.

When I finished, he said, "You are dyslexic, aren't you."

I replied that no one had ever applied the diagnosis to me, but since my Dad was dyslexic, it would be no surprise if I was, too.

He continued, "You have just done a very nice job of describing the cellular chemistry of this reaction, certainly as well as most of our students could do, better than many of them, I would guess. But, you drew a mirror image of the graph. Redraw it and turn it around."

I did so, and everything in the explanation fell into place. Now, I wanted to get away from that blackboard as fast as possible, before making any further errors. I started to lay down the chalk and looked at him questioningly. He indicated for me to sit.

"We do not usually share our impressions with interviewees. In fact, I am probably breaking some kind of rule around here, however, I want to tell you what I think. A portion of our students are from privileged backgrounds, some going back for generations. Many of these students: have never held a real job, have never been anywhere in life that wasn't a guided tour, and have no experience with the world most of their future patients live in. Considering your background, I think you would make a wonderful addition to this class... and, I can't believe how hard you have worked to get here.

"I'm just a nobody around this place. I don't know that my opinion counts for anything, but I am going to recommend you for admission, and I wanted you to know that."

The interview was over. I think my knees were literally shaking as I walked out into the hallway. He offered to help me find the way back to the Admissions Office. I thanked him but declined. I wanted to get out of his sight before I did or said something to cause him to change his mind.

. . . .

Walking through the Ward Building, I touched the student lockers lining the halls, the wrought iron stair railings, and long-ago plastered walls that had seen so many famous physicians and scientists in their time. I began to let myself feel like I might belong here. The sensation was overwhelming... but there was a lingering problem, Dr. Berry. My second interviewer had claimed to have little influence (although I suspected he was downplaying the respect his colleagues actually held for him). However, Dr. Berry was clearly the big dog in the yard. Without his support, it was doubtful the mountain of institutional policy would move. I *had* to do a better job of winning him over! Maybe I should write a letter... not enough time. Besides, my grad school roommate, Mike, the marketing whiz, had convinced me of the truism that, in persuasion, personal performance almost always beats the written word.

I slowly climbed the steps back to the Admissions Office, trying to think of a plan. The same young lady was still there and asked if my second interview had concluded. I nodded affirmatively.

She smiled brightly and said, "Well, you're all through then."

I asked to see Dr. Berry for just one more minute.

Her smile faded immediately. "Why do you want to see him?"

I explained that the second interview had gone very well, but I didn't feel as if the interview with Dr. Berry was as positive. I was hoping to say just one more thing to try to explain myself.

"Well, this is highly irregular. I don't know if..."

I could see him at his desk down the hall. She couldn't beg off with the excuse he had left for the day.

"All right, I will ask. But, I don't know that he will agree to see you. We *never* do this."

406

Her look, and the tone of her voice, suggested I wouldn't even make it to the batter's box.

She returned quickly, "He will see you, but just for a few minutes."

"Thank you," I replied, with the most sincerity I had applied to those two words since the first time I got laid.

. . . .

I stepped through Dr. Berry's partially opened door, hesitantly.

"Yes? What can I do for you? I need to leave shortly," was his curt greeting.

"I will only take a minute, Sir. Thank you for seeing me again.
I don't feel that I did a very good job of explaining my particular strengths, or why you should take a chance on me."

"Oh, you did well enough. It was a satisfactory interview."

Still very non-committal.

I took a deep breath and began. My undergraduate grades aren't even close to the level of your students, and my MCAT's are just satisfactory. But, I don't think those things measure my abilities accurately. I have actually performed in the real world of medicine, and doctors who observed me in that setting are the people who talked me into trying this improbable quest. I don't know how that can be measured with a test, but if I may, I would like to tell you a story to illustrate my point.

An attractive young female graduate student, studying cultural anthropology, was spending the summer on a Native American reservation out West. Her goal was to learn the customs and daily activities of this particular tribe.

Dr. Berry leaned forward in his chair with a slight smile.

During her observations, the student had noted the Great Chief of the tribe spent much of his time sitting cross-legged in front of his teepee. Towards the end of the summer, she was completing some odds and ends of her data collection. By then, she felt fairly comfortable with the tribal members. Gathering her courage, she approached the Chief, asking if he could help clear up some confusion in her information.

He agreed to assist.

"Well, Chief, I have observed the custom of your people, when meeting a stranger, is to hold your right hand upward with the palm facing forward and offer the greeting, 'How.' "

The Chief confirmed this was correct.

"But, Chief," the grad student continued, "I have also noticed that when tourists are visiting, and a young woman approaches, you hold up your hand in the traditional manner but say, 'Chance.' "

The Chief replied, "Me know how. Me want chance!"

At this point, Dr. Berry burst out laughing. I thanked him for seeing me and quickly left the office.

. . . .

The next week was torture. From Monday morning on, I was afraid to leave the house, for fear I would miss the call. The days dragged by. Finally, Thursday afternoon, the phone rang.

"Hello?"

"Hello, this is Dr. Berry."

"Yes, Sir."

"I wanted to call you myself," he explained.

Oh, no! A thought raced through my brain. His next line will be that he is very sorry to say, they just can't make an exception to existing policy. I braced myself for the worst.

"You know Jim, my administrative position here at the medical school really isn't very much fun. It seems like I spend most of my time talking to young people who are in trouble or aren't happy about the subject matter in a class, or don't like one of their professors. I rarely get a chance to deliver good news. So, I wanted to make this call myself.

You have been accepted into the sophomore class of Northwestern University Medical School."

Until the day I die, I will never forget those words.

. . . .

And, that is how a brain damaged, hyperactive kid with dyslexia got into Northwestern University Medical School.

Tail of the Dog

Reflections

In the final analysis, my first-grade teacher was right. I am brain damaged. Where she got it wrong was in assuming that the atypical neural pathways which resulted in my syncopated method of thinking and learning meant that I was hopeless, destined for failure, and undeserving of any effort at instruction.

The story of how I overcame my educational disadvantages may be unusual, but the learning disabilities I possess are by no means unique. Those of us who do not think and learn in the manner school systems have decreed as "normal" probably represent 15-20% of Americans.

Although I speak from the perspective of ADHD and dyslexia, many other children and adults, who may or may not fit into an existing diagnostic or neurophysiologic category, are subjected to the same inaccurate assessments and restriction of educational opportunities that I experienced. The label may have changed from "minimal brain damage" in 1953 to "children with special needs" in 2018, but the same stereotypes, prejudices, and scientific ignorance still confront most people like me, sixty-five years after I entered school. Over that span of time, the fact that neurologic diversity exists in how people process information and express their thoughts has been clearly established. Yet, the brahmins of mental health cling to labels of their own creation for the patterns they regard as other than "normal." Their labels are uniformly pejorative. If you are a kid who fidgets in his seat at school and becomes distracted when bored, you have attention deficit *disorder*. If you can't form letters into words or recognize words in print by the age of six, you have a learning *disability*. If you are unusually good at pattern recognition in complex designs or identifying the contradictions in what others say or write, but you also have trouble with the order and pronunciation of words in English (one of the most difficult and structurally nonsensical languages on the planet), then you have *dys*lexia, or possibly, autism spectrum *disorder*. But you are almost never identified as gifted, or even normal, while in school. You are disordered, deficient, disabled. You are abnormal.

Who are we really; this group of educational misfits? I think Temple Grandin, Ph.D., has provided the most useful general descriptor so far. She calls us, as a group, *atypicals*, as compared to the *normals* or *neurotypicals*. Steve Silberman has added the descriptive *neurotribes*, in his book of the same name. Yes, these are just words... but at least they have not yet acquired the negative connotations associated with the names we are usually called.

We hear, absorb, and process information by different neural pathways or sequences than neurotypicals, and frequently have difficulty articulating our thoughts in easily understandable or socially "acceptable" ways. These variations in neural processing are then judged, rather than the content and intellectual quality of our responses. Labels are subsequently affixed to categorize our inferiority, and the perceived abnormalities used as justification to deprive us of the educational resources we need and deserve.

. . . .

I wish I could say that my experience in school is a relic of the past and no longer relevant... I cannot. Although the Edwardsville school system that I attended now enjoys a national reputation for excellence, many other schools continue to struggle to provide a quality education for all of their students, and some systems actively resist efforts to create meaningful opportunities for students who are judged impaired.

We live in an increasingly competitive global environment. As a society, I don't think we can afford to continue under-educating one fifth, of our next generation. We need all-hands on deck, performing at their peak potential capacity.

Shortly after I began medical school at Northwestern, I had an impromptu conversation with Jack Snarr, Ph.D., the Associate Dean for Student Programs. He inquired as to how I was acclimating to this new environment and reassured me of their confidence in my abilities. Then he said, "We believe our responsibility as faculty and administrators is to provide our students with the tools necessary to become the best that they can be. If there is ever anything you need, to assist you in that process, please come see me."

I think this standard should be the acknowledged expectation of all teachers, administrators and school boards. We can, and must, do better. Every kid should have an IEP (Individualized Education Plan).

. . . .

I now have seventy years of experience living with a rich genetic amalgam of atypical traits. This book is not intended to be a "how to do it manual" for *atypicals* or their families. However, on this subject, I cannot resist indulging in the annoying habit of old people to offer unsolicited advice to those who are younger. Try to think of it as insight.

For parents and families, three things are of paramount importance: patience, understanding, and consistent support.

- Life is never easy for us... It probably won't be easy for you, either.

- Most of us understand that we are more difficult than normal children, even though we may not be able to articulate our appreciation of your efforts.

- Although our attempts may be difficult for you to fathom, and don't always work out as intended, we do try to please you.

- Our performance will often be quite variable from day to day and task to task. This unpredictability can be exasperating and inexplicable to those around us. Please try to understand that it frustrates us at least as much as it does you.

I can't speak for the other atypical tribes, but for those of us with ADD/ADHD, mentoring is enormously helpful. I have been blessed with a series of mentors in my life. Looking back at these individuals, I see one commonality amongst all of them. They were unequivocally on my side. They wanted me to succeed and expended the effort to help me in any way they could. The world can be a pretty tough place for us to navigate. Knowing you aren't alone in a corner feels like having a life-preserver in rough seas. Admittedly, not everyone has the skill set to be an effective mentor. If you are one of those who do not, you can still assist in finding others to serve in that capacity. And remember, mentors are different than spouses; it is acceptable to have more than one at a time. (That said, spouses can, and often do, serve as very effective mentors.)

For my younger brethren in the atypical tribes, these are some of the things I have learned:

- First, reject the assumption that you have a disease or a disorder or a deficit. Not everything that is different is a disease. At a fundamental biological level, our DNA possesses variations from the most common pattern. In the rainbow of human genetic diversity, we are a slightly different hue. (This is not meant to imply that well-chosen medications aren't effective for some of the challenges associated with being atypical. They are.)

- Be proud of who you are. Do not succumb to the negative perceptions of others when they judge you unfairly. Believe in yourself, even if others do not. For me, a line from "The Desiderata" has always been the most comforting, "You are a child of the universe, no less than the trees and the stars; you have a right to be here."

- Keep in mind, ADHD, dyslexia, and other atypical traits we posses are not excuses; they are explanations. Most of us can do almost anything, provided the test question, the description of the task, or the interpretation of our response is formatted appropriately. However, success will also require hard work, and may involve more complexity than is experienced by neurotypicals.

- One of my friends is fond of saying, "It isn't always easy being me!" If you are atypical, you will immediately identify with that observation. Accept it. This is the price we pay for the gifts we possess.

- Mother Nature is more benevolent than you may realize. We have some impairments, but we also have abilities that most *normals* lack. We see things, hear things, and perceive things they will never get to experience. Society is filled with people who are varying shades of gray. *Atypicals* contribute to making this world a colorful and multidimensional place. I would never willingly trade my own unique brand of weirdness for life as a *normal.*

- In spite of the prejudices and inequalities you face every day, try to be kind to *normals*. We ask them to accept us for who we are, so we should accept the reality that: we often baffle them, annoy them, and inadvertently threaten them with our abilities. Remember, they weren't lucky enough to be born *atypical.*

And finally, I recommend optimism. In explaining my own successes, I must take into account its role. Over the course of my life, I have frequently disappointed people who are important to me. Most days, I have not behaved or performed as well as I might have, in part due to the quixotic nature of my atypia, and in part due to sloth and torpor. But, almost every morning, I get up and try again. Sometimes, that has yielded surprising results.

Postscript

The author graduated from Northwestern University School of Medicine in 1977 with the degree of Doctor of Medicine. Although the policy of the Medical School was not to divulge the class rank of graduates to outside entities, individuals were informed confidentially of their standing. In a class of over 170, Dr. Turner ranked within one or two students of the median.

His first year of post-graduate residency training was in Emergency Medicine at Akron General Medical Center, Akron, Ohio. This was followed by a two-year residency in Internal Medicine and two-year fellowship in Critical Care Medicine at the University of California, Davis, Medical Center in Sacramento, CA.

Upon completion of fellowship training, he was invited to join the U.C. Davis faculty. In addition to teaching medical students, residents, and fellows, Dr. Turner served as Medical Director for the EMT-II training program, as Medical Director of the U.C. Davis Lifeflight medical helicopter program, and as a member of the Human Subjects Review Committee, which was responsible for oversight of all university research using human subjects. He also organized and staffed a consultation service providing Critical Care medical services to the Neurosurgical Intensive Care Unit and the Intensive Care Unit for Special Surgery.

In 1989, Dr. Turner transitioned from a full-time faculty position and briefly served as the Chief Executive Officer and Medical Director of a small, inner-city hospital. This effort was followed by a consulting practice in Critical Care Medicine at private hospitals in the Sacramento, CA area. During the course of his professional career, Dr. Turner served as a member of, or chaired, numerous medical quality assurance and administrative oversight committees at the local and regional level. He also participated in clinical research trials of new medications and biologicals for the treatment of severe infections, pneumonia, acute respiratory failure (ARDS), and ICU sedation.

In 2003, he was nominated for a Northern California Heroes in Medicine Award. In 2004, a survey of 3,000 physicians in the Sacramento region named him as the Critical Care specialist most physicians would call if their own family member required intensive care services.

Dr. Turner retired from daily responsibilities as an ICU staff physician in 2012 and currently divides his time between his home in Northern California and the family farm near Greenville, IL. He continues to provide analysis and advice for complex medical cases, quality assurance issues, and the logistics of health care delivery.

Dr. Turner is available for speaking to groups
Please contact: james@burningbarnbooks.com

Acknowledgements

In addition to the many people mentioned in the stories above, a number of others have provided indispensable support during the three years in which this book slowly took form. They know their contributions, individually, and I am deeply mindful of how essential their assistance was. I am forever grateful.

Heather Turner Killeen, PhD.

Deana Starrs

Will Chambers

Adele Barsoti

John Champlin, M.D.

John and Lisa Schwarz

Daniel Wilcoxen

Will Turner

Jane and Rick Hilliard

John Darnell

Roger Darnell

Natalie Rush

Robin Kruzik

Bill Bratton, D.D.S.

My high school classmates:

John Speciale

Mary Jo Hoover

Marilyn (Stolze) Marsho

De (Hurst) Christian

Marie Bensa Dubach

Martha Lamb Harris

Linda Seibert McCoy

Sharon (Price) Meyer

Graphic artist: Adria Starrs

Author photo: Sumit Saurabh, Trishna Creations

In Memorium

On 9 Dec 2018, Mr. Gayle Day passed away. A long-time science teacher at Edwardsville High School, he was for me, and I'm sure many others, inspirational. A great teacher, as well as a kind and gentle man.